Twenty-first-century fiction

Manchester University Press

Twenty-first-century fiction

Contemporary British voices

Daniel Lea

Manchester University Press

Published by Manchester University Press
Altrincham Street, Manchester M1 7JA, UK
www.manchesteruniversitypress.co.uk

British Library Cataloguing-in-Publication Data is available

ISBN 978 0 7190 8149 1 *hardback*
ISBN 978 1 5261 3957 3 *paperback*

First published by Manchester University Press in hardback 2017

This edition first published 2019

for
Liz and James

Contents

Acknowledgements

Katie Craik
Eóin Flannery
Matthew Frost
Jasmine Goody
Simon Kövesi
Nicole Pohl
Rob Pope
Diana Spencer
and all my family.
Thank you.
Liz and James – all I ever wanted from life.

Introduction: contemporary criticism and the untimely

Richard Hoggart opened his autobiography with the words: 'This is an attempt to make, out of a personal story, a sense rather more than the personal' (Hoggart, 1993: xix), and, though it may seem vain, and anathema in a work of criticism, I would like what follows to have some of the flavour of Hoggart's aspiration. For this book is an attempt to understand – to make sense of a body of contemporary British writing from a position of engagement that strives for objectivity but that, like all criticism, ultimately derives from a coming together of professional and personal needs. It was born of a desire to understand what has been emerging in British fiction in the new century and to understand how that relates to the frameworks propagated by critics in what feels increasingly like an intellectual marketplace where the capital of postmodernist theory has been dispersed into ever more fragmented and tenuous ecologies. It is determined by and written from a place of ignorance, with an unnerved sense that this ignorance is insurmountable, but with the optimism that the endeavour will produce a compensatory coherence that will intersect with the views of others and thereby lend to the subject matter something of Hoggart's ambition.

The objective of the book is not to offer an expansive overview of the first two decades of the century but, through close and concerted analysis of the fictions of five writers that have entered the cultural scene largely since the millennium, to identify resonances, contiguities, co-ordinates, and intensities that relate specifically to them but that may also speak across broader concerns in contemporary British fiction. It may already therefore have mis-sold itself to the reader, for the grandiloquence of the title seems to promise what I cannot deliver and have no intention of delivering. The kind of portmanteau project implied by that title requires a synoptical perspective on the past and its literary effects that is particularly difficult when that past is so recent and the effects so multitudinous. Others have striven to offer this longer view of the contemporary British novel and even sought to establish a kind of *in medias res* periodisation that would lend the present a coherent identity, or at least a recognisable character (see Boxall, 2013; Head, 2008; Luckhurst and Marks, 1999; Morrison, 2003; Tew, 2007). But, whilst this book draws on those valuable taxonomical efforts, it deliberately seeks to retain a sense of scepticism towards synopticism which I would like to think of as stemming from the necessary non-attachment of presentism, but which may belong to pusillanimity. For this I make no apologies, and call for self-justification on the numerous failures of vision and understanding that populate the texts under consideration to suggest that, if the contemporary novel is defined by anything, it is its discomfort in ascribing any specific name or nature to the present without comparable anxiety.

Consider, for instance, the work of Jon McGregor, which is beset by the fear of being unable to see things in their entirety, resulting in the narrowing of understanding and emotional engagement to well-worn shapes of domestic ritual. In his debut novel *If Nobody Speaks of Remarkable Things* (2002), a lonely, agoraphobic character experiences, as he stands ready to perform a bungee jump, a moment of crystalline coherence as he observes beneath him 'the whole city [...] shimmering and shining so much that it feels as though he's standing on a diving board over a swimming pool, waiting to somersault and twist into clear blue water' (McGregor, 2003: 241). After such a moment of clarity, the next step brings a plummet towards perspectiveless immersion in the world, a flattening of vision that is also experienced by the protagonist of Tom McCarthy's *C* (2010a) as he soars above the battlefields of First World War France, ecstatic that the labyrinthine difficulties of his earth-bound life can be temporarily resolved to a series of precise and incontrovertible co-ordinates. These co-ordinates, when programmed into a taxi driver's sat-nav in Ali Smith's story 'The Book Club', take his fare home by the most direct route but cannot map the meandering path her grief takes as she contemplates life without her mother. Similar grief and guilt overwhelm Captain Luke Campbell in the aftermath of his disastrous failure to distinguish friend from foe in Afghanistan in Andrew O'Hagan's *The Illuminations* (2015), a novel about the kind of moral blindness that Sarah Hall's self-obliterating protagonist finds in the depthless darkness of Internet pornography in *How to Paint a Dead Man* (2009).

These are, of course, contingent echoes plucked to support my case that conceptualising anything as obscure as the contemporary will inevitably present problems of perspective. Proximity does not presuppose immersion; nor can it guarantee clarity, so the readings of these authors that will follow are conducted with an uncertain self-consciousness that acknowledges both vision and blindness as part of its method. How can it do otherwise?

In trying to define 'What Is the Contemporary?', Giorgio Agamben argues that 'the contemporary is he who firmly holds his gaze on his own time so as to perceive not its light, but rather its darkness' (Agamben, 2009: 44). Such an individual captures the moment only by a feat of negation; by 'dipping his pen in the obscurity of the present' (Agamben, 2009: 44), s/he shows that writing is a function of sight *and* blindness. But what is the status of the critic in seeking to determine outlines in the crepuscular squinting of others? It is worth remembering that to be a critic means always to be in a condition of untimeliness – the term Nietzsche employs in *Untimely Meditations* (1997; originally 1873–1876) to suggest an out-of-jointedness with the present – but to be a critic of contemporary writing is to feel this particularly acutely. In order to produce a work of credible distance, one seeks to reposition oneself temporarily within all the cognitive and affective structures on which one depends in all the other areas of life so as to be able to go to work on the material at hand with as studied an objectivity as can be mustered. Such is clearly the case for all critics, but, in order to assure others (and themselves) of the clarity of their vision and the completeness of their intellectual decluttering, critics of contemporary writing have to adopt a form of hyper-ironic distance that is unnecessary in the study of other historical periodisations where the effect of untimeliness is already factored into the distance between critic and text. Acutely aware of the risk of partisanship or over-identification, contemporary critics must stand even further back from their material in order to strive for the kind of objectivity that is, in all probability, unattainable.

An additional problem for the critique of contemporaneity in its current set of incarnations is one of nominalism: are we still compelled to categorise the literary production of the new century within the broad taxonomies of period or formal and aesthetic rationale that tend to dominate academic notions of literary history? Whilst the 'contemporary' frequently demarcates work that is produced 'now' – in the sense of the last few years – it is an elusive descriptor that rolls together timeliness and aesthetics. It is, however, a notoriously flexible term that can justifiably point to historical origins in any number of twentieth-century switch-points, the most common being 1945, 1979, 1989 and 11 September 2001. Those dates, closely linked to significant national or global geopolitical watersheds, conform to an embedded model of literary narrative tied to historical aetiology that is dubious at best and that has the effect of balkanising cultural effects into determinate positions that inhibit multivalency. In my own teaching I define the contemporary as the preceding decade, which privileges novelty over historicism whilst being as arbitrarily imposed as any other frame, but for this book the remit extends back to the mid-1990s not as a definitive starting point but to coincide with the early works of Smith and O'Hagan. To a degree this invalidates my titular claim to be focusing on the twenty-first century, but only in the sense that this period is a fixed, calendrical defining point rather than imaginative, taxonomical, or marketing shorthand.

The millennial turn emphasises the tendency to understand literature as a function of history, but, whilst it adds another term to the pile of chronocisms, that pile pales in comparison to the heap of critical and theoretical identifiers that offer themselves up. Much mental energy has been spent in recent years determining the health of postmodernism, and, whilst for many *rigor mortis* has already set in, the idea of what might supersede it is still very much up for discussion. We appear to have reached the point where the experiments in form and style that constituted postmodernism in literature can be labelled as belonging to the twentieth century, whilst we are said to be inhabiting the digimodern, the altermodern, the hypermodern, the metamodern, the exomodern, or, most nonsensical of all, the post-postmodern.[1] If we add to this the anthropocene, the period of postconsensus, the neoliberal period, late capitalism, the posthuman (with its offshoot, sentimental posthumanism), and the re-emergence of a pan-humanism, we are present in an era of truly dizzying uncertainty. That many of the above categorisations can be accommodated within, or are extensions rather than rejections of, the postmodern idea reveals perhaps more about the desire for novelty within the academic humanities than it does about significant changes in the literary landscape. Nevertheless, it is the case that there have been interesting shifts of emphasis in recent years, particularly in American fiction (the work of Teju Cole, Ben Lerner, and David Vann for instance) and around the effects of immediated worlds (Colson Whitehead, Shelley Jackson), the posthuman body (Kazuo Ishiguro's *Never Let Me Go* [2005], Jeannette Winterson's *The Powerbook* [2000]), and the intermediacy of past and present (the work of David Mitchell and W.G. Sebald). But, rather than marking a sea change in contemporary letters, these focuses need to be understood in the context of a great deal of continuity not just with the strategies of the modern and postmodern novels but also with the tradition of liberal realism, which has not only not gone away but has also had a renaissance in recent years, as the writers in this volume attest.

The fetishisation of the newly minted critical sub-category is, in part at least, a product of uncertainty that manifests in a need to shape and order, and corresponds to the visceral fear of not being able to grasp the bigger picture that assails creative and critical writers alike. James Wood addressed this is with his notion of 'hysterical realism', which he describes as 'a perpetual motion machine that appears to have been embarrassed into velocity. Stories and sub-stories sprout on every page. There is a pursuit of vitality at all costs' (Wood, 2001a). The hysterical realist (Wood includes Salman Rushdie, Zadie Smith, and David Foster Wallace in this camp) is terrified by silence and sameness and thus fills her/his page with a profusion of detail and knowledge at the expense of sensibility and psychological depth. This mode of writing supplants the long perspective with the immediate as a way, Wood believes, of deferring answers to the questions of the human condition. Andrew O'Hagan sees the same myopia in the ascendancy of celebrity culture, arguing in his essay 'Saint Marilyn' (O'Hagan, 2008: 65–74) that the frenzy to own part of Marilyn Monroe's estate, which saw someone pay $63,000 for her dog's collar tag, stems from a belief that a meaningful whole can somehow be cogently pieced together from minimally signifying elements.

The unpicking of postmodernism into multiple distinct but interrelated sub-groups is a comparable phenomenon, reflecting the need for a theoretical coherence to account for a host of individualised effects. Theories of the demise of the postmodern and the vitality of its heirs have become a mini-industry within criticism with its own metacritical structure navigating between ethical, affective, environmental, cosmopolitan, narrative, transnational, cognitive, and religious turns that generate their own morphological integrity without too closely approaching a grand epistemological narrative. If we have done away with the postmodern, which in turn did away (at least for Lyotard) with the totality of knowledge, where does that leave us but with a range of intricate theoretical refinements competing to rename something that was always an umbrella term for a host of contradictory practices. This uncertainty – a form of hysterical criticism – gives rise to insistent questions: 'What happens now?', asks the subtitle of Siân Adiseshiah and Rupert Hildyard's (2013) collection of essays on twenty-first century fiction; 'Do you feel it too?', asks Nicoline Timmer's (2010) book on post-postmodernism; and *Beyond Postmodernism: Onto the Postcontemporary* asserts the title of Christopher Brooks' (2013) collection. Each relates the fate of postmodernism to a temporal shift forwards – a state of change in time that anticipates a related change in sensibility – and, though these strap-lines may be only semi-serious, they do reinforce the idea of the linear succession of cultural movements out of and away from their predecessors in a fundamentally timely way – timely here both in the sense of temporally ongoing and expressing a comfort and affinity with the historical moment.

The danger with this trajectory is that it threatens to corroborate – even unintentionally – a view of literary history as progressive, and, though it does allow for backwards flow or the reimagining of formal predecessors, it posits a direction of travel that is essentially teleological and a structure that is hierarchical, qualities concerning which most versions of postmodernism would be profoundly sceptical.[2] But it also further problematises the issue of critical perspective with which I have been grappling. If readers of contemporary culture are expected to stand back sufficiently from their subject matter to visibly legitimise their critical distance, how much distance are they to establish from the kind of criticism that instantiates taxonomical terms such as the post-postmodern, the altermodern, or the didgimodern, which are, to varying degrees, already acknowledging their ironic separation from material that (in turn) acknowledges its ironic separation from a referentiality in which it no longer has faith? Is it productive, or even possible, to be ironic about the post-ironic without disappearing into an uroboros of involutions? If postmodernism was largely seen as a response to the literature of exhaustion, and is accepted as having been itself exhausted, is its wake not equally being overshadowed by an commensurately entropic form of self-referential criticism?

One interesting focus for this set of problems is David Shields' book *Reality Hunger: A Manifesto* (2010), a text that has quickly become a test case of the 'what happens now?' debate. Shields' study of contemporary culture is organised around a series of aphorisms that bemoan the draining of the authentic from artistic production in the twenty-first century. For him the ascendancy of a kleptomaniacal recombinant culture that reworks existing forms only through pastiche or direct sampling is indicative of a pathological self-interment beneath the strata of the already known and already exhausted. The joyful plundering of the archive that constituted postmodernism's playbook has turned in the present to a jaded retreading of simulation's simulations, leaving us desperate for something real. 'We want', Shields asserts, 'to pose something nonfictional against all the fabrication – autobiographical frissons or framed or filmed or caught moments that, in their seeming unrehearsedness, possess at least the possibility of breaking through the clutter. More invention, more fabrication aren't going to do this' (Shields, 2010: 81). Shields' antidote to this manufactured artificiality is, firstly, the introduction of a real that is autobiographical and anecdoctal and, secondly, the repositioning of textual attention to the spaces of inbetweenness that are productive because their liminality renders them least formed, least stable, and therefore least exploited. The 'lyric essay', which is Shields' term for the written version of this intermediacy, is a provocation to the essayist to start 'imagining things, making things up, filling in blank spaces, or leaving the blanks blank' (Shields, 2010: 27) and to the novelist to introduce the unashamedly personal and factual. Combining fact and fiction without submitting to the pressure to distinguish them, acknowledging the inseparability of subjectivity and objectivity, and articulating reason's emotionality are crucial in Shields' project to flow against the tide of modernity's desire to purify the specious imagination from reliable facticity. He thus demands a hybridity that embraces both modernity's utopianism and postmodernity's scepticism, a mashup in itself, but one that undermines the teleology of criticism's fondness for 'post' prefixes.

Madness lies in the hall of mirrors that informs the current critique of critique, and I largely want to avoid those infinite regressions in this book, not because I consider them intellectually invalid but because, for me, they represent a disciplinary practice that is too sterile. The critic is ultimately, and rightly, responsible for displaying that s/he has adopted an objective approach, but how far back can s/he be expected to stand in order to gain perspective on something in which s/he is inextricably bound? For all its quirks, Shields' manifesto proposes a connectedness between the artist and the materiality of production that counteracts the movement to neophilia and abstraction rather than commitment and rootedness. This book will not offer anything as hubristic as an alternative way of reading the contemporary, and may look old-fashioned in many of its critical methodologies, but it will also not excuse its embedness in a cultural moment from which it cannot be excised. To consider oneself distinct enough from the present to be able to map and summarise it strikes me as problematic, but the need for meaning-making is as much an imperative of criticism as it is of the fiction it takes as its subject. As such, like any study in its vein, this book will be diagnostic in appearance and intent, and like any diagnosis it will look for patterns of symptoms that point to an underlying condition – or perhaps more appositely to a set of cohering topoi. But, if the work is diagnostic, it seeks to avoid prognosis that always implies the kind of teleology that I have queried in relation to formations such as post-postmodernism. Instead, and if we are to employ the progression metaphor, I offer a pause in the journey to explore in depth a number of points of interest along the way. This may or may not mean very much in the long term, but it will valorise a particular kind of looking without seeking to understand every brush stroke in the bigger picture. My approach is thus a mixture of depth-reading and stylistic and formal analysis that tries to draw some (not many) conclusions about some (not many) of the issues with which some (not many) contemporary British writers are preoccupied. Primarily my task has been to listen to resonances, to note correspondences, and to suggest contiguities. This will not build into a composite picture of contemporary British fiction, but it is not intended to and, in my opinion, cannot do so.

My aim in offering all these caveats is, in no way, to plead special circumstances for myself or for any critic of contemporary writing, but to interrogate in a roundabout way a point put forwards by Robert Eaglestone in his essay 'Contemporary Fiction in the Academy: Towards a Manifesto' (Eaglestone, 2013). Eaglestone argues that, though 'issues of literary judgement and value are now integral to the discipline of literary studies as problems[, ...] to express explicitly a value judgement in a formal setting – a journal article or a conference paper – is almost taboo' (Eaglestone, 2013: 1098). Where it might be nonsensical to claim that James Joyce is not a writer of world historical significance, the same cannot be said for David Mitchell, Zadie Smith, or indeed any of the writers contained in this book. It would be a brave critic who claimed world historical significance for any of these, but not to do so involves, as Eaglestone points out, an 'intellectual contortion' (Eaglestone, 2013: 1098). All academics working in contemporary literature make implicit and explicit judgements about the values (historical, formal, aesthetic, pedagogical) of the texts they ask their students to read, or on which they choose to write and publish papers. Yet there is always a self-imposed pressure to question those choices, or, at the very least, to emphasise the contingency of the selection and the validity of any alternative combination of texts, for we labour under the self-reflexive and democratising legacies of postmodernism, which make any such choices political, and thus potentially suspect.

An unwillingness to make value judgements is an understandable response to post-deconstructive literary studies – the infinite recession of questions about what would constitute value is usually deterrent enough – but it cannot help feeling like a rather perverse refusal of responsibility. Whether or not we are comfortable with it, academics are gatekeepers of social and cultural values, values understood outside the academy, I suspect, as a whole lot less fluid and negotiable than those of us in the profession would like to imagine. Estimations of literary worth are being made all the time, and in increasingly diverse contexts, leading Eaglestone to ask: 'what differentiates a geek or a journalist or member of a reading group from an academic?' (Eaglestone, 2013: 1090). Would it be entirely wrong to suggest that only the latter is intellectually conditioned to be unsure of her/his judgement? Unlike the others, the academic has a significant amount to lose in terms of reputation if her/his judgement proves to be misguided, underinformed – 'wrong'. Though the linguistic turn largely ghettoised the notion of 'getting it wrong', turning judgement into an exercise in relative comparison, such a fate haunts a book like this, which, with all its excuses, nails its colours to the mast by offering up Sarah Hall, Tom McCarthy, Jon McGregor, Andrew O'Hagan, and Ali Smith as contemporary voices from Britain that I believe have something worth listening to.

In the light of all that has been said above, what can this possibly mean? Firstly, and most importantly, this is not an attempt to project these writers as part of a twenty-first-century canon, even though that is undoubtedly what it might look like. To some extent that work has already begun – each of these writers has been nominated for the Man Booker Prize, and Sarah Hall (in 2013) and Andrew O'Hagan (in 2003) have been included in Granta's Best of British Novelists lists, which, whilst perhaps not as influential as they were, still have a significant cultural (and no doubt commercial) cachet. Smith is increasingly garnering a critical following, and essays on both McCarthy and McGregor have recently appeared in serious journals of contemporary criticism. Interestingly, when, in 2012, *Modern Fiction Studies* devoted a special issue to 'New British Fiction', four of the ten essays in the volume addressed McCarthy's work (O'Donnell, 2012). No doubt some form of canonical celebrity will attach itself to some of these writers in years to come, but the objective here is not to suggest that they are worth reading to the exclusion of other writers of serious literary fiction currently practising. Though it would have changed the critical pathos of the volume, those foregrounded here could have been replaced by any of Monica Ali, John Burnside, Rachel Cusk, Bernardine Evaristo, Michel Faber, Niall Griffiths, A.L. Kennedy, Hari Kunzru, Andrea Levy, David Mitchell, Helen Oyeyemi, David Peace, Will Self, Zadie Smith, Adam Thirlwell, Alan Warner, or Sarah Waters.

That said, it would be wrong to suggest that those addressed in the coming pages were the first out of the contemporary fiction bingo machine. Each has produced a significant body of work since the millennial turn, has maintained a consistent quality across her/his work, has written with depth and skill about the experience of living in the new century, and has, whilst largely working within a realist mode, sought to experiment with form and style in ways which unite the narrative explorations of the twentieth century with a twenty-first-century structure of feeling. Each has also been relatively free of the 'next big thing' tag that has attached itself to Monica Ali, David Mitchell, and Zadie Smith – although this may be changing for Tom McCarthy and Ali Smith. The dubious pressure that comes with what is effectively a marketing ploy taken up by those with cultural influence and ultimately embedded in the academy may make for neither unselfconsciously liberated fiction nor sound critical judgement, so, in identifying the authors for consideration here, I have selected those whose reputations have been, and are being, built less pyrotechnically. My critical judgement as to their posterity value might be no sounder, but I hope it has been only minimally influenced by publishers' hyperbole.

I have not striven for representativeness in my selection, a decision that has produced significant qualms of political conscience in terms of both ethnic and national exclusiveness. There are no Welsh or Northern Irish writers here just as there are no British Asian or Black British writers, but there is no sense in which I am seeking to vocalise a specifically white Anglo-Scottish range of issues, or privilege one version of Britishness over another. Britishness is largely used instead as a categorical frame for these writers, within which they function but with which they engage in non-direct ways. O'Hagan's fiction comes closest to a consideration of what Britishness might currently mean as he charts the birth pains of a devolved Scottish nation, and, whilst a notion of emplaced identity underpins the work of Hall and McGregor, it is expressed most commonly through their engagement less with the idea of the nation than with specific regions of England – Cumbria in Hall's case, the East Midlands in McGregor's. Smith I cast as the most universal of these writers, for, though Scotland features quite prominently in a number of her fictions, place tends to operate as a backdrop for the enactment of a domestic realism in which the contours of the self are mapped in shared, often private spaces. Smith is also aware that, in the age of the Internet, identity as a rooted, embodied, and conscious construction is one of many possible ways of being, and McCarthy's similar awareness leads him to dispense with the notion of identity as anything more than a cluster of bodily affects and external vectors in a networked, globalised age that renders the national obsolete.

The question might justifiably be asked as to whether, therefore, the concept of a specifically British fiction is a valuable focus or indeed a workable critical paradigm in the context of trans-cultural, globalised informational exchange. The rise in the popularity of world literatures written in English, allied to the avenues for trans-national discussion opened up by digital technologies, would seem to render the consideration of an exclusively British fiction wilfully narrow minded. Recent critical treatments of specifically British writing, such as Peter Childs' and James Green's *Aesthetics and Ethics in Twenty-First Century British Novels* (Childs and Green, 2013), tend to emphasise the flows and inheritances of empire as transforming the nation into a nodal point of culture in a global network rather than regarding it as a site of unilateral signification.[3] If such accounts reflect cosmopolitan shifts in British reading tastes – and the popularity of Chimamanda Ngozi Adichie, Roberto Bolaño, Yiyun Li, and Orhan Pamuk amongst others would certainly suggest that they do – then my focus on texts largely set in and about Britain, by white writers largely born and living within the British Isles (McGregor was born in Bermuda), may have the smack of provincialism, if not a phoney, retrograde nationalism.

However, as Tim Parks has argued in his collection of essays and journalism *Where I'm Reading From*, whilst the internationalisation of literary fiction, with the consequent soft modelling of a global canon, has the hallmarks of a utopian good, it can have the reverse effect of making national literatures appear parochial unless they engage with the geopolitics of the global community of readers. He quotes Bas Heijne, a Dutch essayist, as arguing that world literature 'invites us to see our own cultures as foreign and minor' and that writing that purposefully aims to speak to audiences across national boundaries renders us 'ever more self-referential and less genuinely engaged with any society' (Parks 2014: 64). It is an interesting counterargument to the idea of a global cultural convergence, and one made in similar terms by Emily Apter (2013), who resists the homogenising commodification of world literature on the grounds of untranslatability and language's resistance to cultural substitution. Parks argues that the profit principle still heavily influences the translation of literary fiction into English, and it might be argued that the opening up in 2013 of the Man Booker Prize to global writing in English – rather than writings solely from the British Isles and the Commonwealth – and the growing status of the Dublin IMPAC prize, whose nominations are assembled from public libraries around the world, reinforce the commercial impact of the novel, which can be culturally translated across borders but which may compromise contact with the traditions of its originating locale. Parks bemoans his own experience as a teacher of creative writing whose students want to write the novel of universal appeal and consequently mix Chinua Achebe with Primo Levi whilst knowing little of what connects Elizabeth Bowen, Anthony Powell, Barbara Pym, and Evelyn Waugh (Parks, 2014: 74).

The abundance of global literary endeavour (both translated and untranslated) demanding serious attention, allied to the marketability of the experience of globalisation as a literary theme, and the changing ways in which books are increasingly bought and consumed, has the impact of rendering all but a few of us poorly read. What Eric Gans (2007) calls the 'archive' of contemporary material that deserves consideration is so vast – and accelerating away from us with the mass digitisation of extant and previously out-of-print texts – that only the most robust spirit would not feel some degree of inadequacy that s/he had not read as widely as her/his conscience would demand. To write of the British novel in this context is, I suspect, to court criticism of being an outmoded and exclusionary cultural Luddite, unable or unwilling to keep abreast of the accelerating flows and rhizomatic extensions of trans-national cultural production. Of the second part of this accusation I would almost certainly be guilty, not as a deliberate failure of curiosity but rather as a consequence of the sublime too-muchness of my immediate being. Visits to bookstores or to Amazon's Borgesian library have increasingly been accompanied by an unsettling vertigo as the piles of books recommended by my browsing history or suggested by editorial teams – the books I feel (or am made to feel) that I should have read – build up mountainously around me, largely unread, and unreadable not only in my available time but also in more lifetimes than I have been granted. Add to this the wealth of periodicals, blogs, literary wikis and Web resources, journals (both disciplinary and interdisciplinary), tweets, reviews, opinion pieces, and email alerts, and the piles begin to teeter dangerously, threatening me with a Forsterian demise, or at least a paralysis of inadequacy.[4]

This effulgence is, in part, a historical consequence of the explosion of the Western canon in recent decades, which has decentred cultural hierarchies and legitimated narratives previously subjected to hegemonic silencing. However, when vigorous marketing policies on the part of publishers and the technological innovations that enabled digital transmission and consumption are added to the mix, it is clear that the experience of reading is changing rapidly and dramatically. In fact, the coincidence of theoretical, capitalistic, and technological imperatives on a global scale is a hallmark of twenty-first-century culture and has articulated the archival pressure in new ways.

Eaglestone points out that the problem with the contemporary archive is not simply quantitative; it is rather a matter of its openness. Where the Victorianist may deal with a relatively circumscribed set of primary materials, open to new discoveries and rereadings, the contemporary scholar has no delimited base of pre-filtered resources on which s/he can judge with any degree of certainty because the archive is continuously being refreshed with new matter. Moreover, these additions demand the constant review of existing material because 'every new work of art changes the relations of all the past ones' (Eaglestone, 2013: 1095). Of course, this is true of all frames of literary study, but one problem that faces the contemporary researcher in particular is the provisionality of reaching critical opinions on writers who need to be revisited with each subsequent publication. Over the course of writing this book, all the novelists have produced further work that has required frequent rethinking and redrafting in the certain knowledge that, at whatever point its reader opens it, it is likely to be obsolete. Such is the self-evident nature of a field that gains in dynamism what it sacrifices in hindsight.

Andrew Hoberek (2007) introduces a different dimension to this problem by exploring the ways that qualitative judgements of post-postmodernist texts (to employ his term) are confused by the increasingly prevalent intermingling of genre and literary fiction. This results, he believes, from the symbiotic infusion of genres such as the graphic novel and fantasy into the mainstream as a result of the greater value ascribed to popular culture by postmodernism's anti-hierarchicalism, but it is augmented by the increasing number of literary figures producing genre titles. Hoberek focuses primarily on American exponents of this latter phenomenon, such as Michael Chabon and Jonathan Lethem, but a comparable list of British examples would include Iain Banks, Andrew Crumey, Bernardine Evaristo, Neil Gaiman, Steven Hall, China Miéville, Courttia Newland, David Peace, Christopher Priest, Sam Taylor, and Sarah Waters. A correlate in the world of crime fiction would be seen in the (barely) pseudonymous work of John Banville as Benjamin Black, and previously of Julian Barnes as Dan Kavanagh.[5] Though the effect on contemporary fiction has been democratising, acknowledging the porosity between forms and highlighting the anachronism of vertical definitions of high and low literature, it is difficult to disentangle the aesthetic drivers of this phenomenon from the pressures of a multi-platform commercial market in which competition has produced a flattening of style associated for some with the uniformity of middlebrow realism.

Hanif Kureishi, Tom McCarthy, and Will Self have all vocally criticised what they see as the draw towards mainstream conventionality that the middlebrow represents: the 'jolly good read, with a beginning, a middle and an end, and sympathetic characters that they [the reader] can identify with', as Self (2012) describes it.[6] The middlebrow still represents for them, as it did for Dwight Macdonald in 1960, an artistic inauthenticity that pretends 'to respect the standards of High Culture while in fact it waters them down and vulgarizes them' (in Mallon, 2014). Though the term has undergone some degree of reclamation in recent years, and has become capacious enough to include many that would see themselves as practitioners of literary fiction, it still retains a cultural odour that marks it as formally conservative and intellectually undemanding.[7] Kureishi, McCarthy, and Self identify the middlebrow with a particular brand of lifeless writing that has emerged through the increasing popularity of institutional creative writing courses, which, in their opinion, spin money for those institutions whilst producing a 'naïve and uncritical realism' and the kind of write-what-you-know mantra that passes for a 'doctrine of authenticity' (McCarthy, 2014a: 21).

Kureishi's estimate that 99.9 percent of his students are untalented is surely a little unfair, but Self's point about the model for teaching creative writing no doubt has some validity: 'Perhaps you can take a mediocre novelist and make them into a slightly better one, but a course can't make someone into a good writer. Ian McEwan and Kazuo Ishiguro both did the UEA (University of East Anglia) MA, but they were both innately good anyway' (Self, 2012). Of course, practising writers such as these – all of whom have at points been paid for their expertise by universities or institutions – would say this. They are conscious of their public profile and the precious vulnerability of their market traction, but the broader point that their spikiness reveals so strikingly is the concern that there is now a concentration in the middle ground of diverse writing communities which might previously have been more decisively and hierarchically stratified. The cross-writing by established literary novelists that Hoberek identifies exerts a downwards pressure, whilst the professionalisation of amateur writers in an era of online forums, self-publication, and self-marketisation exerts a countervailing pressure upwards, producing a crowded and ever more competitive middle ground across which it is difficult to navigate with any degree of certainty with regard to quality and durability. In this situation the archive of contemporary fiction becomes ever more uncategorisable, for how is it any longer possible to make the kinds of distinction between literary and non-literary value in a band of horizontally spreading cultural products that maximise their market appeal through a narrow set of universal themes (loss, exile, memory, community) and well-crafted but unchallenging aesthetics?

This is, to a degree, an exaggeration, but the place of the serious social novel, or the novel of ambitious formal experiment, has become, in the context of this broader and flatter literary landscape, uncertain and precarious. The artful novel that challenges traditional formal conventions has always been marginalised in British letters, but it has become increasingly so in recent decades, and particularly within the generation of emerging writers that are succeeding Salman Rushdie and Jeanette Winterson. The direct inheritors of Anthony Burgess, Angela Carter, John Fowles, and Ann Quin are few, though those authors' influences are legion, and it is perhaps not insignificant that a figure such as B.S. Johnson has undergone a serious revival in literary criticism in recent years. Retrospection throws the present into perspective, and the current interest in the flowering of experimentation that followed the *nouveau roman* indicates a lack of comparable contemporary material and/or a critical wariness about the originality of what there is. Whilst Will Self's *Umbrella* (2012) and its follow-up *Shark* (2014) represent attempts to extrapolate modernist techniques into a consideration of consciousness across the long twentieth century, and the manipulations of narrative structure in David Mitchell's early works (particularly *Ghostwritten* [1999] and *Cloud Atlas* [2004]) display the legacy of postmodernist forebears, British fiction in the twenty-first century has not been characterised by a strong willingness to 'make it new'. Indeed Mitchell and, to some extent, Self have become recognisable figures of a contemporary literary establishment rather than outliers of radical deconstruction, their work fast becoming staple fixtures of teaching and critical canons. Lee Rourke (2008) – whose own novel *The Canal* (2010) is an intriguing study of existential boredom – believes that literary avant-gardism now sits more comfortably in the world of conceptual art than with publishers concerned primarily with their bottom line, and certainly imprints such as Book Works' Semina, which has produced the work of Stewart Home, and Metronome Press, through which McCarthy published his first novel, *Remainder* (2005), represent rare outlets for the kind of crossover publications that would likely be shunned by more mainstream presses.

What the above suggests is that, although a taste for the avant-garde remains in contemporary fiction, it has been subject to processes of commodification that have drawn all but its wilder incarnations beneath the umbrella of the commercial and the middlebrow. The effect of this has been to further blur the visible stratification of cultural production, eroding distinctions between high and low, conventional and radical, literary and generic in ways which make the determination of a contemporary structure of literary feeling difficult to isolate. Timotheus Vermeulen and Robin van den Akker elucidate this to some extent through their notion of metamodernism, which they conceive as an oscillation between modernist and postmodernist concerns with neither surpassed nor dominant. As a consequence, they regard the co-presence of sincerity and irony as two perfectly plausible orientations for a culture that gravitates between 'hope and melancholy, between naïveté and knowingness, empathy and apathy, unity and plurality, totality and fragmentation, purity and ambiguity' (Vermeulen and Van den Akker, 2010: 6) without settling on one co-ordinate. Whilst I do not expressly wish to privilege any critical position that I have previously questioned, metamodernism offers a helpful means of explaining the way that postmodern strategies of pastiche, parody, anti-teleology, ontological playfulness, and anti-hierarchicalism have become embedded in the everyday discourses of Western-oriented representation. Once the radical becomes enfolded within the popular in the way that irony has become the intellectual touchstone for a generation of consumers encouraged to fashion *ex nihilo* subjectivities, it becomes unremarkable and customised. But, as Vermeulen and Van den Akker suggest – and as Zygmunt Bauman (2000) has amply demonstrated through his work on 'liquid modernity' – this is not a fixed pole through which new identities can be sedimented but rather a temporary stop in the oscillation between equally valid, but seemingly contradictory, formations. By this token, the twenty-first-century reader can comfortably regard a work of fiction with cynicism *and* credulity, outrage *and* ennui, optimism *and* despair without needing either a cohering sentimental narrative, or any balance between these states.

How might this continuous condition of inbetweenness assist us in our reading of contemporary fiction? The dynamic of oscillation that characterises the metamodern depends not on regularity or counterbalancing pendulum swings but on competing forces of attraction that draw away the affective force before it settles, and it seems to me that there is a corollary here with the drag of the middle ground, which pulls together the literary and the generic, the avant-garde and the conventional, and the cynical and the sentimental, producing not a static or homogenous mass but an unpredictable, amorphous zone that speaks to a contemporary condition as 'both-neither' (Vermeulen and Van den Akker, 2010: 6). How this manifests in practical terms is evident in the fact that Mitchell's *Cloud Atlas* can be simultaneously radical *and* conventional, David Peace's 'Red Riding Quartet' can be both literary *and* crime fiction, Gordon Burn's non-fictional novel *Born Yesterday* (2008) can be both narrative success *and* failure, and W.G. Sebald's writing can flow seamlessly across history, fiction, memoir, art history, and photographic collage. It is also the reason why the recent fashion for Shields' 'lyrical essay' has quickly gained credibility in the work of writers such as Ben Lerner (*Leaving the Atocha Station* [2011] and *10:04* [2014]), Karl Ove Knausgård (*My Struggle* [2009–2011]), and Shields himself (*The Thing about Life Is that One Day You'll Be Dead* [2008] and *How Literature Saved My Life* [2013]). All these texts exhibit qualities of the 'both' and 'neither' that cannot be separated and that gain their dynamism from the tension that follows their juxtaposition.

The novelists contained in this volume display this oscillation to a degree, and, whilst I would not go so far as to suggest the metamodern as a cohering thread, there are good reasons for reading many of these works within its spirit of indeterminacy. It is, for instance, discernible in how Ali Smith continuously exploits the instability of language and the deferral of fixity and yet never once abandons the idea of love as an irreducible absolute. It is there in Tom McCarthy's philosophical appropriations from Blanchot, De Man, and Derrida to deconstruct the Tintin books by Hergé – the intentionality is thoroughly serious and comic, not in the sense of pastiche that might be levelled at Frederic Tuten's speculative fiction *Tintin in the New World* (1993) but as a thoroughly committed engagement that is nonetheless conscious of, and content with, its ironic effect. It is also there in McCarthy's willingness to use the *Bildungsroman* with all its subjectivising baggage in *C* whilst constructing a central protagonist that can be described as a character only in the most generic sense. The two are not incompatible for all their contradictoriness, and such is the case too in Sarah Hall's dialectic of humanity and nature. For her, the forces that demand a distinction between human beings and the world they inhabit are always weaker than the forces that join them. Hall's fiction may vocalise a Romantic sensibility, but it is always paired with the consciousness of environmental catastrophe that haunts the twenty-first century. Other examples suggest themselves in the work of O'Hagan and McGregor, but, without labouring the point, it is clear that the material under review here exhibits an interesting set of extensions on existing representational tropes and methods. It would be wrong to identify these as new developments or radical departures from the fiction of the 1980s and 1990s – all such periodising breaks tend to function as critical shorthand – but there does seem to be a constellation of contiguous concerns that is prompting the need for sensitive critical mapping.

If the acceptance of a both–neither ontology is liberating in one sense, it is disabling in another, for, as Peter Boxall argues, the literature of the post-millennium is preoccupied by a sense of indeterminacy, where 'late time' transitions to an, as yet, unshaped understanding of temporality:

> The turn of the millennium is figured, time and again, and in a wide range of different fictional and theoretical forms, as the calendrically convenient bridge between these opposite historical conditions, as if the passage from one century to the next doubles as a transition from old to new, from the last world historical order to one as yet unimagined. (Boxall, 2012: 682)

Boxall believes the millennial turn was seen as a symbolic moment of passing in which the concerns of the late twentieth century, associated with entropy and demise, gave way to the new century's embryonic enthusiasm, which has nevertheless been characterised by a historical disorientation as writers struggle to 'work out how to respond to a time that seems suddenly recalibrated' (Boxall, 2012: 698). The break with the historical past was violently realised on 9/11, an event that Boxall believes, along with mass uptake of informational technologies, marks the twenty-first century's break with the temporal succession, forcing space and time into new relationships that map confusingly onto new global political realities. This historical split with the past is to a large extent notional, but is no less significant for that, as it instantiates the formation of a specifically twenty-first-century cultural mood associated by Bauman (2000) with the liquefaction under hyper-technologised consumer capitalism of modernity's solid structures of subjectivity, nation, and industry. Liquid life dispenses with the burdens of consensus and moral duty to the other in favour of individualised, monadic needs that can be fulfilled only through the mechanisms of capital and that are understood through the same narratives of precarity and flexibility that dominate financial markets. Self, Bauman argues, is the commodity with which we bargain in the twenty-first century, and marketisation, or self-branding, must be as incessant and uncompromising as the 24/7 temporality that has come to dominate the contemporary episteme.[8]

One of the effects of this syncing of identity with the organising structures of a sleepless capitalism is exactly the spatio-temporal disorientation that Boxall identifies. Stripped of the rooting influences of solid modernity, and inexorably embedded within the exponential acceleration of technological hypertrophy, the individual reaches 'escape velocity from the gravitational pull of any grounding in reality of history such that we are left floating in weight-less, directionless space' (Luckhurst and Marks, 1999: 2). In this non-space of 'unbounded, timeless intensity' (Virilio, 1991: 15), the co-ordinates that govern embodied, material, human life become increasingly speculative, sub-ordinated to the few sense-making narratives that are available to us, narra-tives that are increasingly anti-humanist and homogenising.

*   *   *

The purpose of this introduction has thus far been to give an overview of some of the challenges facing the critic of contemporary British fiction, rather than a directive roadmap for interpreting the work of the writers whom I have selected for study. To attempt the latter would, I feel, vali-date a cohesive and specious paradigm of contemporary British fiction that it would be pointless to either seek to extrapolate across a wider group of writers in early-to-mid career or to weave through the amorphousness of the contemporary. Rather I restrict my readings to a circumscribed set of practising novelists to identify their personal responses to the contemporary moment and to seek commonalities and undertows which may be in the process of solidifying into cultural tropes and to which it may be fruitful to return in future years. Looking across these writers, there are certainly shared concerns, and in what remains of this introduction I will briefly out-line three that appear to me particularly resonant: materiality, connectivity, and authenticity. These are intended as little more than prompts, but hope-fully they reveal common strains.

Materiality

Interpreted in the broadest sense of the relationships between the physi-cal stuff of the world and the individuals with whom it comes into contact, materiality is a strikingly recurrent concern of these novelists. This is perhaps most evidently articulated in response to the liquefaction and virtualisation of social relations that has rendered the physical dimension so abstract in the digital age. On what levels of communication does the physical heft of touch operate in a world where interaction is increasingly mediated by technol-ogy? For the homeless protagonist of Ali Smith's *Hotel World* (2001) and the drug addicts of Jon McGregor's *Even the Dogs* (2010) physical contact with another human being has become so rare, so overlain with aggression, that the act of being touched with kindness is experienced as an electrifying reminder of their own physical tangibility. Where their marginal status in the social realm is pressed upon them by their exclusion from the material economies of transaction and bureaucracy, a more profound separation from a sense of humanness is effected through the physical and moral disgust that they engender in others. They are visible only when they correspond with the orderliness of capital, to the extent that Smith's Else sucks filthy discarded coins to give herself a (literal) taste of normality. Material embodiment exists for them, as it does for O'Hagan's missing characters, such as Maria Tambini in *Personality* (2003), only in the fleeting moments of visibility, the recognition by others not just of their presence but also of their needs. Maria, a fictionalised version of the teenage performer Lena Zavaroni, literally fades from view as the anorexia sparked by the anxiety of her celebrity status consumes her self-confidence as swiftly as it eats away much of her body. She becomes a shadow in her own story, increasingly spoken for by those who manipulate her talent for their own gain, eerily reminiscent of Kafka's hunger artist and of the revenant fresco painter of Smith's *How To Be Both* (2014), who has had to erase her gender identity to ensure that her art is accepted in fifteenth-century Italy.

Ghosts populate Smith's work, just as the missing flit through O'Hagan's, and the excentric haunt the margins of McGregor's provincial settings; they are manifestations of immateriality totally in consonance with a vision of the physical world that seems increasingly incorporeal. If reality has receded behind the computer screen, always happening elsewhere amongst the networks and matrices of global connectivity, the embodied observer, tied to place and time, is rendered insubstantial by comparison. Sarah Hall's *How to Paint a Dead Man* (2009) employs an apt metaphor to convey this: its grief-stricken protagonist sits in a darkened room in front of a flickering screen surfing through alarmingly obscene material in a desperate and fruitless search for something sufficiently visceral to connect her to her body. This is paralleled in the inherent irony with which the Internet is mislabelled the 'Intimate' in Smith's *There But For The* (2011) and in the way in which the trace residues in the Turin Shroud form a negative imprint of a human body so impalpable in comparison with the webpages describing it that McCarthy's narrator navigates at the start of *Satin Island* (2015). In all these examples, being-in-the-world is subordinated to the artificial, vicarious experience of a dematerialised and mediated reality with which the characters have only the most tangential relationship.

For all this, and as a response to the virtualisation of reality, the physical world makes its presence felt in contemporary fiction through a brutality and unmalleability that resists the weightlessness of the Internet. When Miles occupies a room in his dinner host's house without explanation in *There But*

For The; when Peter Caldicutt's leg is trapped overnight on the moors by a fallen rock in *How to Paint a Dead Man*; when the ground rushes to meet the parachutists in *Satin Island*; or when Major Scullion's legs are blown off in a skirmish in Afghanistan in O'Hagan's *The Illuminations* (2015), the brute physicality of the material world reasserts itself as a reminder that stuff cannot be outmanoeuvred completely; the 'real' real is non-negotiable. The return of the real has been heralded in contemporary theories of aesthetics – notably by Hal Foster (1996) and Catherine Belsey (2004) – and has seen a limited renaissance in contemporary fiction in Britain with Niall Griffith's *Sheepshagger* (2001), Ross Raisin's *God's Own Country* (2008), and Evie Wyld's *All the Birds, Singing* (2013) being notable examples of where the overpowering realness of the natural threatens human control. Sarah Hall's work particularly highlights this now uneasy relationship between the human being and nature, one in which archaic forces can be contained (*Haweswater* [2002]) but cannot be controlled (*The Wolf Border* [2015]). For all their pretensions, human beings are part of the materiality of the world they strive to dominate and are consequently intuitively and intellectually married to its survival. The virtual dimension does not, she reminds us, fully clean the dirt from beneath our fingernails. And this responsibility to acknowledge the familial proximity of immediate, local quiddity of material life comes across repeatedly in the fiction under review here. For all the abstraction of social relations that the twenty-first century delivers us, the necessity of the well-intentioned hand on the imperfect body of another is never diminished.

Connectivity

That hand is placed on the body of Eleanor at the conclusion of McGregor's *So Many Ways to Begin* (2006). It is the affecting culmination of a life of disappointments where the connections between people, places, and things have come under considerable but unspectacular strain. McGregor's carefully calibrated emotional scenes always present duty and desire in a balance that verges on collapse but is held together by the threads of empathic connection. These might be the threads that spread out over the city in *If Nobody Speaks of Remarkable Things*, holding all the diverse and lonely inhabitants in a common web, or the thread that follows the decrepit body of alcoholic Robert from flat to morgue, to autopsy slab, to coroner's court in *Even the Dogs*. McGregor's fiction highlights the unregarded connectivity that underlies an atomised, individualistic age, reminding his reader of the duty of care that comes with humanness. It is a duty expressed even more fervidly by Ali Smith, whose fiction is replete with instances of disconnection: the lovers separated by missed train connections, disrupted phone calls, door-slamming arguments about the trivial and serious alike, all ultimately shaped within the interrupted duologues that constitute relationships. Much of Smith's writing has a very straightforward question at its heart: how does one human being ever understand another? The answers are, however, far from straightforward, and over the course of her writing career she has sought to wrestle into words the contradictory impulses that dictate connection with the other. Informing her work, though, is the conviction that knowing the other demands and deserves commitment and stamina – connectedness is the equivalent of a lifelong contract signed without reading.

This unnegotiable duty viscerally reminds readers that the technologically ascendant episteme may throw humanness into a new relief but does not negate it. Anti-humanist fictions, such as those of McCarthy, may increasingly regard the individual as a function of *techne* – a node in the contemporary discourse network – but, on the evidence of the fiction considered here, portraying the ethical dimension of intersubjective connection remains the dominant purpose of the novel. Granted, the meaning, value, and affective impact of that connection is obscured by the liquefaction of social relations in late capitalism where patterns of predictable praxis orient libidinal desires, but the need for a worthwhile and profound set of relationships with others is not diminished. The problem that afflicts so many of the protagonists of these fictions is their ignorance of what shape and flavour those relationships should take. From McCarthy's ciphers, unsure about whether cynicism is any longer a worthy aesthetic value, through O'Hagan's celebrities, lost in the hall of mirrors generated by their simulcast personae, to Hall's misfits, who throw themselves into relationships with the land to escape the depthless fissures of sociality, these fictions present characters in search of meaningful shells that they can inhabit and from which they can negotiate the complexities of the world. The dissolution of fixed subject positions under the pressure of globalised consumer capitalism is reflected in a contemporary dramatis personae characterised by uncertainty, precariousness, provisionality, and, unsurprisingly, anxiety.

In search of a rootedness in which they have little conviction, many of these protagonists enact the performance of self through the Internet's architecture of connectivity. The reassuring safety-net connotations of the Web's metaphor, its numinous promise of answers to undreamt questions, belies its limitations as a tool of connection, for, as Mark discovers in Ali Smith's *There But For The*, the Internet's charm is also 'a kind of deception about a whole new way of feeling lonely, a semblance of plenitude but really a new level of Dante's inferno, a zombie-filled cemetery of spurious clues, beauty, pathos, pain, the faces of puppies, women and men from all over the world tied up and wanked over in site after site, a great sea of hidden shallows' (Smith, 2012a: 159). For U, the narrator of McCarthy's *Satin Island*, the Internet is the answer to all his questions without being the means by which he can connect those questions into an epistemological mainframe. He works for a mysterious boss whose crowning virtue is his ability to persuade others that they are connected. Connected to what is never elucidated, but for U the specifics are less significant than the experience of being connected 'to a world of action and event, a world in which stuff might actually *happen*; connected [...] to our own age' (McCarthy, 2015: 41). On the one hand, then, connection is a powerful metaphor for a contemporary sensibility of opportunity, liberality, anti-hierarchicalism, and interdependence, but on the other hand it is also chimerical, superficial, and mendacious, a promise of return that delivers only the most generic answers to the most specific questions. It is no surprise that Sarah Hall's protagonist in *How to Paint a Dead Man* undoes herself not with Internet pornography but with a reckless sexual affair where the smell and taste of the other are at least tangible.

Authenticity

Related to the previous concerns, authenticity features most strikingly in contemporary fiction in the question of what the real can any longer connote in a period not only of image saturation but also of widespread sophistication in the reading of the simulacrum's artificiality. In his 2002 novel *Dorian: An Imitation*, Will Self crowns a discussion of the inauthenticity of the post-theory age with the line 'not everyone knows fuck all about Foucault' (Self, 2002: 213), an acknowledgement that the radicalism of deconstructionist social anthropology had found an (albeit limited) place, by century's end, within the cultural mainstream. If the endless regurgitation of cultural production has become a discursive commonplace in the twenty-first century – as the omnipresence of remixes, mashups, and recombinants would suggest – then the notion of the authentic as a point of deep origination should be fast losing its relevance as a marker of value. Yet, on the evidence of the authors considered here, and many more not covered by this volume, authenticity is a significant concern of twenty-first-century writing, not just as a point of flight but also as a credible point of return.[9]

Authenticity tends to carry with it a nostalgia for an unspecified and inchoate wholeness rooted in an archaic and simpler conception of the real, but the way in which it tends to feature in my selection of writers is as a form of mythical precondition that has no place in truth but that nonetheless exerts a formidable idealism. The knowing inauthenticity of postmodernism's self-reflexivity has produced a sedimentation of ironies (deliberate and circumstantial) with which the twenty-first century is grappling to discern a model of authenticity that is both self-conscious *and* natural. This delving through layers is evident in a novel such as O'Hagan's *The Life and Opinions of Maf the Dog, and of His Friend Marilyn Monroe* (2010), where the last three years of Monroe's life are played out through the narration of her Maltese terrier, himself channelling Tristram Shandy. O'Hagan's Monroe, like his Lena Zavaroni, is trapped within the spectacle of the character she performs, knowingly producing a false universe around herself and yet convinced that beneath her confection lies a woman of authentic substance that the outside world will not stomach. O'Hagan layers one reflecting narrative surface on top of another, crushing Monroe beneath the weight of her own simulacra but at the same time, elevating her death to the status of quintessential late twentieth-century spectacular tragedy, and thereby rescuing her from the accusation of complete inauthenticity.

Similarly, the Smart family in Ali Smith's *The Accidental* (2006) are beset by layers of middle-class affluence that render their engagement with the world detached, automatic, and, to employ Astrid's term 'sub-standard'. She is only comfortable viewing the world through the lens of her expensive camera, bought for her as a sop by her guilt-filled parents each concentrating on their own self-immurements. Her mother, at work on a children's historical book series entitled 'The Genuine Article', is anything but, whilst her father seduces his university students with the Eliotian mantra of impersonality. All are trapped by their individual and several inauthenticities until the mysterious arrival of Amber, who variously drags and cajoles the family into enlightenment. The Smarts typify a late-century ennui that has absorbed and validated postmodern cynicism and cannot, when the irony has worn thin, find anything to take its place. Authenticity is forced upon them through Amber's interventions – she confiscates and destroys Astrid's camera, for instance – and they are repurposed through hardship into agents of moral action. Interestingly, as in many of Smith's narratives, it is intercession rather than epiphany that initiates the learning process, but this confirms the embeddedness, the sedimentation of inauthenticity as a contemporary mode of being. At play, however, is not the existentialist question of whether or not inauthenticity represents a flight from an exigent authentic, because, as represented here and in other texts, authenticity is a viable option only as an abstract ideal that can be recreated but never created.

Such is certainly the case in Tom McCarthy's *Remainder*, the most extensive treatment of authenticity that we will encounter. For the novel's narrator, injured in a freak accident, putting his life back together involves a stringent determination to reconstruct his experience of the world authentically – authentic not to a pre-existent actuality but to an idealised reality that can be inhabited seamlessly, and without thought. Imagining and then actualising his world in intimate detail allows the narrator to avoid the 'detour that sweeps us around what's fundamental to events, preventing us from touching their core' (McCarthy, 2007: 244), but, as his mania for recreating and controlling the external world grows in both detail and scope, he experiences the infinite recession of authenticity beyond the reach of materiality. The novel concludes with a botched bank-heist recreation that is transformed into a genuine robbery, completely eliding the space between authentic and inauthentic. Unlike O'Hagan and Smith, McCarthy rejects the sentimental narrative of authenticity. For him it is part of the carapace of a suspicious humanism that celebrates integration and development over dispersal and repetition. O'Hagan and Smith may be sceptical about what authenticity might resemble in the contemporary moment, and both recognise that it is probably indistinguishable from its negative, but neither dismisses the value of the authentic as a horizon of subjectification. Where McCarthy sees the authentic as another version of the inauthentic, both O'Hagan and Smith retain a romantic belief in the overcoming of the inauthentic and the consequent restitution of the genuine, if impalpable, article.

*   *   *

These three areas are not intended to highlight a rigid structural or methodological model for what follows; they are, at best, stones dropped in the waters of contemporary fiction, whose ripples cut through many of these texts and many more not covered here. Nevertheless, they represent notable vectors of interest that flow across mediums and forms in contemporary culture and that may assist in determining to some extent the structure of feeling that underpins the present age. Working with such a limited range of writers in such a prescribed historical frame is likely to produce a thesaurus of related concerns which it would be foolish to denote the 'spirit of the age', but it would be equally foolish to dismiss as random the persistence of such concerns. In the readings that follow, these issues occur repeatedly, but so do many others, and I have not striven to offer an inclusive critical architecture that privileges or precludes countervailing discussion. I have, rather, tried to make sense – albeit heuristically – of what is an increasingly theoretically over-determined field. That, I acknowledge, has produced largely liberal readings of liberal books but has, I hope, gone some way to fulfil Hoggart's prescription. Embedded as contemporary critical readers are within the cultural mindset on which they comment, lack of perspective is an inevitable by-product, but there is something to be gained – and learnt – from being in the presence of a collection of authors and their texts without succumbing to the compulsion to take too many steps backwards.

Notes

1 For digimodernism see Kirby, 2009; for altermodernism see Bourriaud, 2009; for hypermodernism see Lipovetsky and Charles, 2005; for metamodernism see Vermeulen and Van den Akker, 2010; for exomodernism see McGurl, 2011; for post-postmodernism see Nealon, 2012. Not to mention cosmodernism, performatism, postpositivist realism and the New Sincerity, for which see Konstantinou, 2013.

2 David James' work is a notable exception in this regard. His recent studies in the legacies of modernism have re-examined modernist experimentation in contemporary writing. See James, 2012a and 2012b.

3 Childs and Green focus in particular on the work of Nadeem Aslam, Hari Kunzru, David Mitchell, and Zadie Smith.

4 Nielsen Book records that 133,224 books of all genres were published in the UK in 2009, which according to the *Guardian* had increased by 2013 to 184,000. See www. nielsenbookdata.co.uk/uploads/press/NielsenBook_BookProductionFigures3_Jan2010.pdf; Flood, 2014b.

5 This is, of course, not solely a feature of the contemporary period. Graham Greene and Anthony Burgess are two notable twentieth-century examples of those who have crossed genre, both experimenting with the spy novel – *The Quiet American* (1955) in Greene's case, *Tremor of Intent* (1966) in Burgess'. Ian McEwan followed their lead with *The Innocent* (1990), a Le Carré-inflected thriller set in Cold War Berlin.

6 See also Flood, 2014; McCarthy, 2014a.

7 See Brown and Grover 2011; Driscoll, 2014; Edmondson, 2010.

8 John Crary's *24/7* explores this acceleration in the context of its effects on sleep patterns. He argues that the advent of online commerce has removed the barrier to 24-hour consumption that had been enforced by regulations on shop trading hours, creating a situation in which there is no single point in time when one could not be consuming. One effect cited by him is the reduction in average sleep for a North American from ten hours in the early twentieth century to six and a half hours in the early twenty-first (Crary, 2013: 11).

9 See for instance the work of Rachel Cusk, Steven Hall, Ben Lerner, and Joseph O'Neill. See also Lea, 2012a.

1

Ali Smith

If one were to describe the writing of Ali Smith in a word, it would probably be 'but'. Though this might seem an inelegant and reductive way of summing up the playfully carnivalesque work of Smith, the contingency of 'but' encapsulates a stand-out quality of her fiction that might be termed 'conjunctional'. Smith's novels and short stories are always concerned with the pivots that balance alternative perspectives and worldviews, and gain their richness from the divergence from singularity that is implied by 'but-ness'. If what precedes the 'but' is a forceful statement of subjective point of view, that which succeeds it brings depth and polyvocality and, crucially for Smith, opens up the creative possibilities of ambiguity. As one of the main characters in her 2011 novel *There But For The* comments: 'the thing I particularly like about the word "but" [...] is that it always takes you off to the side, and where it takes you is always interesting' (Smith, 2012a: 175).[1] Being taken off to the side, detoured, disoriented, or derailed are adventures to which the reader of Smith must get accustomed, for her style, though often directly personal in its address, is characterised by a quirky roundaboutness that demands a continuous openness to others' ways of seeing the world. That those ways often embrace the voices of children, outsiders, the dead, or inanimate objects points us back to the liminality of the 'but', which sits between, conjoining disparate stories and forging difference into a grammatical coherence. As the title of one of her collections of stories suggests, our narratives are always, and never, whole.

Smith's first collection of stories, *Free Love*, was published in 1995, and, over the course of three further collections (*Other Stories and Other Stories* [1999], *The Whole Story and Other Stories* [2003], and *The First Person and Other Stories* [2008]) and six novels (*Like* [1997], *Hotel World* [2001], *The Accidental* [2005], *Girl Meets Boy* [2007], *There But For The* [2011], and *How To Be Both* [2014]), she has established a reputation for narratives of wit, perception, and vocal virtuosity. Stylistically her writing embraces fragmentation and multi-perspectivalism to reflect the crumbling of singular, authoritarian voices in contemporary discourses. Her narratives are filled with contrasting points of view, invoked in a restless marriage of difference and competitiveness, each seeking the privilege of primacy. These voices explain the world as it appears to them, but none are allowed the satisfaction of authoring the truths of others' experience. Instead Smith relishes the argumentative grist of another's perspective, queering the singular with the plural. Her novels and many of her stories tend to be constructed as duologues or multilogues, with characters' differing versions of the world built around shared events or experiences. The real point of interest is not the victory of one voice, though that is often how her characters understand it, but the profusion of various registers, *paroles*, tones, vocabularies, accents, and pitches that feed into the ambiguity inherent in speech and communication.

The ways in which human beings fail, or refuse, to understand the other have been a consistent concern of Smith, but undercutting this antagonism is the recognition that such difference is the grounding for positive human experiences such as love, empathy, and duty. Limitation and liberation are conjoined in Smith's writing, as is evident in narratives which sweep from the sublime to the banal, the bombastic to the bathetic, and the formal to the ludic. Smith's writing is thus characterised by that balance that I am calling 'conjunctional'; her narratives are often heartbreakingly tender in their treatment of loving relationships and yet frank in their acknowledgement of the losses that intimacy brings with it. Equally, they are resonant with a melancholic pain at the lost potential of unlived opportunities, but rambunctiously chaotic and untrammelled in their optimism and invention. In short, there are always at least two sides to any Ali Smith story.

Given that Smith is a writer that situates polyvocality at the heart of her politics and aesthetic, and one that critiques the lifelessness of contemporary literary theory, it is ironic that the academic response to her work has chosen to interpellate her through critical tropes that emphasise her discursive limits. To critics, she is notable largely for her lesbianism, her feminism, and her Scottishness, all tried and trusted anchors for current identity debates and yet all equally limiting to readings of Smith's work, which stand outside the politics of otherness. Her nationality is a case in point. A significant portion of writing about her work has so far been published in anthologies of essays and criticism of Scottish writing (Germanà, 2012; Lumsden, 2000; Murray, 2006; Williams, 2006), which not only identifies her explicitly with her national concerns but also privileges a particular kind of reading of her politics. Smith is frequently bracketed with those who espouse the kind of Scottish identity that loudly asserts its opposition to Englishness and metropolitanism, and yet her fiction sits uncomfortably within such a frame. Whilst Scotland features as a geographical setting in a number of her novels and stories, it is rarely the direct subject of her writing, nor the political driver for her poetic vision. Smith's wrestling with the human consequences of otherness thus becomes overshadowed by her own otherness in a way that hinders consideration of the significance of her voice within contemporary writing.

The short stories

Smith's stories display an acute awareness of the pain of individual loneliness and the cost that is involved in combatting that existential emptiness by placing other people and other things in our lives. From *Free Love* onwards, she has portrayed the emotional and moral difficulties of connecting with an other and has repeatedly emphasised the fragility of understanding that overshadows even the strongest and most intimate of human bonds. The voices that emerge from her stories are often conflicted, fearful, melancholic, and in thrall to the hurtful memories that have defined and limited them. Yet, at the same time, these voices are also often hopeful, daring, altruistic, and open to the possibilities of transformation that being touched by the other can bring. Finding momentary common ground with a would-be combatant, or sharing the unspeakable sadness of another's life through wordless physical contact, infuses Smith's stories with a humane acceptance of life's trials and guarantees the existence of meaningful depth. Smith's vision is thus precariously balanced between pessimism and optimism: pessimistic that the price of being in the world will be too high, but optimistic that the moments of transcendent connection and empathy will compensate for the erosive action of subjectivity. Like her longer fiction, some of the stories critique the nature of individualism in a contemporary world where intimacy has given way to solipsism, but often they address more universal concerns with love and its failure, death, the search for meaning, the human compulsion to tell stories, and – encompassing all of these – the problems of connecting with other human beings.

This issue is both a thematic and formal one for Smith, as she regards the short story as a quintessentially dramatic form that reveals the synaptic flash of connection in its structural demands. In an interview on the short story with her friend Kasia Boddy, she repeatedly emphasises brevity as a moral component of the form, stressing that short fiction creates an interrogative space between connection and disconnection both in its structure and its expectation of characters:

there is always an answering back and that answering back is really exciting. [...] Dialogue is absolutely life. The whole of life happens in dialogue. [...] And response is the place at which we get to be our most human and playful. [...] When you've got two minds engaged, they open up whole worlds, incredibly vast new worlds, and beyond that, there's a multilogue as well which is that the worlds in themselves start to connect. (Boddy and Smith, 2010: 73)

Smith's point is that the minimalism of the short story allows for a pared-down emotional expression that always indicates the existence of convoluted and dialogic interchanges. The story never simply describes a narrative arc towards closure but is rather 'always some kind of middle or beginning' (Boddy and Smith, 2010: 68). This open-endedness works against the fixity of the novel's characterisation by focusing on the transformative power of the evanescent and the epiphanic. Smith's stories perform this receptiveness to reshaping through narratives where endings and beginnings are the same thing; where moments of connection in relationships are undermined by chasms in understanding; where generic or formal conventions are invoked only to be subverted; and where one's perspective is challenged by the legitimacy of the non-speaking voice. This leads to narratives that celebrate the spaciousness of the universal at the same time that they nurture the uniqueness of the exceptional. Smith's writing is largely domestic in setting, but the resonance of small actions across history, geography, culture, and politics is far from quotidian.

Free Love (1995)

Smith regards her first collection as the least cohesive of her career (Boddy and Smith, 2010: 68), yet many of the stories gravitate around ideas of connection. The title story, 'Free Love', establishes the tone by describing how a sexual encounter with an Amsterdam prostitute helps the young female protagonist beyond the awkward anxieties of teenage becoming, and similar chance collisions between worlds are presented repeatedly throughout the text. 'A Quick One' describes the ending of a brief sexual relationship; 'Jenny Robertson Your Friend Is Not Coming' details an uncomfortable evening spent with the friend of a friend when something more intimate was expected; and 'The Unthinkable Happens to People Every Day' offers another serendipitous fusion of childish innocence with adult jadedness. The story concerns a burnt-out TV producer's journey to his home in Scotland and his chance encounter with a nine-year-old girl, who, by challenging him to throw a rock into a loch, reconnects him with the positive, compassionate part of his personality, which has become lost. These narrative vignettes focus the reader's attention on the contingency of human interaction, but, in two of the most successful stories in the collection, 'A Story of Folding and Unfolding' and 'Cold Iron', Smith explores how such momentary encounters can expand to fill and determine a life.

'A Story of Folding and Unfolding' conveys the sum of a lifelong relationship and the desperation of loss through the metaphor of women's underwear. Not long after the Second World War, a nosy electrician and his mate titillate themselves by looking through the lockers of female military personnel, commenting salaciously on the condition of the underwear they find. The final locker contains garments that are 'smooth, arranged and unrumpled, folded with talent' (Smith, 1995: 16), ordered by a name that the electrician memorises, and a person he subsequently marries. Years later, he sits on his marital bed surrounded by his late wife's unfolded underwear helplessly asking 'What am I supposed to do with all of this?' (Smith, 1995: 14). This oblique account of love tolled through the forging of a shared intimacy works both with and against the moments of snatched enlightenment present in other stories. The delicacy of love built over time and its precariousness are contrasted with the less significant encounters, but these moments of connection are not denigrated by comparison; rather they represent in crystalline fledgling form the possibility of a love that might sustain.

'Cold Iron' is a comparable story of grief, but that experienced at the loss of a parent. It explores how the last days and hours of dying fuse the momentous and the prosaic into an interpretational dissonance as the narrator seeks to come to terms with the various disconnections that her mother's death represents. Throughout there is an iteration of the distance between the narrator and her dying mother – physical in the sense that she is parted from her at the end, emotional as she struggles to place her mother's life into order and context – and a sense of the vulnerability of life. Like 'A Story of Folding and Unfolding' and 'The Book Club' in *The Whole Story and Other Stories*, which also deals with the loss of a parent, the story portrays the sturdiness of the material world in comparison with the fragility of human memory and experience, but, as with the balance between momentary and lifelong relationships, there is a distinct lack of judgement about the relative values of the physical and emotional. Instead the story balances the banal and revelatory properties of the domestic. The everyday world of things is not in opposition to the subject but rather contains a capacity for transcendence that can illuminate the inner experience and ground consciousness in the concrete. The final image of the story is thus one of contrasting despair and hope: 'Myself I'm hanging on, leaning on the rail that overlooks the sea on either side of me, I'm picking up bits and pieces for my house. I'm thinking it out, I'm working out the story' (Smith, 1995: 85).

ALI SMITH

Other Stories and Other Stories (1999)

Though less intensively than the later collections, *Free Love* explores the mystery of how relationships happen, the angles at which people's lives connect, and how those collisions develop (or fail to develop) into something more meaningful. Smith is no heady romantic; her conviction in a transformative love accepts the innumerable tiny setbacks, irritations, niggles, and fractures that characterise love as an organic and lived experience with seasons of growth and recession. But, out of all these fluctuations, something can develop which blends difference and sameness, habit and spontaneity, conjunction and fragmentation into a profound connection that can only be described as humane. Consider, for instance, a story such as 'The Theme is Power' from *Other Stories and Other Stories*, which concentrates on personal catastrophes narrowly avoided, played out against a backdrop of global tragedies unavoided. The narrator's decision as an adolescent not to be solicited by a friendly but potentially dangerous stranger is set against the failures of moral judgement on a strategic level that have led to war and death on a grand scale. The personal and the political fuse to create a deep sense of insecurity about the luck of living in a bubble of peace and protection, but the story concludes with a statement of commonality that goes some – but not all the – way to counteract the instability of living:

> Under the covers you take my hand and turn it around, put your fingers through mine, interlocked, and you fall asleep like that, holding my hand. That's all it takes. One glance, one sidelong blow from you, and a rock as big as a room explodes into little bits of gravel. [...] I lie in our unpaid bed and trust you, carelessly, precariously, with my whole heart. (Smith, 2004: 136–137)

There is a sincerity here that prevents Smith's prose from sliding into sentimentality; the smallness of a gesture of harmony amongst the chaos of uncontrollable events affirms the power of intimate connection, but 'precariously' identifies its contingency. The world cannot be made safe, Smith implies, but shared moments of tenderness and compassion can temporarily make us believe in the possibility.

Perhaps more than any of the other collections, *Other Stories* worries about the fragility of the individual in a toxic world of disconnection and misrecognition, where relationships are exploitative, care is perfunctory, and there is always so much more to be known. One of Smith's domestic invasion stories, 'Small Deaths', literally engages with the idea of toxicity as an infestation of insects is eradicated by a chemical repellent horribly destructive to human health, whilst another, 'The Hanging Girl', addresses the desensitisation to pain within contemporary representation – a topic to which Smith would return in *There But For The* and *How To Be Both*. 'Okay So Far' is a

TWENTY-FIRST-CENTURY FICTION

more subtle story that balances ignorance of the lives of others with a crushing sense of the tenuousness of our connections to our selves. It is another story where a chance encounter opens up emotional anxieties that have been silenced for years as two women travelling across North America grow concerned about the safety of a young child seemingly travelling alone. The child is translated in their eyes into a metaphor for their own vulnerability: they are far from home and see in her aloneness the miracle of their survival into adulthood. Later, the narrator relates for the first time a story of her own childhood in which she narrowly escaped injury, emphasising not only the fragility of life but also the persistence of childhood within the adult body. The body does not outgrow the past, Smith claims, but always contains a childhood kernel of unmanageable anxiety that is dampened rather than forgotten by time. The recognition of her own helplessness propels the narrator into a form of loneliness that is resolved only by the sharing of her partner's comparable fear of the world. As they lie curled protectively in each other's arms, the narrator wonders how they 'have come so far. It frightens me to think how far we have come and how fast we've gone, how little we've noticed of it' (Smith, 2004: 103). This is a statement of resilience and survivorship, but it is also a recognition of how easily that ballast can be eroded; after all, as the story's title indicates, the characters are only okay so far.

'Okay So Far' is like many of the stories in *Other Stories* in that it identifies storytelling as a means of recuperating the self through another's narrative. However the volume also contains a number of stories where the subject of connection is addressed through the opposition of differing accounts. One such is 'More than One Story', which details the perspectives of an older man and an eighteen-year-old girl. The protagonists observe each other neutrally – he sitting in his potting-shed, she sun-bathing topless on a flat roof – their interest only mildly piqued by the presence of the other, but, in reverie, both drift back to defining moments of sexual discovery, and the comparability of their memories suggests that, despite their age, their genders, and their inability to perceive the other as anything more than the sum of their outward appearance, the two have a great deal in common. Despite their potential affinity, each is compelled by the limits of her/his perspective into regarding the other as an object from which s/he is completely divorced. For all the moments of pure connection in Smith, there are numerous instances of such intersubjective disjunction – many, as in Smith's first novel, *Like*, more aggressively oppositional.

They remind us that Smith's writing is dominated by a voice, and, though that voice is frequently that of a first-person narrator, we are never allowed to forget that the dialogic element inherent in speech disrupts any utterance – however authoritative. Smith has described *Like* as 'a nasty warring book'

(Murray, 2006: 222), and it is undeniable that, for all the moments of loving transcendence, her fiction more commonly pitches voices into conflict. *Other Stories* contains six of what Smith calls her 'you-me' stories (Murray, 2006: 220), which deliberately collide differing accounts – often, as in 'A Story of Love', through a squabbling wrestle for control. When she came to write *The Whole Story and Other Stories*, this 'you-me' technique became a structural imperative.

The Whole Story and Other Stories (2003)

In interview with Isobel Murray, Smith commented:

> I knew there were more [you-me stories] to write for *Whole Story*, and I knew they'd be different; they wanted to answer themselves back, as it were, to be multivocal, multilogue. I love more than one voice. I love the coming in of all the voices: there's no such thing as a single voice, not unless you're alone on a desert island and then there's always Friday or your reader! There's never just one voice, one story, one way to tell or see things. This is crucial. (Murray, 2006: 220)

Through the 'you-me' stories, *The Whole Story* deliberately builds dialogue into a structure that echoes the circularity of the conversation. The collection contains three stories related to each season of the year, with one 'you-me' tale for each sub-group. By this means, the structure proceeds through 'separate moments but at the end of the book, [you] have come a full cycle, a full rhythm' (Murray, 2006: 223). This conceit serves several thematic purposes, but it allows Smith to 'hold things in a cycle', which offers 'a different kind of progression from chronology' (Murray, 2006: 223). The cycle is important because it connotes completion, something that is rare in the short story form and even rarer in Smith's work, which revels in open-endedness. But completion here does not imply resolution or even conclusion; instead the end point is always also a starting point, a returning of attention and energy back into the cycle. The 'you-me' stories illustrate this structural principle well as they consist of two distinct first-person voices recounting, from opposite perspectives, their summation of a crisis in a relationship. The broken-backed structure of these narratives, which consist of duologues rather than dialogues, reflects the insurmountable otherness of those that are most familiar, but, for all their ambivalence and confusion, they suggest a completion based on the 'whole' story being heard. As fractured and oppositional as many of these stories may be, there is also the conviction that they reflect the truth of human relationships, which are defined less by straightforward linear development from a beginning to an end than by processes of continuous rebalancing, retuning, and restarting. Endings and beginnings are as fundamental to the human cycle as they are to the seasonal.

The most striking stories in this regard are 'May', 'Being Quick', and 'The Start of Things'. In 'May' the first 'I' protagonist falls in love to the point of obsession with a tree, finding in it the perfect quintessence of all the beauty and authenticity of being that she struggles to find elsewhere in the world. The tree represents an example of pure essence that somehow rises above the status of language and description. When the narrator tries to describe it, she recognises that it exceeds the possibility of metaphor: 'The blossom was like – no it was like nothing but blossom. The leaves, when they came, would be like nothing but leaves. I had never seen a tree more like a tree. It was a relief' (Smith, 2003: 57). The focus here is the authenticity of the tree; it does not require representation or translation in any way into the register of language; it simply is. This is entirely unlike the narrator, who admits: 'It was me who was like something other than myself' (Smith, 2003: 57). Where the individual is self-alienated, the tree is self-identical. In some ways the tree is thus the antidote to the flux of emotional life that is represented in the narrator, and also possibly the antidote to the narrator's madness, as she spirals away from the fixity of self-knowledge. The tree is a simple manifestation of sameness: 'People passed back and fore behind it. Mothers went past it to fetch children from school, brought them home from school the other way. People came home from work all round it. The sun moved round it in the sky' (Smith, 2003: 59).

The first narrator's increasingly detached state of mind contrasts strikingly with the second narrator's psychological rootedness. What comes across most strikingly from the narrative of the partner is the partner's tolerance, willingness to accept, and willingness to love in the face of extreme alienation and provocation. As we will see in 'Being Quick', where the first voice is identified with a form of irrational solipsism, the second (rational) speaker moderates the intense experience of disconnection that the former goes through by providing understanding and acceptance but without ever questioning the validity of her worldview. The moderating speaker does not seek to draw the irrational one back into the realm of reason, or to have her conform to a particular worldview, but instead the partner allows the speaker to speak and to tell her story. 'May' concludes with the second speaker choosing to join her partner in lying under the tree. Regardless of the madness that has enveloped her, the second voice draws them back within a form of narrative embrace by providing a listener and a responder. This human charity and love does not necessarily palliate the madness but it does provide it with human context and shape.

'Being Quick' similarly explores the dynamic between a narrator in a profound state of alienation from the world around her, and her partner, ready at home to resume domestic normality. After believing that she has encountered the manifestation of death at a London station, the first narrator is trapped in a hell of other people on a train halted by a suicide on the line. The torment of forced social interaction allows Smith one of her customary moments of comedic discomfort, but the wall-to-wall phone conversations explaining the delay also emphasise her fear that modern technology has generated a profound withdrawal between human beings that is only masked by an ersatz and superficial connectivity. The narrator feels:

> numb, anaesthetized, and I knew for the first time as I sat staring blankly out and the realization of it broke cold on my skull [...] that I hadn't ever cared at any point about anything other than myself and that I had no idea how to change this or make it any different. (Smith, 2003: 32)

After several ill-received attempts at conversation, the narrator leaves the stationary train and begins following the direction of the rail lines. At this juncture the point of view shifts to the partner, who receives a late-night phone call from the initial narrator appraising her of these events and of the random thoughts by which she has been beset. Though naturally troubled by her partner's distractedness, the story's second voice maintains a tender and non-judgemental concern similar to that described in 'May'. The emotional distance between the two voices, emphasised by the physical distance created by the phone line, is nonetheless underpinned by an openness to understanding the need of the other, and a tolerance of their different worldviews. The anxiety and need for reassurance experienced by the second point of view is temporarily suspended in a gesture of committed altruism which expresses Smith's view that connection is as much about sacrifice as it is about reciprocity.

In stark contrast to these two narratives of loving care, 'The Start of Things' portrays the numerous cruelties of which love is made. It begins with the seemingly definitive concluding statement: 'It was the end and we both knew it' (Smith, 2003: 195), but the story goes on to show how endings and new beginnings are intricately and cyclically entwined. The story maintains the 'you-me' format of two first-person narrators involved in a serious domestic dispute, but also contains a central, italicised section told from a third-person-plural point of view which details the post-argument reconciliation in bed together, fuses the voices into indistinction, and indicates the continuation of the relationship beyond the end. This spatial and vocal harmony contrasts dramatically with the first-person accounts, which vigorously contest the ownership of material belongings in childishly selfish ways. The house, with its entrances and exits, becomes the metaphorical focus for the story's emotional disconnection as one of the protagonists locks the other out. The outsider watches the insider taking ownership of what is shared: 'You opened the fridge and took out the milk. It was me who'd bought that milk; I had bought it at the shop the day before and you just using it like that made me angrier than anything else' (Smith, 2003: 197). The glass that divides the banally routine from the seemingly life-changing symbolises the invisible barriers that underpin even the closest relationships. We are returned once again to the disconnection that characterises otherness and that, in intimacy, is such a disturbing reminder of our aloneness. Later the couple recall an episode when they became separated inside and outside a tube train: 'And we were miming at each other through the doors of the train, I say, and then the train began to move and you were saying something through the glass but I had absolutely no idea what it was you were trying to tell me' (Smith, 2003: 200). Comic yet revealing, this incident encapsulates the ambivalence that Smith believes dictates our engagement with the other.

The point that Smith seems to be making in *The Whole Story* is that love is all about starts and endings, all about competing voices and differences that can never be understood, let alone breached, but at the same time it is also about the myriad moments of caring and moments of anger that make love worthwhile. The love that Smith describes is convoluted and destabilising because it involves the surrender of oneself to another who does not understand, and it demands a commitment to connect with another. That commitment is not a predicate of love but an ethical choice that human beings have to make or not make. Smith's fiction – both short and long – presents connection with the other as a challenge to the boundedness and self-interest of the individual. It is an offer to explore beyond the known, to leave oneself open to the randomness of possible connection and disconnection. As she says in conversation with Boddy:

> There's something which is really exciting and something which is the same about the places of connection and disconnection. They're about either acceptance or decision to connect or to be part. [...] They are like a kind of interstice, they're like the stitches. Even the disconnections are the things that hold things together. (Boddy and Smith, 2010: 69)

Understanding the whole of the other is as impossible as understanding the whole of the self, but to live in the way that Smith seems to advocate requires a deliberate decision to reach out, however tentatively, to the possibility of connection.

If the fruitful wholeness of connection is one dominant theme of this collection, then the story of this wholeness is another. Books and stories are insistent motifs in *The Whole Story*, as they are in everything that Smith writes. Many of her stories – 'Text for a Day' (*Free Love*); 'A Story of

Love' (*Other Stories*); 'The Universal Story' (*The Whole Story*); 'True Short Story'(*The First Person*) – deal directly with literary subjects, asserting the shaping influence that narrative has on the ways in which we organise the world and understand how to behave in it. Fundamentally, Smith writes about the value of words; she is a crafter of narratives in which wordplay is central not only to the diegetic energy but also to the thematic investigation. Puns, neologisms, jokes, metatextual references, and ellipses dominate her stories, but, above and beyond this technical attention to the vitality of words, Smith's writing also creates characters of books, joyously identifying our relationships with them as some of the most significant and fulfilling of our lives. 'Text for a Day' follows a character in crisis who literally disassembles her library – tearing out page after page after they have been read – in a bid to reattach herself with the unrepeatable experience of discovery. 'True Short Story' has the narrator debating the value of the short story form with her friend Kasia as a means of helping the latter through debilitating bouts of chemotherapy. 'The Universal Story' in *The Whole Story* constructs biographies for the contents of a second-hand bookshop, detailing the books' experiences with consecutive owners and the ways in which the intersection of life and literature affects both. Each story about a book's history is enshrined in another story, a form of endless *mise-en-abyme* that indicates the continual resonances of stories through each other and through their tellers/readers. Smith's book/story is like her relationship: always open to fresh interpretation and analysis but also subject to surprising transformation and redirection. In 'Believe Me' in *The Whole Story*, we see how this transubstantiation of word and person can occur:

> because I can read you like a book and because the thing about a beloved book, if it's a good one, is that it shifts like music; you think you know it, you've read it so many times, of course you know it, of course the pleasure of it is in how well you know it, but then you hear, in the background, the thing you never heard in it before, and with the turn of a page you see a combination of words you know you've never seen before, you thought you knew this book but it dazzles you with the different book it is, yet again, and not just that but the different person you have become, the different person you are now, reading it again, and you, my love, are an excellent book for me, and then us both together, which takes some talent with rhythm, but luckily we are quite talented at reading each other. (Smith, 2003: 146)

Reading and loving are thus closely related for Smith; they both come with costs and benefits and they both offer ways of understanding the world. Throughout her collections, books act as forms of distraction, forms of consolation, forms of shaping the past in new ways, and forms of ordering the difficult lives we live. This can be seen in 'Erosive', where the narrative structure of a story about loss is reordered in order to better comprehend the shifting nature of grief, and in 'The Book Club', where the ordering of the story and the ordering protocols of a sat-nav device overlap as metaphors for control of the disorienting realities of the physical world.

Narrative is alive for Smith, it is organic, and, as a consequence, it has the ability to be disruptive and disorderly, challenging the formal ascription of meaning. 'The Shortlist Season' is a story about a visit to an art gallery that juxtaposes the formalising narrative of pinning art within frames of meaning with the carnivalesque disruption of narrative inherent in daily life. The story's narrator watches with horror, giving way to pleasure, as a small child runs her hand all over cordoned-off and pompously annotated paintings. As with her mocking treatment of academic literary study in *Like* and *The Accidental*, Smith loves undermining esoteric pretensions and the territorialisation of the story by 'official' culture. For her stories are neither fixed nor containable, and display the danger of imaginative sterility once narrative is used for a specific purpose. Instead, narrative is most vital, intriguing, and perceptive when it is allowed to form itself outside the imperative of order. Language offers potential for the unsaid to be articulated in any number of ways, but narrative which is shaped is always susceptible to dominance and the tyranny of meaning. Smith is instead all about the 'but', the pivots that are inherent within words and the transformative potential for seeing things differently that they allow. This is ultimately why stories are so important to the cyclical structure of *The Whole Story*; reading – of one's own life, of another's, of books, of life as a narrative – is a process that is both linear and profoundly non-linear. Stories always spiral into other stories and suggest fresh ways of reading the world and others. They are part of an organic process that is simultaneously progressive and retrogressive and that involves telling, listening, re-evaluating, and retelling.

The First Person and Other Stories (2008)

Smith's fourth collection of stories received a more guardedly positive reception from reviewers, for some of whom, such as Sophie Gee, the characteristic whimsy and subversion of literary culture 'are no longer jolts from the margins; they are comfy and relaxed, too much at home' (Gee, 2008). Paradoxically, Gee considers this a sign of Smith tending too strenuously towards the literary, but one can see her point; mannerism can quickly grate and cross over into pretension. Fatema Ahmed similarly criticised Smith for balancing her narratives too heavily towards spiralling helixes of quirkiness at the expense of narrative movement (Ahmed, 2008). There were many positive reviews, but a significant number acknowledge that the devices familiar from the previous collections are beginning to wear thin. It is certainly true that, whilst containing many accomplished stories, *The First Person* as a collection lacks some of the cohesion and originality of the earlier volumes. The fantastical imaginative extrapolations of couples lying in bed and telling each other the stories of themselves have become, if not predictable, then over-familiar, and, without the organising principle of a collection such as *The Whole Story*, *The First Person* feels slightly repetitive.

'True Short Story' is perhaps the most striking, and, in its introduction of Smith's friend Kasia Boddy and Boddy's journey through chemotherapy, begins a skein of argument about the truthfulness of stories that reappears in a number of stories in the collection. The story begins with the narrator overhearing the conversation of an older and a younger man sitting in a café and, perhaps surprisingly, discussing the relative sexual merits of the novel and short story, with the former described as a 'flabby old whore' and the latter as 'a slim nymph [...] in very good shape' (Smith, 2008: 4). The incident allows the narrator to make a diegetic leap to the hospitalised Boddy, an academic and expert in the short story, and to introduce the idea of contrast as a form of play. As a patient, Boddy is subject to the pathological determination of a mirthless disease and to a hospital system which is characterised by an institutional *chiaroscuro*: when the narrator phones her she waits 'for the automaton voice of the hospital phone system to tell me all about itself' (Smith, 2008: 5). The same systematism is reflected in the decisions made by health professionals about their patients' care, most pointedly in Boddy's case over whether to administer the effective, but costly, breast cancer drug Herceptin. The unenviable choices about who should and shouldn't receive the treatment are shrouded in defensive acronyms such as PCT (primary care trust) and NICE (National Institute for Health and Care Excellence), and Smith's resistance to authority butts against these euphemisms with undisguised ironic emphasis: '"Primary". "Care". "Trust". "Nice"' (Smith, 2008: 11). Each term is punctuated not just to highlight the distance from reality of these terms in the context but also to open those terms out to the many and varied meanings that each one contains.

For Smith, language is captured and perverted by authority and is used to mask small truths such as the two-centimetre tumour in Boddy's breast, whose undeniable and irreducible reality defies description. Yet the story suggests that the only answers to these truths, and the hard twists of language made to cover them, are the lies of stories. Smith is not romantic about the healing power of imagination here, but rather she suggests that the invented is all that can be offered in the face of the indifference of things as they are. Words transform reality through their refusal to be monologic, so, in telling

Boddy of her experience in the café, the nymph transmutes between a dirty joke, a fishing fly, and ultimately the mythological story of Echo, which is retold by Smith as a tale of answering back against an immovable power. 'True Short Story' becomes a celebration of the litheness of a form and of the possibility of responding to the seeming immutabilities of the physical world with a defiance born of humour and multiplicity. However, the story never claims that such strategies are anything more than compensation. Narrative, imagination, and a creative unwillingness to accept the way things are will not prevent them being thus, but such devices at least provide a temporary respite and the sense of a small victory.

Of the other stories in *The First Person*, the three interconnected tales 'The First Person', 'The Second Person', and 'The Third Person' are also concerned with voice, both grammatically and thematically. Each of them tackles, from different positions, not only the problem of knowing the other but also the temptations of speaking for, over, and about the other. They are elucidated well by Smith's epigraphs for the collection, which include Katherine Mansfield's 'True to oneself! Which self?' and Grace Paley's 'The First person is often the lover who says I never knew anyone like you The listener is the beloved She whispers Who? Me?' (sic). Speaking in the first person is always fraught with nominative insecurity, but, the stories suggest, that derives (at least in part) from an ill-controlled desire to speak for the other to shape her/his pictures of us. In 'The Second Person', Smith opposes two squabbling lovers, each recounting what the other is 'like' and each upsetting the other with her/his analogy. One is the 'kind of person' who would make nonsensical impulse purchases out of unrealistic ambition; the other is the kind of pedant who points out to a pianist all the historical nuances of the songs he is playing. Of course each protagonist is like and unlike these character sketches, but each sees in the other's story her/his own self-doubt cut together with the fear of how the world sees her/him. Neither sees the romantic sub-text that the other implies, the open-hearted acceptance of another's enlivening and maddening totality; in the heat of an argument, they hear only the singular, accusatory 'you'. The story ends with reconciliation and the uplifting, wry 'You're something else, you' (Smith, 2008: 134), a phrase that encapsulates the knowing acknowledgement of the other's strangeness and the recognition that we are equally mysterious to ourselves.

'The Third Person' opens with a characteristically vivid metaphor for the strangeness outlined above: a relationship, Smith claims, is like being trapped in a small room with another person and a piano which is just too big to make moving around comfortable. This comic image captures well the clumsy intimacy of many of the relationships she describes, and the story then unfolds to explore the epistemological trouble involved in being in the position of the third person. Presented as a series of unconnected vignettes, the story involves moments of anxious doubt: a petty theft on holiday, a theatre visit for a couple nearing the end of their relationship, a man's fear of being observed as he is cruel to a cat. In each case the perspective is singular, the thought-processes of the other an unreadable blank, and the reader is left with a clear sense of the piano in the room that underpins all intimacies – closeness and awkwardness are inseparable.

Shifting voice once again, 'The First Person' plays on the double sense of first person as both a point of view and an agent (the first person to do something). As with many of Smith's stories, it involves a couple in bed imagining how they will tell the story of their relationship to others, and there is a sweet tenderness to the banter as they tease each other with the accusation 'you're not the first person to ...'. Yet this slight defensiveness, the warning to the other not to get above her/himself, is touchingly countered by the novelty that fresh love brings; it is a wariness in performance only. Actually the narrator experiences a stripping away not just of her cynicism but also of her identity to reveal her first-personage in an Edenic sense: 'You have peeled the roof off me and turned the whole library into a wood. Every book is a tree. Above the tops of the trees there's nothing but birds' (Smith, 2008: 196). Love, in its most idealised incarnation, is retroactively trans-formative here, turning a spirit calcified through experience back into youth-fulness and anticipation. And this reversion to first-ness brings with it a new, but welcome, awareness of the self as strange and mutable. The story, and collection, ends with the brightness of a surprised revelation of what the self can become: 'I don't know what I'll think tomorrow or the next day, but this is what I think right now. It's the best thing that could happen to anything I ever imagined was mine' (Smith, 2008: 207).

The novels

Many of the issues we encounter in Smith's stories are evident in her longer fiction, and there are significant repetitions in idea, motif, structure, and tem-per across forms, indicating a relatively circumscribed set of literary concerns. Though she champions the short story for its litheness and narrative agility, the 'flabby old whore' of the novel has nonetheless garnered her greater critical rec-ognition. Her novels draw heavily on the structural precision of her short sto-ries, routinely shying away from dominating single-person narrators in favour of multiple viewpoints, set, not directly in competition, but alongside each other. This technique of narrative cross-talking continues Smith's commitment to the imaginative fecundity of acknowledging the perspective of the other.

Like (1997)

Smith describes her first novel, *Like*, as 'a nasty warring book [...] a book of two sides [...] squaring up to each other all the time' (Murray, 2006: 222), and there is a certain consonance between this and many of her 'you-me' stories in the forceful insistence by the protagonists of the justice of their readings of the world. A novel of two parts, the first relates the story of Amy, an ex-English Literature lecturer who has mysteriously lost the ability to read upon the birth of her daughter and has retreated to Scotland and to relative isolation. The second part is told from the perspective of Ash, whose brief childhood friendship with Amy has developed into an abiding and obsessive passion in later years. *Like* works backwards from the mysteriously limited life of Amy in the present to the days of Amy and Ash's friendship in Cambridge, and contrasts the ways in which each constructs her personal history. At the same time it is, in the words of Kirsty Williams, 'a love story about the need to be accepted, the desire to love and be loved and the price paid when we try to erase or ignore love's impulse' (Williams, 2006: 175).

Such a description paints a rather softer picture of the novel than might appear to be the case. *Like* is a war of words and a war between versions of what words can do. Its battleground is the usefulness of language for describing the complex reality of the emotional life, and the divide between the two women might be seen as the divide between simile and sameness. Amy's closed emotional apparatus and her refusal to acknowledge the possibility of the feelings that she might have for Ash, or to recognise the love that Ash feels for her, create a sense of metaphorical substitution through which she distances herself from the world of feeling. Simile depends upon an identification between two things, a similarity but not an exact replication; to be 'like' something is not to be of it but to be a comparison and thus at a distance. Amy's repressed feelings become transformed into linguistic and literary surrogates, shaped and ordered as a means of keeping the world at a safe and manageable distance. She does not feel able to pin down her emotional life, or to express it in ways that are precise, committed, or unretractable. This reveals itself in her academic distrust of language's ability to represent anything real. She embraces the ideas of the linguistic turn and the slipperiness of the signifier. The treatment of language as nothing more than a code that only has relevance in certain semiotic contexts deflects her from the experiencing of life as a wordless urgency.

By contrast, Ash's relationship with language is one of visceral intensity. She believes in the living power of words to reflect the world of feeling precisely; for her, far from emerging from the social negotiation between semiotic codes, words are born through the drama of the human being's interaction with the world. Metaphor is inadequate to the task of encapsulating this drama, as we see in Ash's description of the night she and Amy spend sheltering in a ditch. Amy asks Ash to describe what the beat of Amy's heart is like, to which Ash can only answer: 'It's like, like – I said, and I stopped. I couldn't think what it was like, it was Amy's heart, it wasn't like anything else' (Smith, 1997: 342). This realisation parallels that in 'May' and suggests that the world is beyond the descriptive power of language and cannot be brought into a relationship of equivalence. For Ash, words are not simply mental constructs but are embodied and are shaped by the body too. She can confidently assert that, were her bones to be snapped open, they would reveal the letters A, M, and Y, and her discovery on breaking into Amy's college rooms that she is absent from Amy's diaries is as much a physical blow as a psychological rejection because it means that she is 'symbolically absent in Amy's life' (Williams, 2006: 172) – she has no place within Amy's signifying register.

Smith's treatment of language in *Like* reveals an interesting contradiction that is evident elsewhere in her longer fiction: on the one hand, she is committed to the idea of language as forever open to playfulness and transformation, and regards this as a fundamental aspect of language's anti-authoritarian ability to avoid cliché and hierarchy. Stories are told and retold, language is formed and reformed, and words are shifted from their accepted moorings to take up temporary residence in other semantic regimes. But, on the other hand, there is a palpable regret in her work that language does not perform the task of describing the individual's experience of the world with any degree of accuracy. Words, for all their potential, are endlessly frustrating and imprecise and cannot access the authentic in a way that is ultimately meaningful or restorative. This tension is often, in Smith's hands, productively managed and turned into narrative food for thought, as we see in her second novel, where she allows meaningful and meaningless discourse to sit side by side.

Hotel World (2001)

Smith announced herself fully to the critical and reading public with the publication of her second novel, *Hotel World*. It is, unusually for Smith, a novel that wears its politics openly, offering a forthright condemnation of globalising capitalism and, in particular, the kind of inequalities that are engendered in a society in thrall to money. That said, though this novel is peculiarly strident in its social commentary and lacks some of the humour of Smith's other work, it retains a humane sensibility at its core. Its moral is epitomised by its treatment of passing time and by the phrase 'Remember you must leave', which, along with the variation 'Remember you must love', establishes *carpe diem* as the urgent imperative. The story revolves around the character of Sara Wilby, a chambermaid at Global Hotel, who was killed when the dumbwaiter into which she squeezed herself to win a bet plummeted to the bottom of the building. Sara's ghost haunts the narrative, bookending the accounts of others connected to the hotel and reminding the reader – 'Yes, you. It's you I'm talking to' (Smith, 2002: 31) – of the brevity and insecurity of life. The direct order to embrace the fickle, finite, and unquantifiable joys of living is made in the face of the monolithic determinism of capitalism represented by the hotel. Here, as so often elsewhere, we have Smith's humanism set against the intractable materialism of the postmodern world. In many ways, *Hotel World* is a novel about the desire for restitution and coherence, but before that can be achieved there is a whole lot of fragmentation to negotiate.

Hotel World is a novel characterised by fragmentation. This can be seen in the sharing of the narrative across five female voices – Sara (in the first and last sections), Else, Lise, Penny, and Clare; in the elliptical linguistic structures that these characters use to express themselves; and in the partial experience that each has of Sara and of her demise. It can be seen most potently in the broken body at the bottom of the lift shaft, a constant reminder of brokenness at the heart of superficial coherence. The hotel is all about meeting expectations, smooth efficiency, and the kind of experience which reinforces the guests' conviction of the benign quality of the corporate world. Yet at the centre of the building is a hole that generates horror and lack of meaning; it is a void in space and in hermeneutics. This metaphor of emptiness at the heart of a rigidly determined and policed space speaks well to Smith's criticism of the hollowness of capitalism, not just in a moral sense but as a system for providing order and meaning that encompasses all members of a society. Without a place within the economic rationality of Blair's Britain, the narrative foci of *Hotel World* are equally robbed of their own places within the signifying regimes that go with it.

As a homeless person, Else is the physical surplus of a rapaciously utilitarian society that pushes to the extremes those who cannot, or will not, participate in the free circulation of capital. As her name suggests, she is the disregarded leftover from the process of selling and buying, not fully material and unrepresentative of anything other than residue. As such she represents an indeterminate something else that cannot be fitted into the social or economic orders of signification. She is identified with small change, the pennies and tuppences that are superfluous to the ambitions of a society with grander ideas of exchange, and thus ejected to join the human waste on the fringes of capitalism. For those who disdainfully toss her the ballast of their pockets and purses, money is notional, purely a means to various ends, but Else's relationship with it is physical and conducted in the here and now. She can describe the feel of each coin on her tongue, the taste of the encrusted grime that has accrued from their past owners, the weight of the pound coin as it sits in her mouth. This ingestion of the literal filth of capital stimulates a disgust that emphasises Else's abjected status within not just the social order but also the social imaginary. Her place is provisional, a visible irritant to a smoothly functioning system, and she is consequently moved on by the police, temporarily removed from sight and from the need for explanation.

Else's abjection is presented not just in her position on the fringe of social action but also in the interaction with others that she is forced to undergo. Without an economic status, she is in no position to determine how others regard her and cannot dictate the terms of conversation. Her place outside the hegemonic signifying order renders her a non-person in the eyes of many who either deliberately fail to acknowledge her or believe that she deserves the contempt due to an offence to financial propriety:

> Move along now, Else, we can't have this; you know we can't. (a woman) Ever thought of working for a living? The rest of us have to. We can't all just loaf around like you. (a woman) (whispered) Now I'm telling you straight and I'll only tell you once. You want a good raping, and you're for it. You let me see you in here again and you'll get it. I mean it. That's a promise, not a threat. You hear me? Hear me? Eh? (a man, at the station) Can't you get it through your thick skull that decent people hate scum like you? You're scum of the earth. You spoil it for the rest of us. The scum of the fucking earth. (a woman, at the station). (Smith, 2002: 43)

Alongside a vituperative disgust for those who have 'escaped' the drudgery of work, there is a darkness here that reveals the abhorrent fascination of the abject. For those who do not follow the rules, the rules do not apply, and they are fair game for the kind of dark fantasy that is kept in check by proper status. For those, Else is a carrier of contamination who threatens the purity of the system and must, therefore, be made safe through objectification. With the numerous sexually exploitative solicitations, Else experiences other kinds of desperation from those barely keeping up appearances in a game over which they have no control. From the evangelists seeking to save her to those seeking to bond as outsiders without proffering material assistance, Else encounters the full spectrum of public reactions to her as a form of sub-human currency. Only Lise extends her a genuinely humane hand, offering her an illicit night of comfort and security in the hotel, a hotel identified with a different kind of surplus, as the number of vacant rooms attests.

Like Else, Lise is a victim of the relentless and restless energy of capital. Badly paid and poorly motivated, she services her reception duties with an automaton's efficiency and intellectual engagement, providing the dead-eyed surface sheen to the business of business. But, also like Else, she is marked by contamination. Her narrative, recounted some months after her act of kindness towards Else, shows her confined to bed with a debilitating illness which, though undiagnosable, shares a range of symptoms with ME, from which Smith suffered during her twenties. Her illness sets her outside the frame of normal social reference and as such renders her invisible, as Fiona McCulloch notes: 'Lise's illness is out of sight out of mind and is met with the same discomfort that passers-by feel for the homeless Else or the ghostly Sara, each of them rendered invisible in their otherness' (McCulloch, 2012: 177). Unable to take her place within the functioning economy, she becomes effectively useless – alienated, immobile, passive, and forgotten. Lying in bed, a captive audience for the mindless dross of commercial advertising jingles and slogans, which indicate the continuation of the world without her, she struggles to describe her condition in the terms given her by the 'Incapacity for Work Questionnaire'. Her inability to marry the formulaic blandness of the form with the felt experience of her illness shows that, like Else, she sits outside the signifying frameworks of social discourse. To be out of sight is not just to be out of mind but also to be outside language, and, where the fragmented 'Spr sm chn?' with which Else petitions passers-by indicates her alienation from the fullness of speech, Lise's incompleteness manifests by being spoken for. Whether it is the official questionnaire shaping the nature of her illness, the pop culture cycling endlessly through her brain, or her mother, who is writing an epic poem about her experiences, Lise is displaced from self-description and consequently has no purchase on the *logos* of the material world. If the signifying regime of modernity is tied tightly to the efficiency of capitalism, then those excluded from the money game are at risk of being excluded from representation. Smith's novel explicitly privileges the voices of those at the margins of acceptability, but, at the same time, it acknowledges that the terms for social inclusion might now accommodate an underlying toxicity. Lise's doctor, unable to pin her symptoms down to a specific pathology, concludes that 'It could indicate nothing, it can indicate sheer normality' (Smith, 2002: 89).

Beneath all this fragmentation and dislocation lie the familiar Smith themes of the disconnection between individuals and the otherness of the other, themes that are evident most clearly in the relationship between Else and Penny. Though her name identifies her with the physical materiality of cash, Penny in fact has little to do with the reality of how the world of money works. Her life as a journalist is cosseted by complimentary hospitality, the invisible settling of expenses, and remote transactions based on credit. Unlike Else, she has little use for the raw stuff of money, a fact that is emphasised when, during the chance encounter that brings them together, it is Else who provides the coin to unscrew the cover that hides the lift shaft down which Sara has fallen. Penny is totally insulated from the social inequality that surrounds her, both by the plush respectability of the hotel and by a conservative mindset that disregards all about the world that does not correspond to her sense of personal ease. She is aware of the existence of less privileged social strata and flirts with the idea of experiencing the abject danger they represent, maybe even of exploiting them for an exposé of Blair's Britain. She is, however, only fully comfortable regarding the outside world when she is ensconced within the safety of her bubble of wealth. Lack of money is synonymous with a dirty and morally suspect social condition for Penny and, though titillated by the journalistic potential of deprivation, she is fundamentally afraid of the lack of meaning it represents.

Her encounter with Else thus brings together two totally conflicting visions of money's value. Initially Penny regards it as an opportunity to effect the kind of social investigation of which she believes herself to be capable: 'It was foul and queasily exciting, this humdrum digestive-system exotica of others' lives; Penny was repelled and energized by it' (Smith, 2002: 163). Penny's version of being brought together with another involves a deceitful performance of a slummed-down subjectivity aimed at winning Else's trust. Peddling various stories of a miserable upbringing involving family breakdown and promiscuous sexual relations, Penny identifies herself with the excluded in a shameless parody of personal crisis. She, more than any of the indifferent passers-by, exploits Else because she goes to the trouble of entering the homeless woman's world, only to reassure herself of its degraded otherness. Back in her hotel room, and convinced of her investigative intrepidity, she has no qualms about cancelling the cheque that she has written Else on the grounds that 'If you were poor, you were poor. You couldn't handle money. Money was nothing but a problem if you weren't used to it' (Smith, 2002: 178). This depressing reversion to type and to the easy clichés of wealth inequality displays a darkness at both the moral and the linguistic core of the novel that is aptly metaphorised by the disused lift shaft. Global capitalism is, for Smith, a vortex into which compassion, empathy, and difference are drawn to be nullified by disabling self-interest, wilful blindness, and homogenisation.

Despite the depressing familiarity of Smith's conclusions about the debilitating moral effects of money-greed, *Hotel World* is not a depressing novel, nor does it despair about the possibilities of human beings transcending their material neediness. Drawing back from the abyss, it focuses our attention on the immaterial as a surplus that can escape form and meaning. The ghost of Sara presents an evanescent reminder that not everything is determined by the physicality of the hotel and that the urge to live and love is ultimately as strong a shaping force as money. This might appear hopelessly idealistic, and Sara's dwindling voice suggests the fragility of the call to humanness in the face of more robust material claims, but Smith has made her name reminding us of the viability of difference, and here she calls us to reflect on the error of prioritising things over sentiment. Sara's death has prevented her from discovering the possibilities of sympathy with a girl working in a watch shop, but the fact that that girl's life has been touched briefly and in a beautifully indefinable way offers a powerful antidote to the explicitness of materialism.

The Accidental (2005)

The sharpness of Smith's satirical eye is turned in her next novel on the wilful blindness of Penny's middle-class peers in the face of the increasingly interruptive uncertainties of twenty-first-century living. The Smart family, holidaying in Norfolk, are a catalogue of affluent dysfunction. Smugly insulated from the kinds of keen socio-economic winds that blew through *Hotel World*, they are nevertheless inhibited from connecting meaningfully with each other by the pressures of aspiration and the spectres of failure that dominate their lives. Each is solipsistically engaged in pursuing justifications for their own worldviews and is consequently blind to the desperate need of the others. That is, until the appearance of Amber. Amber exemplifies a familiar trope in Smith's writing: the external catalyst propelled into the world of the narrative in order to make apparent to the protagonists the limits of their ingrained vision. The strategy is used in a number of stories, but it has become increasingly central to Smith's longer fiction, in which outsiders often tie the various narrative voices together. In *Hotel World* the ghost of Sara Wilby hovers over the interconnecting accounts of the other narrators, drawing their life trajectories within a critique of late capitalism's affectless machinery of globalisation. In *The Accidental* and *There But For The*, the outsider is material, but largely without a narrative voice, existing instead as a presence which, through the mystery of her/his motivation, prompts others into the reassessment of their own. By taking up unexplained residence in a casual acquaintance's spare bedroom in *There But For The*, Miles absents himself from the narrative, thereby creating a symbolic hole for others to fill with insubstantial interpretations. His catalytic impact is on those who seek to explain his actions and who, in the process, reveal the visionless poverty of their own motivations. In *How To Be Both*, the spirit of a Renaissance fresco painter is inelegantly propelled into the world of a teenager grieving for her mother; the painter watches over the girl's struggle to accommodate her loss with a mixture of wry self-regard and compassion. Throughout her writing, the force from outside is also a force from inside that reveals to Smith's characters that they have the choice of 'opening [their] world out into wider worlds or different forms or different notions, or whether there's anything beyond the wall you think that's in front of [them]' (Murray, 2006: 195). The outsider precipitates crises of vision in characters' lives but also offers them the possibility of seeing beyond themselves, or beyond the worldviews that have trapped them.

The four narrative strands of *The Accidental* – told by Michael and Eve Smart and their children, Magnus and Astrid – display common characteristics: each character believes that s/he is in some way fake, that her/his experience of the world is ersatz, and that s/he is caught in spirals of inauthenticity. Furthermore, each of them is divorced from the world around them in a way that catastrophically inhibits their ability to empathise with others: Michael, university lecturer in literature, narcissistically flaunts his learning in order to seduce his female students; Eve, an author of popular history books, absorbs herself in the past and in visions of herself as a middle-class have-it-all woman whilst simultaneously struggling with disablingly low self-esteem; Magnus has retreated so far from the world since he perpetrated a school prank that led to the suicide of a fellow pupil that he regards himself as 'Hologram Boy'; and Astrid, deprived of parental attention and guidance, carries with her an expensive camera with which she tries to frame the world into a comprehensible sequential logic. Lost to themselves, each member of the family seeks some form of subjective traction, a grasp on her/himself that validates her/his place in the world, yet all of them have somehow forgotten what being themselves might mean. Individually they dwell in states of desperate self-interest, referring to the world around them only insofar as it confirms their solipsism, and seemingly only aware of the shadow presence of others. Collectively they embody the kind of affective disconnection that Smith associates with postmodernity's loss of faith in the real.

The world of democratic security and liberal peace in which they live is also a world desensitised to threat by the bland superficiality of middle-class homogeneity. It is a world where everything dangerous or disruptive has been pushed to the extremes: politics, morality, justice, and culture have all been flattened into an unquestionable consensus, and anything distasteful – the Iraq war, the growth of Internet pornography, or the commodification of history – is regarded with weary detachment. The Smarts, as their name suggests, are all intelligent, accomplished individuals who know the game of twenty-first-century irony and have adopted – to the point of internal-isation – the idea of themselves as self-determining consumers. Yet each of them has also erected a shield between themselves and the world that medi-ates their engagement and protects them from recognising the consequences of their complacency. Michael's espousal of modernist poetry projects a suf-ficiently avant-garde glamour to allow him to exploit his students, but really his extra-marital activities are a laboured attempt to protect himself from his own intellectual mediocrity. He speaks and thinks in cliché, but does so in a way which is pitched to suggest his ironic awareness of the fact:

> Deeply exciting, though, cliché was, as a concept. It was truth misted by overexpres-sion, wasn't it, like a structure seen in a fog, something waiting to be re-felt, re-seen. Something dainty fumbled at through thick gloves. Cliché was true, obviously, which was why it had become cliché in the first place; so true that cliché actually protected you from its own truth by being what it was, nothing but cliché. (Smith, 2006: 59)

Michael's vanity expresses an anxiety about the used-upness of the 'already known and been and done and postmodern-t-shirt regurgitated' (Smith, 2006: 60) world, and it is one shared by Eve, whose name may suggest authentic origins – her first husband, and the children's father, was Adam – but who is equally trapped in a cycle of reproduction. Her series of historical fictionalisations of real people is called the 'Genuine Article', yet Eve has become so totally separated from any sense of her own authenticity that she conducts aggressively interrogative Q&A dialogues with herself that simply confirm her low opinion of herself. Ageing, a growing disconnection from her children, and a suppressed disgust for her husband have emphasised Eve's self-alienation and brought into sharp focus the thwarted expectations and compromises that her life has involved. Her self-defence is a mantra about the excessive demands on contemporary femininity:

> It is very very hard work indeed [...] to be a woman and alive in this hemisphere in this day and age. It asks a lot, to be able to do all the things we're supposed to do the way we're expected to do them: Talent. Sex. Money. Family. The correct modest intel-ligence. The correct thinness. The correct presence. (Smith, 2006: 85)

Though poignant, this is just as much a self-deception as Michael's philan-dering, and it is just as much a cliché that prevents Eve from seeing herself as having a choice about her way of life.

Their parents' inability to break free from habitual thinking has inhibited Magnus and Astrid in shaping themselves within the world. Circumscribed by lies and conveniences, they have grown to adolescence with a sense that the world needs to be ordered and made safe for it to be bearable. Magnus' guilt at his fatal prank has resulted in such a serious self-alienation that he can no longer regard his body as an expression of his interiority: 'The real Magnus is this, now, massive, unavoidable. The real Magnus is too much. He is all bulk, big as a beached whale, big as a floundering clumsy giant' (Smith, 2006: 38). Become abject, Magnus seeks in mathematics a paradigm for controlling the emotional disconnection he experiences, but predictability and rationalism elude him. The balancing of life's elements into comprehensible equivalences, by which he has learnt to manage his existence, fails him when he is faced with a crisis of emotional literacy. Unable to relate to either of his parents or to find any suitable metaphysical framework for his depression, Magnus is reduced to inarticulacy, from which he feels he can escape only through suicide.

For Astrid the world is either 'substandard' or 'dead', typical teen hyperboles possibly, but inflected with a pathologically vehement rejection of the material world. Her curiosity about the world around her tends towards the macabre but is neither structured nor encouraged by her parents, who have little time to indulge her associative flights. Instead they buy off her neediness with an expensive camera in the hope that it will channel her energy into a solitary pursuit. Her disaffection is consequently transferred to photography, just as Magnus' has found an outlet in the Internet. However, photography feeds her tendency to regard the world at a remove and with the eye of a disengaged observer who records rather than participates in life. It further isolates her because she understands the world not as a fluid interchange of subjective and objective realities but as a series of frames which can be edited into an orderly narrative representation. Her 'Beginnings' project involves photographing successive dawns in the hope of identifying the precise moment at which the day starts, a venture which should be read both as a reaching for a point of certainty and as the expression of a desire to exert an authorial control over the world of things. Her undertaking is, however, forever compromised, and her stability undermined, by relative perspective – Astrid cannot determine whether the day has a definite beginning or starts only when each person opens her/his eyes. Her plea for a point of reliability in the objective world is thus as unanswered as it is in the subjective realm of her family.

The novel's photographic metaphor highlights the problem of vision that bedevils the Smart family: they regard their experience of the world as the negative to a rewarding, meaningful, and connected positive print. They are convinced that their shadow existence – the family are routinely described in terms of darkness – is predicated on a happier, fulfilled obverse which is obscured from their vision by an obdurate fate. But Smith's treatment of the image suggests that there is a more fundamental breach between the appearance and reality than the family would recognise. The Smarts are a twenty-first-century family: media-savvy, technologically adept, and conscious of the whirlwind of simulacra that constitutes the contemporary relationship with the referential world. Yet, for all their cynicism, they also retain a residual conviction that the world should be as it seems – they are, for instance, disappointed that the Internet pictures of the holiday home that they have rented do not correspond with the reality. Their ability to behave unironically whilst maintaining a fashionable irony speaks to a discomfort with postmodernity's scepticism, but it fails to acknowledge the changed terrain on which the twenty-first century negotiates imagery. *The Accidental* is a novel preoccupied by the way in which technology has flattened the world into a series of impenetrable images that resist exploration or explanation. It is suffused with attempts to capture the material world in such a way that it will be drawn into sympathy with realms of consciousness and affect, but there is such a fundamental disjoint between the internal and the external that the two cannot be brought together. Astrid's photography and Magnus' facility with the Web represent narcissistic, one-directional engagements with the world that defer emotional or moral commitment and thereby preclude any human and authentic experience. Without that dimension, they, like the images they create, are flat and lifeless. Through Amber, they and their parents must be brought to recognise that authenticity requires ambiguity and nuance.

Whereas the Smarts are repeatedly described in metaphors of darkness, Amber is frequently associated with brightness, such as in her first encounter with Magnus, who believes her to be an angel. When she first meets Astrid, she is perceived as a blend of light and dark: 'There is the shape of someone on the sofa by the window. Because of the light from the window behind the person, and because of the flash of light still filling her own eye with reds and blacks, the face is a blur of light and dark' (Smith, 2006: 18). Amber's lack of definition is key to her catalytic impact on the family. She is impossible to locate within any of the rigid organising structures that order the Smart world: Michael's conviction that she is a friend of Eve is as erroneous as hers that Amber is one of Michael's student conquests. She stands beyond definition; her questionable heritage, Scandinavian accent, lack of received social niceties, even her indeterminate age, all point towards her role as an outsider, a shifting signifier that means something different to each member of the family. The intercut sections that frame the chapters identify her with cinematic fantasy: protean and impalpable, yet desirable and attainable.

She is not, in herself, a point of authentic return for she does not represent anything solid or familiar, but she is a force for authenticity. Her interventions provide each person with the opportunity to see her/his relation to the world in a way that demands action. Amber is not primarily a benevolent force, and the crises of vision that she stimulates are, in Michael and Eve's cases, harshly implemented. She reserves her sympathy instead for Astrid and Magnus, to whom she commits herself by drawing out of them the kinds of self-destructive habituation and nascent self-delusion that have blighted the vision of their parents. By refamiliarising Magnus with his body, and more importantly allowing him to sexually experience the body of another, she enables him to recognise that his responsibility for the death of his peer need not blight his life, nor need it destroy his faith in logical balance; instead his logic needs greater nuance, and to acknowledge human sentiment: 'Is there a calculus for sadness?' (Smith, 2006: 241), he asks in a moment of empathic insight. From Amber, Astrid learns 'the importance of civil disobedience and a healthy mistrust in the abuse of language by so-called authorities. Bolstering Astrid's shaky self-confidence, Amber coaches her to talk back' (Breitbach, 2012: 157). Taking her on a trip to the supermarket, Amber points out the proliferating security cameras which guard against displays of anti-consumerist individualism, and encourages Astrid to retaliate by taking photos of the cameras, defying the disapproving glares of the security guards. On their return journey she drops Astrid's camera off a bridge, deliberately tearing away the screen that stands between her and the world. This act has the profound effect of forcing Astrid to acknowledge her place in the world:

> When Astrid gets home and goes upstairs and locks the door behind her in the room, she catches sight of herself in the mirror and her face is so white that she has to look twice. It nearly makes her laugh out loud, how small and white and angry the face in the mirror looks. It nearly makes her laugh out loud that it is actually her. She stares at herself. (Smith, 2006: 119)

By destroying the camera, Amber forces Astrid to trust her own judgements and to reconnect directly with those around her. The important point to reiterate is that Smith's characters have a choice to see the world differently and to connect in a new way. This is a choice that they can either embrace or ignore, but the consequence of ignoring the call to vision is to remain – as Michael does – locked into a web of self-deception and superficial relations. Eve's journey to self-awareness is the most problematic and involves a harsh lesson in the emptiness of materialism. Her self-imposed exile after Amber has stolen everything the family owns is a step towards a nomadic rejection of fixity, in the senses of both middle-class belonging and self-identity. Eve ultimately discards the idea of herself as an insider and adopts an Amber-like ambiguity as she becomes the external catalyst for another family. Such a transformation is a willed choice for Smith and it represents a decision to accept the carnivalesque, the creative, the random as enabling and formative paths to openness. The external catalyst in Smith is thus associated with a productive blankness, an indeterminacy that nevertheless facilitates meaning. It is effectively a presence in absence, which, whether it takes the form of Amber's elusiveness, Sara Wilby's ghostliness, or Miles' semiotic emptiness, spurs others into anxious reflection on their own substantiality.

Girl Meets Boy (2007)

Though I would not describe *Girl Meets Boy* as one of Smith's most significant pieces of work, it is far from being incidental. In fact, it brings together concerns about untrammelled corporate culture, creativity, self-transformation, and the freedom of not conforming to prescribed subjectivities that have dominated her fiction in recent years. The novel was published by Canongate as part of its 'The Myths' series – contemporary reinterpretations of mythological tales. Taking the story of Iphis from Book 9 of Ovid's *Metamorphoses* allows Smith to indulge not only her talent for fanciful reimagining but also her universalising instinct. *Girl Meets Boy* is a light-hearted examination of the ways in which the cultural dominance of certain kinds of being brings with it the implicit acceptance of certain kinds of meaning. Blending the story of individual resistance to the marketing narratives of big business with the development of a covert lesbian love affair, Smith instates ideas of personal and cultural fixity in order to undermine them with a joyful irreverence.

Anthea Gunn works for a multinational corporation on a project to market bottled Scottish water. Her work on the creative team involves being hectored to identify a tiny niche in an overcrowded market by hipster executives peddling worn-out nationalist clichés. Leaving work, she encounters the androgynous Robin Goodman defacing the company's billboards with statements about water being a human right and not for profit. These are Smith's versions of Ovid's Ianthe and Iphis, who according to the myth are both born girls but fall in love and, on the eve of their wedding, Iphis is transformed into a man. Anthea and Robin's love story is rather more conventional, though still shocking in its irregularity to Anthea's sister Midge. It is not just the couple's lesbianism that confounds public conservatism but also their androgynous intimacy. In the long central section in bed – Smith is contemporary literature's greatest pillow-talker – during which Robin relates the myth of Iphis to Anthea, the playfully dilatory delivery marks the creative spirit of their passionate connection. Their constantly interrupted and resumed retelling reimagines the story from a non-gender-specific position where at points both fluidly interchange dominant and passive roles in the narration. This freedom from gendered voice typifies their intimacy and causes Anthea to wonder why on earth would anyone ever stand in the world as if standing in the cornucopic middle of the Hanging garden of Babylon but inside a tiny white-painted rectangle about the size of a single space in a car park, refusing to come out of it, and all round her or him the whole world, beautiful, various, waiting? (Smith, 2007: 105)

The 'tiny white-painted rectangle' represents the limit of vision of those, like Midge and the Pure corporation, that function with a view to the absolute correctness of certain discourses and consequently fail to recognise that the vibrancy of life exists in the interstices between rigid states of being and seeing. Pure, like Global Hotels in *Hotel World*, has aspirations to infiltrate every aspect of consumers' lives, to make it 'natural for someone [...] to spend his whole day, obliviously, in Pure hands' (Smith, 2007: 116), but this kind of monopolisation results, as far as Smith is concerned, only in diminished horizons and miserable automatism. Working against this narrative of singularity, Anthea and Robin's divide-crossing love extends the possibility of otherness at every level of telling and retelling. It is 'the story of nature itself, ever-inventive, making one thing out of another, and one thing in to another, and nothing lasts, and nothing's lost, and nothing ever perishes, and things can always change, because things will always change, and things will always be different, because things can always be different' (Smith, 2007: 160).

Smith employs the mythological framework as a reminder that myths reflect 'the imagination and needs of a society [...] as if they emerge[d] from society's subconscious' (Smith, 2007: 89). She rejects the idea that myths are 'conscious creations by the various money-making forces' (Smith, 2007: 89), favouring instead the liberating disorder of a universal subconscious as a metaphor for the working and reworking of collective narratives. That such stories retain relevance across time, bubbling up occasionally as if communally willed, represents for Smith a pure creative force that resists hegemonic discipline. Instead it is transformative and chaotic, ushering in not just the possibility of difference but the possibility of its acceptance too. Her tale has the optimism of a mythic form that knows itself to be open-ended and expectant of future revisioning. In the same way, she hopes that the full breadth of human being and self-experience will be subject to continuous transformation and social inclusion.

There But For The (2011)

Smith's satirical targets in *There But For The* are familiar from her more recent work: middle-class mores, emotional disconnection, the fetishisation of the image, and the traducing of genuine intimacy by technology. There is also the strain of melancholic reflection on the processes of ageing and decay that has been present throughout Smith's writing career but that claims greater attention here. This is a novel filled with various kinds of death, and it returns frequently to the image of the Greenwich Observatory as a metaphor not only for passing time but also for circularity. Unsurprisingly, there is a mournful tone to the novel, which, for all the customary energy and vitality of Smith's prose, suggests a darker reflectiveness. Certainly her vision of contemporary society is marked by a deep cynicism towards the kinds of change in human interaction that the age of unregulated informational extravagance has ushered in. Far from decreasing loneliness and social exclusion, the Internet, 24-hour television, celebrity culture, and mobile technology have simply generated new kinds of soul desolation where profound connection with others has been replaced by superficial, temporary coincidence. The 'Intimate', as May, one of the novel's older characters, tellingly misnames the Internet, typifies the retreat from meaningful relationships in a culture of obsessive observation and instantaneous 'knowledge' exchange. My ironisation of 'knowledge' is not intended as Luddite scepticism but as an indication of Smith's uncertainty about the kinds of knowing that are possible in our current undiscriminated, free-for-all information culture. Information technology supposedly offers unprecedented and uninhibited access to data from every spectrum of human experience, yet Smith wonders at the extent to which this allows us knowledge of things, and particularly others, with any depth.

As the novel's elliptical title confirms, the missing element is crucial to Smith's portrayal of a society out of touch with itself. There but for the … what? 'The grace of God' is likely to be the most commonly inferred conclusion, but this is not a novel about conclusions, and readers, as much as the characters, are left on the cliff-edge of interpretation, unsure of how to proceed. But the absence of the grace of God in a titular sense also reflects its absence in a metaphysical sense, for *There But For The* is a novel that explores the demands of life without the consolation of a deity. At its centre is Miles Garth, an unspectacular and barely described middle-aged man who comes to the reader fragmented through the narratives of four protagonists who are, in their different ways, lost in the world. Anna, who had a brief friendship with Miles as a young woman, is now a quietly melancholic member of the Border Agency, involved in the dispersal of refugees; Mark, a gay man who befriends Miles at the theatre, is persecuted by the internalised voice of his dead mother, which criticises him in rhyming couplets; May, an elderly woman with dementia, is haunted by the early death of her daughter, whom Miles had known and whom he commemorates every year by contacting May; and Brooke, one of Smith's verbally adept and questioning children, is, for all her precocity, damaged by the self-conscious liberalism of her parents, who, wrapped in their own concerns, fail to notice that she is being bullied at school. Brooke finds in Miles a kindred spirit who stands outside the orthodox ambitions of his middle-class milieu, matching instead her imaginative flights with his own intuitive creations. It is to him that she bonds at the dinner-party set-piece and, after he has locked himself unexplained in Genevieve's spare room, it is to him that she slips notes and receives enigmatic responses. Although these relationships intersect to produce a web of nascent connections, Smith's focus is on the fragility and fragmentariness of the threads that bind people and that are frequently rent by the pressures of contemporary individualism.

That precariousness is illustrated when, during the dinner party, Mark drifts into a reverie on the seductive marketing of human connectedness offered by the Internet: 'Google is so strange. It promises everything, but everything isn't there. You type in the words for what you need, and what you need becomes superfluous in an instant, shadowed instantaneously by the things you really need, and none of them answerable by Google' (Smith, 2012a: 159). Part of the problem with the information revolution lies in its excessive surplus, a surplus that inevitably turns to unfulfillable promise, in Smith's eyes, because it cannot come close to conveying the depth of human experience, nor the diversity of desire. The systemic advantage of the Internet is its proliferative tendency, its metastatic growth, which promises the answer to all desire through sheer informational bulk; but, in embracing its aleatoric non-sequentiality, we are at risk of mistaking breadth of reference for depth of understanding. For Mark, this leads to a hollow, and ultimately soul-destroying, solipsism:

> But the charm is a kind of deception about a whole new way of feeling lonely, a semblance of plenitude but really a new level of Dante's inferno, a zombie-filled cemetery of spurious clues, beauty, pathos, pain, the faces of puppies, women and men from all over the world tied up and wanked over in site after site, a great sea of hidden shallows. More and more, the pressing human dilemma: how to walk a clean path between obscenities. (Smith, 2012a: 159)

It is curious that a writer as celebratory of the anti-hierarchical as Smith would reject the rhizomatic instincts of the Web; in many ways it would seem an ideal metaphor for her anti-authoritarianism. However, the kind of passing attention that the Web tends to facilitate is diametrically opposed to the considered, committed focus that she believes underpins true empathy. For Smith, the 'great sea of hidden shallows' is the consequence of allowing machine technology to replace genuine connection. Or rather to allow it to become an excuse to abjure the ethical choice of connecting with another, for, as I have emphasised previously, real intimacy for Smith demands a morally engaged and humane recognition of the other. Profound empathy cannot be articulated in a moral vacuum; it requires some kind of validating frame which may be metaphysical but which might equally involve a conscious human sympathy with the loneliness of another.

Anna Hardie, an old acquaintance of Miles drafted in by his frustrated hostess to provide some context for his actions, suffers acutely from the kind of contemporary existential invisibility that the loss of profound connection generates. Genevieve refers to her throughout the first section as 'Anna K' as this is how she appears in Miles' phone directory, and her name is mistaken elsewhere in the novel. She is described as having 'exactly the right kind of absent presence' (Smith, 2012a: 61), which draws attention back to Smith's interest in the ghostly but is also a symptom of the contemporary mistrust of the real:

> Maybe there was a new psychosis [...] where you went through life believing that an audience was always watching you, profoundly moved by your every move, reacting round your every reaction, your every momentous moment, with joy/excitement/disappointment/Schadenfreude. [...] But would this mean that people who *didn't* have it were somehow less *there* in the real world, or at least differently there, because they felt themselves less observed? (Smith, 2012a: 8)

At the core of Anna's anxiety, and the novel's scepticism about online profusion, lies the issue of frames, and whether one can interpret the world as real without the application of a determining logic. Whether things exist if they cannot be seen might seem like a rather hackneyed philosophical trope, but it becomes the novel's central conceit once Miles locks himself in Genevieve's spare room. His absence creates a hole in the narrative universe that demands filling; he is ever present but the ambiguous quality of that presence begs explanation and contextualising frameworks. Miles is the core of uncertainty against which the surety of others' motivations and desires are judged, and his constant (obscured) presence is a pointed reminder of the inescapability of strangeness that lies at the heart of subjectivity. Genevieve's comment that 'A stranger is living in our house against our will' (Smith, 2012a: 105) is not just a statement about appropriation but a complaint against the dividedness of self. Smith's fiction repeatedly draws attention to the penumbra of self-understanding and a habituated unwillingness to see beyond what is regarded as comfortable, but often here the attention is directed to the strangeness of growth and change as part of the move towards death. At one point Anna wonders:

> Imagine if people decided at birth never to throw away any of the shoes they wore over the whole course of a life, and had a special cupboard where they kept all these old shoes they'd walked about the world in. What would there be in such a shoe museum, when you opened its doors? Row upon row, perfectly preserved, the exact

shapes we took at certain points in our lives? Or row upon row, rack upon rack, of nothing but old soiled leather, old stale smell? (Smith, 2012a: 58–59)

Smith focuses change on the body here. What kind of continuity, she asks, can exist between the various shapes we take across the course of a life, how do we push out to shape the world around us, and what does the sum of all that being amount to? From her first story collection, Smith has engaged with mortality and the profound disconnection between body and mind that can occur in growing old, and here she articulates the inescapability of the end through the shadow presence of Miles. The unwanted tenant is a metaphor for both the part of the self from which the individual is alienated – the self whose drives and motivations are a mystery – and the process of ageing, which takes up residence and profoundly disturbs the relationship between one's various selves. Even Genevieve, the least self-aware of the protagonists, acknowledges the unsettling psychological effect of Miles' presence:

It is strange having a stranger in the house with you all the time. It makes you strangely self-aware, strange to yourself. It is literally like living with a mystery. Sometimes I stand in the hall and listen to the silence. It sounds uncanny and feels like I imagine being haunted must feel like. (Smith, 2012a: 106)

Like 'living with a mystery' is a very apt description of the way in which Smith understands being-towards-death, and Miles is a reminder of the unknown, who, through the ambiguity of his signification, disturbs the equilibrium of those around him.

Smith's epigraphs for the novel – particularly Stefan Zweig's 'For only he who lives his life as a mystery is truly alive' and John Donne's 'Of longitudes, what other way have we, / But to mark when and where the dark eclipses be?' – draw attention to the customary rejection of the unknown whilst suggesting the attainable richness in the acceptance of the blank spaces in knowledge. What cannot be explained should not necessarily inspire despair as it may enable fruitful interpretations and new meanings to arise. This is a typical Smith sentiment, and it echoes with her invocations in *Hotel World* and *The Accidental* to seize life and to see the world more broadly. Certainly Miles' self-effacement from the narrative allows multifarious productive stories about him to emerge; his lack of meaning frees the imagination from the constraints of causes and effects, and allows Smith to mystify life once more. As his sit-in stretches from weeks to months, and news of his exploits spreads, the house is besieged by modern-day acolytes, drawn to his enigmatic silence as if to the pronouncements of a charismatic cult leader. Rebranding Miles as Milo, those gathered maintain a vigil in the hope of some curtain-twitch or sign of recognition. Smith has great fun at the expense of these would-be disciples, but her point is that, in a period and culture which has largely replaced the metaphysical with the material, we are nevertheless still compelled by the spaces that resist ordering structures of knowledge and quantification. The Internet age is characterised by systems of over-signification and scopic control which run counter to genuine imaginative freedom. Though the prospect of multiple, crowd-sourced answers to any conceivable question appears to democratise and extend access to knowledge, Smith's conviction is that technology is a false god, in that it offers a system for ordering the world but misinterprets the human interest in the edges of the knowable and bearable as satiable by pornography and consumerism. The human being will always be drawn to that which stands outside signification and systematisation but will seek to describe it back into an order of knowledge; only there can it be safe and contained. Yet, for Smith, the ordinary and domestic still have the power to be disorderly and discomforting, producing the *unheimlich* shiver, if they can be removed from the frame of the familiar and absorbed back into the mysterious and metaphysical.

There But For The abounds with an anti-authoritarian spirit that rejects the idea of meaningful frames and dominant narratives in favour of openness and spontaneous connection. Its scepticism towards totalising master-narratives is indicated by the use of MGM's 1939 film *The Wizard of Oz* as an intertext. The wizard is painted as the facilitator of desires, the authority figure who provides an overarching power of meaning, yet he is revealed to be a sham, his power nothing more than an arrangement of smoke, mirrors, and good publicity. Miles' 'authority' is similarly dependent on the expression of others' desire and his own unwillingness to account for himself. His refusal to provide a shape for others' thinking does not, however, mean that he fails to intersect with their lives in profound ways. Anna, Mark, Genevieve, May, and Brooke are all marked by the sadness of their limitations: Anna by the regrets at her disappointed potential; Mark by the continuous nagging cynicism of his dead mother's voice; Genevieve by materialistic concern for the fixings of her period home; May by the way in which the death of her daughter has shaped her life; and Brooke by her difference from and rejection by those around her. For each of them Miles offers a narrative within which to locate their self-reflections, but he also offers ways out of existential angst through meaningful connection to others. It is he, rather than her overbearingly liberal parents, who responds most supportively to Brooke, taking seriously her playfulness and its underlying anxiety. He is also a quiet counterpoint to May's grief, contacting her without fail on the anniversary of her daughter's death. For Mark he extends the possibility of an intimate, fulfilling friendship, and even Genevieve is turned outwards, channelling her materialism into an entrepreneurial adventurism. Less aggressively than Amber, Miles enables the possibility of change and a more willing openness to the blank spaces of experience. In the process he articulates Smith's belief that human beings have a duty to participate fully and consciously in the mystery of their lives, and to commit themselves unreservedly to the reality of others. Whilst the contemporary human condition might be searching for a shape to assume, Smith believes that only in rejecting the orthodox, the enframed, and the authoritarian is it possible to find the kind of soul sustenance that actually confirms a commonality in the face of the unknown.

How To Be Both (2014)

As if one had not had one's fill of precocious children in Smith's fiction, another pops up in *How To Be Both*. George, however, for all her middle-class, adolescent tics, is a more rounded character than Brooke, and is more akin to the truculent teenage self conjured up by the narrator in the story 'Writ' in *The First Person*. George is painted in the sombre tones of the grief that has enveloped her after the death of her mother several months before. Lost in the world, and having to care for both her younger brother and her father, who has sought solace in alcohol, she strives to come to terms with her new status by making small commitments of memory. She arranges photos of her mother around her bed, dances for the length of one song every day as her mother did, and seeks to inhabit her mother's gender politics by repeatedly forcing herself to watch an abusive pornographic film on the Internet. Each act is a ritualistic effort of recuperation designed to bring her mother back to life and to cheat death's unbearable singularity. As the novel's title, and any knowledge of Smith's fiction, would suggest, being one thing only is less desirable than being two, and death *is* cheated, if not quite in the way that George anticipates. For, fighting back through the subterranean rubble and tubers, and emerging into the twenty-first-century world to watch over her, comes the spirit of Francesco del Cossa, an Italian Renaissance fresco painter with whom George's mother, Carol Martineau, was quietly obsessed.

Such is one way of setting up the novel, but *How To Be Both* cannot be described so straightforwardly as a result of a typically playful structural decision. The novel consists of two distinct but interrelated accounts, both identified as being book/part/chapter 'One' and variously ordered depending on the version a reader selects. Half the print-run of the volume was published with the narrative of del Cossa first, and half with the narrative of George.[2] There is nothing in the front or back matter to advertise this device, so the reader falls into an interpretational pattern which is at once likely to be both predetermined and provisional; the happenstance of selecting one copy from a bookshelf rather than the one next to it thus governs the affect-ive, intellectual, ethical, and aesthetic relations that we will form with the text. Smith explained her reasoning behind the decision in interview with Scott Simon for National Public Radio:

> I think it really changes the notion of a narrative to look at something coming first which otherwise might come second. It's a questioning of the very structure of the novel, which is really about, as Margaret Atwood says, one damn thing after another. You know, that's what plot is. It's like a further nudge to the novel to ask about the ways in which sequence and consequence work 'cause I have a feeling the moral of the novel, in a way, is consequence, and that the novel has a very moral form. I wanted to see what happened when we shuffled that notion of consequence. (Simon, 2014)

Elsewhere Smith draws attention to the problem of simultaneity that plot poses, quoting José Saramago's frustrated complaint: 'Why in narrative can't I show things that are all happening at once?' (Lyall, 2014). *How To Be Both* is thus an attempt to circumvent the problem of 'one damned thing after another' by offering an illusion of simultaneity – two interchangeable nar-ratives each dealing with past, present, and future – even though readers are ultimately likely to consume whichever text they choose sequentially. Nevertheless, within the narratives, there is a concerted effort to problema-tise linear diegesis, especially in the use of time. Smith fluidly blends tempo-ral positions, slipping between each frame within the space of several lines and creating, if not simultaneity, then at least a collocation of temporalities. Both effects generate a sense of openness and possibility, for, upon reach-ing the end of the second narrative and recognising that its last page is as inconclusive as the first page of the first narrative, the reader is thrown into a hermeneutic loop that seems infinitely suggestive. It is additionally worth considering Smith's comment above about the moral consequentiality of plot, for Smith has produced, if not a *nouveau roman*, an unconventional, experimental novel which, nonetheless, has a recognisably realist fondness for character and situation, not to mention a strong moral certitude. Smith has amply shown in her collection of lectures *Artful* (2012) her commit-ment to the tradition of the novel and to its need for moral outcomes, and *How To Be Both* does not do away with the idea of consequences as lightly as it plays with form. Instead, Smith's aim is to explore consequences by dis-rupting the teleological arc so that readers experience very different moral outcomes depending on the order in which they read the text, or the number of versions of the text they read. Effectively Smith challenges the idea of plot in a traditional sense without the renunciation of what plot produces. It is an innovative middle way and garnered her the 2014 Goldsmiths Prize for fiction which is 'genuinely novel and which embodies the spirit of invention'

as well as the Costa Novel of the Year award and a shortlist nomination for
the Man Booker Prize of 2014.[3]

How To Be Both is what is sometimes rather leadenly called a novel of
ideas, a phrase which usually implies a lack of drama but in this case points
us towards a feast of hypothetical questions with which the twin narratives
play without feeling it necessary to provide definite answers. Instead the
novel is punctuated by a series of moot discussions which, across the two
narratives, produce a reflective enrichment entirely abjuring firm or singular
conclusions. These questions include: what power does art have to commute
the unavoidable knowledge of death? What is the relationship between art's
value and its worth? Can both the sacred and the profane be artistic? Can
the past, present, and future co-exist within the same time and space? Are
forgetting and remembering necessarily mutually exclusive? Is an individual
tied only to the single body and mind that s/he inhabits? And, in the spirit
of W.H. Auden, does art change anything? These questions appear implic-
itly and explicitly throughout the narratives, but, as much as they are presented as conundrums to be bandied about, often between George and her
mother, they are never closed down in ways which prohibit their recycling.
And indeed, how could they be, for these are complex questions whose discussion is fundamental to human self-realisation and praxis. Smith's structural innovation provides us, however, with an additional barrier on the way
to answers, for the interchangeability of the parallel sections means that
the questions are opened afresh from differing spatio-temporal contexts
depending upon the order in which we read and re-read the text. These are
questions that are not intended to be answered; instead, possible solutions
are offered up, twinned, and entwined across the centuries, creating not an
unfolding of meaning but an enfolding of both question and answer in any
given moment. In so doing, Smith creates an interesting alternative to the
modern narrative which struggles against closure, for she highlights instead
the irrelevance of an end point. Open-endedness is not the renunciation of
closure, she suggests, but an acknowledgement of the impossibility of ending. *How To Be Both* therefore becomes a continuous echo of life's challenges
across people, places, and times, or – like the double helix of DNA, which
becomes such a significant metaphor for George – double and yet single;
finite but infinite; the same but different.

These concerns are neatly encapsulated in the moment of revelation
which seems to have inspired Smith's structural choice, and which is given
to George's mother to describe to her bored daughter:

> when some frescoes in [an] Italian city were damaged in the 1960s in bad flooding
> and the authorities and restorers removed them to mend them as best they could,

they found, underneath them, the underdrawing, their artists had made for them, and sometimes the underdrawings were significantly different from their surfaces, which is something they'd never have discovered if there hadn't been the damage in the first place. (Smith, 2014b: 288)

Carol Martineau sees this serendipity philosophically, teasing her daughter with the pseudo-Berkeleyan riddle of which drawing came first, but what could appear an indulgence cuts to the core of the novel's affective, moral, and structural import. For it forces the reader to set the narratives of Francescho and George against each other rather than reading them as a historical continuity. As with the drawings, the reader is asked to consider which narrative (regardless of historical setting or reading order) comes first, for both engage with the same fundamental set of issues: grief; the desire for a fitting place for oneself; the determination of one's true value; the search for meaning; and the felt experience of friendship. Smith, again in her interview with National Public Radio, commented that she was indebted to Walter Benjamin for this insight:

[Benjamin] says a thing from the past and a thing from the present, when they come together it's not that the thing from the past throws light on the thing from the present or the thing from the present throws light on the thing from the past. It's that in their meeting they bring about a new immediacy, a now-ness, which is even more than present. (Simon 2014)

By this token, concepts such as past and present are not superfluous, but their coincidence gives forth a new dimension of valency which Smith describes in the novel as the condition of being 'both'. This 'both-ness' is highlighted repeatedly in minor descriptive details – the water of remembering and forgetting that Francescho drinks (Smith, 2014a: 142); gold properly burnished, which gives both darkness and brightness (Smith, 2014a: 166); the palace of Schifanoia, which is both light and dark (Smith, 2014a: 235); the obvious gender parallels of women with male names – but it also underpins the representations of life and death that are articulated most clearly in George's narrative. To understand that, it is important to consider her collapse into grief more closely.

As we have seen elsewhere in her writing, Smith has a good eye for portraying the maddening inbetweeness of adolescence. Waspish and yet vulnerable, catholic and yet focused, George represents the combination of childish and adult worlds. Into the latter she has been thrown by her mother's death, but she has not lost the superstition or creative mania of childhood, and, in seeking to explain her loss, she has only these residues and a halting understanding of adult motivations to assist her. She is an intelligent individual whose talents lie predominantly in her linguistic abilities;

she has a grammarian's pedantry, is a Latinist, and has a neat turn of phrase for which her mother pays her. The clinging to the specifics of grammar is an adolescent's contrarian trait, as is George's way of solidifying the world into something correct, shaping it into a regular pattern with which she feels in accord. Moreover, stickling over language endows her with a certain amount of power, and the kind of resistance to authority that her parents value but which, in their own recalcitrant daughter, they find uncomfortably impractical. In the face of sudden and inexplicable death, however, the familiarities of language no longer console, and, as George remarks to her school counsellor, Mrs Rock, 'I don't care any more about syntax' (Smith, 2014a: 200). The security of linguistic minutiae has given way to the silence and blankness of the enormous unknown:

> It isn't about saying. It is about the hole which will form in the roof through which the cold will intensify and after which the structure of the house will begin to shift, like it ought, and through which George will be able to lie every night in bed watching the black sky. (Smith, 2014a: 201)

In this enormity George is searching for something to explain the absurdity of her loss, to shape it into meaningful, recognisable knowledge. She is a seeker – her name was taken from the 1966 song 'Georgy Girl', released by The Seekers – and is someone who rehearses, through imitation and rituals of memory, the connection back to her mother. Yet the incontrovertibility of death repeatedly stymies her, and when she repeatedly catches herself using the present tense to describe their relationship she forces herself to change it to an emphatic and unnegotiable past. Death, it seems, is the hard place against which Mrs Rock is the only alternative. However, the counsellor is as unyielding as her name suggests, a caricature of institutionalised therapies which have little to offer in the face of justifiable sadness other than the kind of textbook mantra that informs George that grief has 'three, or five, or some people say seven' (Smith, 2014a: 191) stages. Mrs Rock either parrots back George's comments in the form of questions or sits in silence surreptitiously glancing at the clock. Whilst there is sympathy in her manner, the 'correct' way to deal with mourning that she has learnt prevents her from ever engaging empathetically with her charge, meaning that the sessions are largely pointless. Grief, Smith suggests through these episodes, cannot be packaged or formalised, and largely resists language's efforts at description. Grief is rather the consequence of the mystery of death, which, in one of her moments of reaching out to George, Mrs Rock explains lacks any of the modern connotations of resolution:

> The word mystery originally meant a closing, of the mouth or the eyes. It meant an agreement or an understanding that something would not be disclosed. [...] But now we live in a time and in a culture when mystery tends to mean something more

answerable, it means a crime novel, a thriller, a drama on TV, usually one where we'll probably find out – and where the whole point of reading it or watching it will be that we will find out – what happened. And if we don't, we feel cheated. (Smith, 2014a: 258)

George is a victim, Mrs Rock implies, of modernity's dread of the inexplicable, and the structures of reason that are erected to mitigate the pain of a truth that is undisclosable trap her in a hopeless search for meaning. Grief is akin, in these terms, to the Minotaur's labyrinth, which becomes a touchstone of George's narrative, a place of loss and isolation that can only be negotiated alone. But, whereas Mrs Rock appropriates the labyrinth as a metaphor to explain the individual's dark, solo journey back to life, George triumphantly points out that the forbidding challenge of the Minotaur's lair was defeated only by the combined efforts of Ariadne and Theseus – woman and man, both and together.

This is significant, for mourning is represented by Smith not as an unbreachable singularity but as an experience of both-ness. It involves a condition of being simultaneously emotionally dead and alive; in pain and yet numb; beyond meaning and yet immersed in it; stuck in the past and present but seemingly without a future; empty and yet full of the past of the lost. Moreover, death is an opportunity for transformation, for becoming something more than the limits of the self; in Francescho's narrative, for instance, it is on the death of her own mother that she assumes the guise of a man in order to learn her trade as an artist. Even more pertinently, Smith's narrative structure proposes the possibility of death and life being co-terminous through another thought experiment, which proceeds as follows: if a person (such as the true Renaissance fresco painter Francesco del Cossa) is recorded at one point in history but then disappears without documentary trace, only to be rediscovered hundreds of years later, is he, for that interim period, alive or dead, or both? The del Cossa on whom Smith based her novel is believed to have lived in the mid-fifteenth century but, apart from his work, did not trouble the historical record until the nineteenth century, when a letter by him to his patron requesting greater remuneration to reflect the higher quality of his work was discovered (Smith, 2014b). Does this constitute a revivification, asks Smith, in the same way that the fictionalised del Cossa comes tumbling into the world of twenty-first-century Cambridge, or was the painter metaphorically alive during the intervening years? It is a version of a Schrödinger paradox which fits in well with the novel's other scientific metaphors, for it suggests (à la Benjamin) that the past and present, the dead and alive, can exist simultaneously in a new form of both-ness. If the frescoes and the underdrawings co-exist but only one is visible, that does not invalidate the presence of that which cannot be seen. Indeed there are numerous instances in the novel of living things being hidden, or made mysterious in the archaic sense – George and her friend Helena hide behind the wall of photos they have created; George puts up posters to hide the crack in her bedroom ceiling through which water seeps; Henry hides from his sister in the garden. Is it feasible, then, that the mother who seems so incontrovertibly dead could actually be conjured from hiding into sight?

There are two answers to this question: one literary, the other visual. The literary was picked up by two of the novel's reviewers and regards George as the creator and narrator of the Francescho section of the novel (Benfey, 2015; Clerk, 2014). Justification for this reading emerges largely from the school project on empathy and sympathy on which George and Helena work collaboratively. Initially electing to use del Cossa as their example, they are faced with the problem of how to effectively empathise with someone so remote in time and so obscure to history. Rejecting the idea of trying to reproduce an authentic voice, they consider endowing del Cossa with their own vernacular, at which George balks, believing: 'You can't just make stuff up about real people', to which Helena responds: 'We make stuff up about real people all the time' (Smith, 2014a: 325). Christopher Benfey (2015) suggests that the phrase 'Just saying', which appears several times in Francescho's narrative, is an identifying mark of George's voice, and one might also point to the abbreviated ''cause' as a similar clue. However, it is George's next reflection that gives most weight to the notion that she is Francescho's author:

> You'd need your own dead person to come back from the dead. You'd be waiting and waiting for that person to come back. But instead of the person you needed you'd get some dead renaissance painter going on and on about himself and his work and it'd be someone you knew nothing about and that'd be meant to teach you empathy, would it? It's exactly the kind of stunt her mother would pull. (Smith, 2014a: 325)

George, as we have established, imitates her mother, so it would be a sensible assumption that she would ironically subvert her own wishes by bringing back to life through narrative a prolix Renaissance painter rather than the mother she so desperately needs. And, by transforming del Cossa from a man to a woman, she not only makes things up about history but also honours her mother's politics and subversive imagination. Whilst this is an alluring reading, I feel that it runs counter to the notion of both-ness that Smith has woven so closely into the fabric of the tale. To see Francescho's narrative as a metafictional outcome of George's grief institutes a narrative structure of precession and succession with George's as the primary account. For me, this goes against the random and egalitarian spirit of the novel which regards the narratives as two sides of the same coin. An alternative, or compromise, reading would suggest that the Francescho section both is and isn't the work of George, which, for all the contortions it requires, is at least consistent with Smith's ludic style.

The other way in which George might be seen to recuperate her mother is through her engagement with the visual, and in particular with the power of the artful. Throughout both narratives, the question of art's worth is tied closely to the expression of power. In the Renaissance section, Francescho's talent is subordinated to the vain whims of her patrons, especially the aristocratic Borse D'Este, for whom the value of art is utterly subordinate to its price. Francescho's labour in the Schifanoia Palace is dictated not only by the order to follow artistic precedents but also by the threat of exposure as a woman and ensuing destitution; she is disempowered by the artfulness of both her imagination and her gender. In the contemporary narrative, the 'artistic' correlative to the frescoes, the pornographic film that George forces herself to watch, is a brutally succinct instance of the market power of the sensational. The two are directly linked by the notion of value, for, just as Borse declares that Francescho is worth no more or less than the other artists, so George's father, in a lather of middle-class righteousness, dismisses the suffering of the young woman in the film with the words: 'She was probably very well paid for it' (Smith, 2014a: 224). What both responses highlight is the masking of suffering by the power of representation; art and its derivatives paper over the cracks in the great unknown just as George hangs posters over the hole growing in her bedroom ceiling whilst secretly allowing the damage to worsen. This consonance between pain and the spectacular is illustrated when George notices the pictures of earthquake victims in her brother's school book:

> There is one picture of a small girl holding a teakettle and standing against a backdrop of aid tents. It's a natural disaster and it looks a bit like a fashion shoot. Well, almost all photos of roughed up places, so long as there are no actual dead people in them, look like a fashion shoot. *Sooner or later*, George's mother said in her head, *the ones with the dead people in them will look like a fashion shoot too*. (Smith, 2014a: 361)

The sepulchral voice of her mother reminds George that art demands a particular type of looking, one which is directed in such a way as to make even the unpalatable seem beautiful, or at least artful. Art is about the focusing of attention, about being made to see in particular ways, and is thus artfully empowered in the dual sense of artistic and the more suspicious sense of manipulative.

Her mother's voice is important here because it points to particular ways of not just looking at but also reading the ways in which art can also be a site of resistance to power, ways that she must learn before she can make her way out of the labyrinth of her grief. By watching the pornographic film repeatedly, George displays a willingness to commemorate her mother's politics, but her reading is simplistic and sympathetic rather than truly understanding and empathetic. George explains to her father that her need to watch the film is to personalise the abuse that she witnesses:

> *This* really happened, George said. To *this* girl. And anyone can just watch it just, like, happening, any time he or she likes. And it happens for the first time, over and over again, every time someone who hasn't seen it before clicks on it and watches it. So I want to watch it for a completely different reason. Because my completely different watching of it goes some way to acknowledging all of that to this girl. (Smith, 2014a: 224)

Watching the film, she believes, generates a connection with the woman, offering at least a token acknowledgement of the humiliating disempowerment endured. It thus grows from a creditable ethical impulse, but, like the digital format in which it is distributed, George's viewing is automatic, repetitive, and identical. Regarding the pain of others (to use Susan Sontag's phrase) is a reaching towards something that matters, an attempt to feel like/ for the girl in the film, but George's repeated viewings are merely sequential rather than profound – she simply watches the film over and over without getting any closer to understanding the suffering that the girl endures. It is as if George thinks she can ethically reboot the experience of both herself and the girl with each click of the play button. She is aware that what she is watching is appalling (unlike her father, who simply rejects it viscerally), but she has no way to connect with the individual on the screen, and so repeating the experience is traumatisation without any kind of emotional consequence. She is merely seeing.

By the time that she is playing truant to sit in front of del Cossa's portrait of Saint Vincent in London, she has learnt to read rather than purely see. If her viewing of the film is digital in its horrific replicability, her experience here can only be described as analogue, for the source material subtly mutates with each viewing, as does its viewer. The painting focuses attention in an entirely different way to the exploitative film or earthquake book, pulling the viewer's gaze in a way which is exploratory and enriching. George notices 'the stone road [...] which seems to be changing from road into waterfall', then 'a Jesus at the top in a sort of gold arch', then 'the saint is standing on a little table', then 'very small people in the background behind the saint's legs' (Smith, 2014a: 341–342). Unlike the titillating immediacy provided by the pornography, George engages with the painting over time, forming and refining an aesthetic sense as she does so. It is this attention to looking, to seeing the nuances of the piece, which allows her to master a fully mature, affective response. Importantly, she doesn't – and does not need to – understand the numerous significatory levels of the painting; knowing is suspended in the face of the aesthetic. Instead it is the experience of the work as a felt, bodily and emotionally connected response that enables her to appreciate its exemplary qualities.

These skills of subtle looking and reading she has learnt from her mother, to whose passion for art's ironical properties she is drawn despite herself during their trip to the Schifanoia Palace. Carol Martineau revels in what is hidden or quietly resistant in representation; she seeks below the surface for the deviations of the imaginary underdrawing, for it is through the anomalies between the manifest and the latent that she believes the value of a work of art emerges. Her own artistic practice mines this irony to reveal the duplicitous shallows of contemporary culture. Her 'subverts' – disruptive Internet pop-ups that mock the vanity and hypocrisy of political leadership – break through the white noise of a celebrity-driven culture to coruscate the simplifiers and sclerotic hierarchs of mediated production. The most successful of her subverts depicts

> a baby Blair [...] in a nappy and so on but standing fully-formed and otherwise naked on a shell (not the beach kind, the missile kind) with Thatcher all puffed-out cheeks blowing his hair about and baby Blair with one hand over his crotch and the other coy at his chest and the caption underneath: The Birth of Vain Us. (Smith, 2014a: 205)

This image is a neatly worked echo not only of Botticelli but also of the rebirthing of Francescho as a man. Carol embodies a contrarian unwillingness to accept the received (or as George puns 'deceived') wisdom of the world, and celebrates resistance in all forms, even in her daughter's exasperating pedantry. Art, in her view, should disempower those who would only have the world as it is, and there is a clear narrative echo in the small acts of subversion which Francescho builds into her paintings at the Palace. Smarting from the Borse's refusal to recognise her greater worth, she makes subtle additions and emendations to the mythological panorama which ridicule his claim to be the embodiment of justice. The irony is further sharpened in that he is unaware of the irreverence because he is too busy pompously addressing the hordes of citizens who have actually come to the Palace to admire Francescho's caricatures.

What George learns from her mother is the power of the image to disconcert authority and to bring back into the realm of the comprehensible that which has seemed to be outside it. Similarly to Astrid in *The Accidental*, she discovers not only that the limitless enormity of reality needs to be masked by representation but also that the gaze of the mysterious, whether it be the unbearable pain of mourning, the fear of being isolated, the imponderable question of her sexuality, or the cruelty of others, can be faced and returned without damage. Surrounding herself by images of her mother is one form of Platonic self-empowerment, and learning to read the narrative of the visual is another, but in her pursuit of Lisa Goliard she gains a control which allows her to begin to 'maze the minotaur' of her own grief.[4] Lisa is the novel's true mystery and one which is, suitably, never resolved. She could be an agent of surveillance assigned to scout Carol's subversive activities, or she could be the book-making friend with a straightforward erotic interest that she seems. The mystery is largely irrelevant, but the fact that she represents such a significant, if amorphous, threat to George isn't. Lisa's presence runs through both narratives like a traumatic memory, one that still inspires 'Guilt and Fury' (Smith, 2014a: 245) in George. She is the third element of the relationship between George and her mother, the one that George unconsciously reveals to Mrs Rock before retracting (Smith, 2014a: 256) and that is associated with the word 'liar' throughout. George's inability to come to terms with her mother's (possibly homoerotic) relationship with Lisa, and her inability to accept that her mother had a life outside the family, adds another level of conflict to her grief. The hole of unknowing disables her completely, and it is only through pursuing the woman she believes to be Lisa, sitting outside her house, and taking numerous photographs of her curtained windows that George is finally able to exert a modicum of control. Whatever Lisa's relationship with her mother, George is powerless in the face of not knowing, but, as with her mother's subverts and Francescho's frescoes, her images disrupt the authority of ignorance and allow her to face the mystery without needing to understand it. This may not recuperate her mother physically, but it enables her to resurrect her spirit.

How To Be Both is such a distillation of Smith's thematic concerns, stylistic tics, and formal mastery that it is difficult to imagine the novel having been written by anyone else. Its content richness means that the assessment here has necessarily focused only on salient aspects of the text, and it is certainly a work that will repay close and extended attention in future years. In one of the hands-off notices that literary critics frequently receive from reviewers, Tom Adair in *The Scotsman* described its likely fate: 'Sooner or later this quirky, doppelganger book will be purloined by the universities, footnotes spread around like ticker-tape, and the ghosts of Burke and Hare in the wings awaiting their moment to grab it' (Adair, 2014). If, as a critic, I am a life-denying, grave-robbing pedant, then I am at least, with George Martineau, in good company.

Coda

Given the musical associations of the term, and the homophonic potential of its translation as 'tail', it seems particularly appropriate to end this chapter with a coda rather than a conclusion. Smith's tales are often constructed like musical scores with themes developed through repetition, counterpoint, dissonance, and harmony. Frequently they circle back through modulated versions to a dominant motif before losing themselves in spirals of creative extemporisation, igniting the page with sonorous verbal variations. Her fiction is also full of musical interludes, such as the bagpipe band that haunts Violet in 'Scottish Love Songs' (*The Whole Story*), the intricate interweaving of *Fidelio* and *Porgy and Bess* in 'Fidelio and Bess' (*The First Person*), and the extended discussion of the origins of 'Somewhere Over the Rainbow' in *There But For The*. It is this musicality that often gives Smith's fiction a quality of airiness and a melodic rather than a diegetic progression. She writes prose that threatens to escape the page, flying in a fantasy of verbal inventiveness that trills and skeins with the sheer joyousness of language's mutability. And yet, thematically, Smith's fiction is often pitched in a minor key and marked by dark, distressing tones. Repeatedly she writes of grief that is world-destroying; too many of her texts contain parental figures slipping away from their children to suggest a consciousness untroubled by a deep anxiety about ageing and loss, and the death of the mother is a particularly recurrent trope. But the sense of imminent loss is ever present in her fiction in many other registers too: the security of relationships is always overshadowed by the likelihood of their demise; the benevolence of the other is always queered by the caprice of that other's desires; the drowning out of difference by a mono-lingual and authoritarian homogeneity is a constant threat. The extravagance of the improvisation is thus counterpointed by the seriousness of the underlying theme, and it is the productive entangling of this duality that most characterises Smith's fiction. Smith's writing world teeters between limitation and liberation but she ultimately accepts this compromise with a rueful shrug and the knowledge that comedy and tragedy are inseparable melodies in the song of human experience.

Notes

1 In her review of the novel, Sylvia Brownrigg claims that Smith 'can give the word "but" such a star turn that you wonder why you'd ever taken it for granted' (Brownrigg, 2011).
2 The edition on which I based my reading has del Cossa followed by George.
3 See www.gold.ac.uk/goldsmiths-prize/about.
4 Construction based on George's discussion with Mrs Rock in Smith (2014a: 364).

2

Andrew O'Hagan

Like George Orwell, a figure who is referenced repeatedly in his work, Andrew O'Hagan is a novelist, journalist, essayist, and reviewer who continues to balance his time between fictional and non-fictional writing when his critical and popular success as a novelist might encourage him to dispense with some of his commitments. To date he is the author of five novels, *Our Fathers* (1999), *Personality* (2003), *Be Near Me* (2006), *The Life and Opinions of Maf the Dog, and of His Friend Marilyn Monroe* (2010), and *The Illuminations* (2015); a non-fictional account of Britain's missing person phenomenon, *The Missing* (1995); and a collection of essays, *The Atlantic Ocean: Essays on Britain and America* (2008). In addition, he is a regular contributor to *Esquire*, the *London Review of Books*, the *New York Review of Books* and the *New Yorker*. In 2011 he was also engaged to be the ghostwriter of Julian Assange's autobiography, but the collaboration ended acrimoniously with O'Hagan describing the Wikileaks founder as 'a little mad, sad and bad' in an article published in the *London Review of Books* in 2014 (O'Hagan, 2014). Whether, at some point, that book sees the light of day in another format remains to be seen, but it would not be surprising for O'Hagan has a penchant for exploring what he describes as the porous 'parameters between invention and personality' (O'Hagan, 2014: 51). In both *Personality* and *The Life and Opinions of Maf the Dog, and of His Friend Marilyn Monroe* (*Maf*) he has examined the precarious balancing act involved in managing a celebrity persona with the maintenance of a coherent sense of private selfhood, whilst, in a more minor key, he ruminates on the dubious fame found by the killers of Jamie Bulger and the serial killers Fred and Rose West in *The Missing*. Given his journalist's nose for the popular appeal of stories of disciplinary transgression, and his novelist's interest in the hubris of self-projection, Assange would seem to be a prime O'Hagan subject, not least because the politics surrounding the divulgence of classified state data and Assange's avoidance of questions of sexual misconduct amply illustrate for O'Hagan contemporary culture's problematisation of the borderline between public and private spheres.

O'Hagan has, in fact, consistently incorporated into the form of his writing a sense that the traditional distinctions between the public and private are increasingly unsustainable in an image-obsessed world where the logic of performative subjectivity holds sway. His work has always walked the line between fiction and non-fiction, blending reportage and drama in a mélange of high and low culture tragi-comedy. And, in truth, these categories do not best describe a writer comfortable in the interstices of literary forms. O'Hagan has the moral vision of a nineteenth-century realist, the psychological depth of a modernist, the political bite of a social documentarist, and the philosophical eclecticism of a contemporary cultural theorist. Add to that a journalist's work ethic and we have the closest thing to a twenty-first-century Orwell that British letters currently has to offer. Stylistically, his writing is characterised by metaphorical precision, dialogic vibrancy, and a lyricism that often stands in stark contrast to the subject being depicted, such as the description in *Be Near Me* of an Ayrshire beachscape with its broken bottles, plastic-bag jetsam, and a smell 'so high it reminded me of the French poet's lily that soaks up blue antipathies' (O'Hagan, 2007: 64). Reviewers have heaped praise on the meticulous attention to the poetic harmony of his writing[1] though for some, O'Hagan's linguistic intensity can, at times, distract from the subjects with which he is engaging.[2]

The most commonly occurring theme in the work under consideration here is the complex constitution of selfhood, and, in particular, the ways in which identity is made rather than makes itself. Though, particularly in *Be Near Me* and *The Illuminations*, O'Hagan addresses the existential condition of the isolated consciousness at moments of moral crisis, he customarily positions that drama within the broader context of social, political, or cultural life in millennial Scotland.[3] He balances the personal and the public by employing his principal protagonists as litmus indicators of social trends: Jamie Bawn (*Our Fathers*) on the fate of Scottish socialism, Maria Tambini (*Personality*) and Marilyn Monroe (*Maf*) on celebrity culture, David Anderton (*Be Near Me*) on the Scottish distrust of outsiders (the English in particular), and Luke Campbell (*The Illuminations*) on post-9/11 ideological conflict. The characters are not specific representatives of these ideas, but they are products of their milieux and thus reflect, and inflect, the prevailing socio-cultural landscape. In all his novels O'Hagan's interest lies in the ways his protagonists have been made by the environments in which they have grown up, whether those influences be familial, cultural, topographical, or ideological. The unfortunate lives of Fred West's victims are recounted with genealogical zest in *The Missing*, just as the story of Jamie Bawn in *Our Fathers* cannot be told without recourse to digressive historical forays into his antecedents' lives, deeds, and political ideals. The present is not just contextualised but realised by the past, given meaning only as part of a long inheritance of communal interaction that contains equal measures of unity and division.

The effect of this interrelation of space and time on subjectivisation is profound and, in large part, damaging. O'Hagan's chief characters are in a constant struggle for self-determination against forces that seem bent on containing, limiting, moulding, and defining them in terms of the community rather than the individual. Anderton, Bawn, Campbell, and Tambini restlessly search for a position of self-made solidity and stability in the face of extreme pressure to be what the family, the community, or the world at large would rather they were. Whilst Anderton is immediately cast as the barely tolerated outsider by his community, life experience has already alienated him from himself, forming him into a person that he didn't expect to be, a kind of self-loss that is as puzzling to him as it is distressing. Luke Campbell searches for personal illumination amongst the lights of Blackpool's Golden Mile, struggling to rationalise the loss of control that caused him to murder a group of Afghan children, whilst his grandmother slides towards a forgetful senescence beside him. Bawn and Tambini are imaginatively distorted by the environments in which they have been raised: Maria is the product of a pushy, hyper-critical mother whose determination to make the most of her daughter's talent destroys Maria's fragile sense of self. In *Our Fathers* it is the same: Jamie is a man seeking self-determination away from the influences of his father and grandfather, but, in practice, he cannot develop his own isolated subjectivity without being constantly reminded of the legacies of a potent familial, political, and ideological tradition. Exiling themselves will not allow either to escape the formative influences of the past or of the family; it merely defers the recognition that self-determination can only come through the acceptance of both what they have and have not chosen to be.

The past is never far away in O'Hagan's work, and at times it broods over the present with an accusatory malevolence; insistent, inflexible, and ineradicable, demanding its debts are honoured and its broken promises redressed. Such a tyrannical prohibition against forgetting hard-fought battles for identity and expression is characteristic of recent Scottish history for O'Hagan, who has consistently critiqued the versions of contemporary Scottishness available to him as a writer and commentator. If his characters undergo crises of identity, then they reflect in miniature the problematic question of Scottish selfhood that was much debated in the lead up to the referendum on Scottish devolution in 1997, the elections for the new Scottish parliament in 1999, and even more vigorously around the independence referendum of 2014. Though he largely chose not to publically air his views on the latter test of the relationship between Scotland and the rest of the UK, O'Hagan was voluble on the matter of devolution, which he believed represented a moment of collision where the hopes and expectations for the future were brought up against the entrenched cynicism of a politically pessimistic generation.[4] The prospect of, at least limited, self-determination brought about an anxious questioning of exactly what kind of nation Scotland wanted to become and, with it, the forced acceptance of what Scotland is.

In an article written for the *Sunday Herald* around the time of devolution, O'Hagan declared that, before taking too many steps as a new country, it was necessary for Scotland to re-assess its past: 'Modern nations need to reconcile the common memory. They might feel the need to look into themselves with a passion of civic intelligence – and then move on' (O'Hagan 1999a: 1). This moving on requires not just an acknowledgement of 'what has been bad in Scotland' (O'Hagan, 1999a: 1) but an acceptance of its integral part in the fashioning of the nation. In 2002 a scathing O'Hagan wrote:

> Scotland is presently – and quite horrendously – failing the test of its own modernity. Much of its life is, by and large, a mean-minded carnival of easy resentments; it is a place of bigotry, paralysis, nullity and boredom; a nation of conservatives who never vote Conservative; a proud country mired up to the fiery eyes in blame and nostalgia. It's not nice to think about but it's there, this kind of Scotland, and everybody knows it's there. (O'Hagan, 2008: 24)

Here and elsewhere O'Hagan demands that his fellow citizens address their attitudes towards, and historical involvement with, the rest of the UK, an involvement that has brought them wealth and opportunities that would have been impossible as a small, independent country.[5] The strain of brooding Scottish nationalism that fans cross-border anomie may abhor the idea of acknowledging this debt, but it is only by accepting the totality of the nation's past and foregoing dyed-in-the-wool resentments that the true optimism of devolution can be realised. O'Hagan writes with passion about the schizoid Scottish temperament, about growing up to see a new Scotland emerging from the destruction and decay of the post-war years – one of 'white rooms', 'shining towers', 'maisonettes' with 'the sound of earth-movers outside the window' – but he is always conscious that this newness is indivisible from a troubled and conflicted past, a past that is intrinsic to the very mindset of the nation. This duality, this pastness of the new, can only be reconciled, so O'Hagan argued in 'Scotland's Old Injury', by 'a new way of thinking, a new kind of relation to the old, a way to live, a way to make itself better than the badness that's been and the badness to come' (O'Hagan, 2008: 30). As we shall see, this being 'new in an old-fashioned way' (O'Hagan, 1999a: 1) echoes through his fiction in his construction of both the nation and the individual.

The Missing (1995)

Until the publication of his first novel, *Our Fathers*, in 1999, O'Hagan's reputation had been built upon his journalistic and non-fictional work. This found its most extended expression in *The Missing*, a part-autobiographical, part-investigative treatment of the rise in the number of missing persons in late twentieth-century Britain. O'Hagan maps his boyhood memories of lost acquaintances onto a social history of post-war Glasgow, before broadening his focus onto the national picture of loss and recovery, concluding with an account of Fred and Rose West's multiple murders, which were uncovered in Gloucester in 1994. The text's blending of memoir and reportage is not entirely even or successful, but does point towards O'Hagan's willingness to creatively imagine his participation in Scotland's post-war social rearrangements, aspects of which he would later draw on in his fictional work. Underlying the text's engagement with the realities of life amongst the missing is a more metaphysical concern with the nature of missingness itself. Why people go missing transmutes into a more abstract question of why things, ways of life, beliefs, securities, and empathy go missing, are lost, or become forgotten. The sections detailing the O'Hagan family's settlement in Glasgow from Ireland and O'Hagan's upbringing in the era of tenement clearance and housing schemes speak resonantly of the city that was lost in the name of social progress: 'The Glasgow my grandparents grew up in no longer exists: it has disappeared. I suppose my sense of the family's missing history has always mingled with a sense that their world is missing in other ways too' (O'Hagan, 2004a: 14).

The cityscape with all its complicated intertwined histories and dependencies is intricately tied to the family's self-identity, and its loss is both intimate and municipal in impact. Whilst his family are rehoused in the formidable newness of Glasgow's hinterland, the reconstructed city retains a mystique of the lost past, one that is written into the landscape and familiar bodies of its inhabitants: 'Glasgow sounded like Granda to me; I'm sure they were one and the same' (O'Hagan, 2004a: 4). The solidness of the city masks a public and private insubstantiality, a simultaneous being and absence, and as such reflects *The Missing*'s concern with the shading of the visible into the invisible. At root O'Hagan is perplexed by the disparity between the solidity of documented life and the ethereality of lives lived at the margins, beyond even peripheral vision. How can people or places go missing from sight and yet still be seen, O'Hagan asks, and how can so many simply drop off the register when the register so diligently records their presence? Ultimately *The Missing* leaves its reader with a sense of vulnerability; the individual's grasp in the world of the seen is precarious and the links that hold her/him to time, place, and people are no guarantee of continued recognition.

O'Hagan's desire to understand the many faces of loss in *The Missing* is echoed throughout his fictional (and at times his journalistic) writing. He has consistently struggled to define that quality of missingness that he sees to be endemic in post-war British society and culture. Whether it is characters who are missing to themselves such as Maria Tambini, David Anderton, and Luke Campbell; a celebrity culture robbed of all authenticity (*Personality*, *Maf*); or the gradual erosion of communal ideals in the face of a selfish individualism (*Our Fathers*), O'Hagan's work repeatedly returns to points of disconnection where characters lose their way, values become discredited, and dreams begin to unravel. Published in 2008, O'Hagan's collection of essays and journalism, *The Atlantic Ocean: Essays on Britain and America*, offers some interesting aetiologies for these tropes in his work. Missingness is a condition of contemporary British society, he argues in the introduction, for throughout the 1970s and 1980s Britain 'had already given up both its industries and its idealisms and much of its community to a brand-new notion of the individual' (O'Hagan, 2008: 1). The hard-line Thatcherite challenge to centralised trade union authority within industry allied to a right-wing free-market neoliberalism that encouraged individual entrepreneurialism changed not only the physical landscape of Britain but also its psychological cartography. The privileging of the individual over the communal has come to seem an ideological default that condemns as out-moded such traditional identifiers of social belonging as class, community, and ethnicity. Furthermore, the monadic imperative of Thatcherism with its replacement of a collective utopianism by a call to ethical egotism has led, O'Hagan argues, to a bankruptcy of idealism where the notion of the general good has been supplanted by the generally popular.

This ethos of populism reached its apogee under Tony Blair's New Labour administration (1997–2007), where the pre-eminence of individual choice, allied to a fast diminishing sense of social obligation, brought forth a culture where prurience, self-regard, and political disengagement replaced ideological commitment, community spirit, and mindfulness as ethical lodestars. The rise of celebrity culture, to take one example, with its casual and apparently arbitrary elevation of unremarkable individuals to the level of public notoriety, perfectly exemplifies O'Hagan's belief that populism 'is taken to stand for common sense; a communal blaming and self-pity is held in our culture to answer most persuasively to the call of truth' (O'Hagan, 2008: 6). The metaphysical weight of truth has been downgraded to the status of personal speculation and delectation, rendering individuals and communities coreless, morally aimless, and with an ability to communicate togetherness only through the orchestrations of the mass media's version of reality. 'Margaret Thatcher may have wrecked our former sense of community', O'Hagan argues, 'but she created a temperament for other forms of mass communion based on spite, many of which seek to mobilise collective feeling at 54p a minute' (O'Hagan, 2008: 14). The wraith-like disappeared of O'Hagan's first work represent a broader cultural anxiety: neoliberal Britain, he suggests, is missing to itself.

Our Fathers (1999)

Like *The Missing*, *Our Fathers* concerns itself with the lost and unrecoverable by focusing on the damaged idealisms of three generations of one Ayrshire family. It is a novel about the debts that are owed to the ideals, values, and errors of preceding generations, and the ways in which those sometimes unpayable debts can weigh heavily on the shoulders of the present. It is also a novel about the reconciliations with history that Scotland must make as it moves into an era of devolved self-determination. The problems of moving on through a rational acceptance of the legacies of the past are very much at the heart of *Our Fathers*, a novel where the looming pressures of past ambitions are balanced as precariously as the decaying tower blocks that form its most insistent metaphor.

The narrative is recounted from the perspective of Jamie Bawn, structural demolition engineer in his mid-thirties, who returns to Ayrshire from Liverpool to visit his dying grandfather, Hugh, from whom he has become estranged. Hugh Bawn is the novel's central character in many ways, a cantankerous idealist who, in the wake of the Second World War, brought into being his plans for social improvement by the sweeping away of Glasgow's most impoverished tenements and the rehousing of their inhabitants in swiftly and cheaply constructed tower blocks in the city's outskirts. In one of these blocks, Hugh is now dying, his vision of municipal utopianism badly damaged by the dilapidation of the jerry-built housing schemes, schemes which, with an inevitable irony, Jamie is tasked with demolishing.

Ideologically the two men oppose each other. Hugh is an unreconstructed socialist convinced of the moral as well as physical benefits of his housing projects, whilst Jamie, whose socialist credentials are more New Labour than Old, is a pragmatist who looks with rather pained scepticism at the dreams of his grandfather's generation. Political differences have led to conflict and distance, and Jamie's admiration for Hugh's dogmatic progressivism has turned, over time, into exasperation at the inflexibility of his vision for the future. The crumbling housing schemes attest to the foresight of that vision, but also to its intemperately rushed implementation, bringing with it accusations of cut corners, shoddy materials, and backhanders. In late life, these accusations have returned to dog Hugh, and Jamie finds himself instinctively defending if not his grandfather's methods then certainly his motives.

Hugh's faith in the benefits of social progressivism is rooted in the belief that the past can be escaped, that we should be future oriented and relieved of our dependence on outmoded and hindering models of selfhood. The high-rises that he builds are manifestations of this bristling confidence:

> A face of iron looking out to the future, over the fields and the roads below, and so firmly her mouth was set on future glory. The high-rise future. A land of pure belief and honest work lay somewhere up ahead, where swooning towers would dot the land. (O'Hagan, 2000: 68)

Though architectural in immediate execution, Hugh's progressive agenda is basically ethical in its ambition: 'We must make ourselves all over again', he asserts, to which the narrator (focalised through Jamie's consciousness) adds the telling phrase, 'Rub out the past' (O'Hagan, 2000: 119). To embrace the future requires, in Hugh's estimation, the elimination of the past. This utopianism is clearly presented in the novel as a continuation of the Scottish enlightenment tradition allied to a strong urban socialism that has dominated the twentieth century: Jamie recalls school lessons drilling home the achievements of the industrial revolution with the imprecation 'The work of our fathers might give us hope' (O'Hagan, 2000: 30), and the litany of streets around his home commemorate the lives of Scotland's socialist lineage: 'Keir Hardie Drive. John MacLean Drive. Sandy Sloan Drive. James Maxton Drive. [...] Street after modern street, named for the receding glories of dead socialists' (O'Hagan, 2000: 45). It is from this uncontestable valediction of the past, with all its spurious ideological baggage, that the adult Jamie feels he must fly in order to be master over his own identity, but O'Hagan suggests that exile does not necessarily provide a simple path to self-determination: what's bred in the bone remains there to direct and influence the course of one's life. The novel's primary vehicle for articulating this struggle between past and present, and in particular the process of passing down from one generation to the next, is the family.

As its title suggests, *Our Fathers* is fundamentally concerned with fathering, but on a national as well as an individual level. Jamie is parented by Hugh and his wife Margaret because his own father, Robert, is a brutal alcoholic who regularly beats his wife and bullies his son. Robert is himself in flight from the clarity of his parents' ideals and the strain of social optimism that they represent. His escape to England and self-loss in drink and depression is a renunciation not only of his parents' aspirations but also of those of the nation. Robert wishes to sever the umbilicus of Scottish patriarchalism by 'seeking an end to the question of himself' (O'Hagan, 2000: 5), but, in refusing to be made in the shape of his ancestors, he is consequently unmade by an anger and hatred of the world around him. Yet, by rejecting the summary transference of patriarchal authority offered him by Hugh, Robert effectively tries to reject the past only to find that it runs deeper in him than he had expected. This is made clear early in the novel when Robert's self-disgust is explicitly linked with the entropic slide of the nation:

> My father bore all the dread that came with the soil – unable to rise, or rise again, and slow to see power in his own hands. Our fathers were made for grief. They were broken-backed. They were sick at heart, weak in the bones. All they wanted was the peace of defeat. (O'Hagan, 2000: 8)

Robert (who in name at least recalls two national icons – Robert the Bruce and Robbie Burns) is connected to the landscape; he, to borrow a metaphor used by O'Hagan in 'Caledonia Dreaming', carries 'every complication of the soil in [his] shoes' (O'Hagan, 1999a: 1). But it is a rotten, infertile soil that he treads and one that is diminished by his pathetic defeatism.

Faced with two versions of the Scottish patriarch – the idealistic, politically motivated activist, prepared to sacrifice the individual to the idea, and the violent, alcoholic, self-pitying bully who cares for none other than himself and has no faith in ideas – Jamie initially strives to steer his life by different co-ordinates from both of these. He is literate, articulate, and strong enough to cut the ties with both father and mother when living with his father's casual brutality becomes intolerable. Practical by nature, he is drawn, as a child, to the kinds of academic disciplines that require reason and order. Science offers him a way out of the chaos of his life through regulation and a broader perspective based upon timeless and universal laws. Physics, or more specifically its definition as 'the study of pressure and time' (O'Hagan, 2000: 27), becomes a powerful, recurrent phrasal motif employed to indicate the process of sedimentation that governs not just the physical world but individual and collective behaviours of people. But, despite his grounding in the positivism of science, Jamie is characterised by a geographical and psychological nomadism: his birthplace, Berwick-upon-Tweed, has historically changed ownership between the English and Scottish on numerous occasions, and is presented here as a borderland, an indeterminate space over which neither country has ultimate claim. Jamie's identity is similarly contested, defined more by borderlines (Hadrian's Wall; the seashore he adores) and the empty spaces of demolition than either the triumphantly present concrete beacons of Hugh or the inert, hate-filled living death of Robert. Arrived at early middle age and sure only of his unwillingness to emulate either his real or surrogate fathers, he is thrown into his own crisis of transmission when his partner, Karen, becomes pregnant. Unable to bear the possibility of perpetuating either of the uncompromising poses of fathering that he has learnt, he persuades Karen to abort their child, engendering a climate of tension and insecurity between them. Like his father he has sought to break the chain of familial inheritance and as a result can only exist as an exile from belonging.

Throughout the novel, Jamie undergoes a struggle for place from a position of placelessness; he must arrive at a self-identity that will accommodate, but not be overwhelmed by, the legacies of his forebears, but at the same time he must acknowledge the inexorable pull of the landscape and history on his moral and ideological rudder. As he nurses his grandfather through his final days, he notices the effect on his body of his time spent in Scotland: 'My arms seemed thinner. It was as if, in some strange way, my body was going back in time, becoming a child's body again. All the power had gone out of me' (O'Hagan, 2000: 186). Such a physical disabling speaks not only to the infantalising effect of being around his surrogate parents but also to the impact of Jamie's environment on his sense of self; he is once more overshadowed and dominated by the omnipresence of Scotland's contradictoriness. O'Hagan's point here is that identity is shaped by an environment that includes not just the influence of history and politics but also the physical landscape, art, literature, and music. By this token, selfhood is determined rather than chosen, and agglomerate rather than monadic; the self is the mould rather than its content. Hugh's grand vision for the Glasgow poor was not simply to rehouse them but to reform them by literally providing new vistas for perceiving the world, and, in a nod to this, Jamie ruefully remarks: 'We shape the buildings, afterwards they shape us' (O'Hagan, 2000: 69). It is his consciousness of how he has been moulded by Scotland that makes him so unwilling to return; coming back threatens his sense of self by confirming its existing latent presence in him, leaving him with the unpalatable decision of remaining forever an exile or reconciling himself to the models of masculinity offered by Hugh and Robert.

It is the latter he seeks to do, first in his care of Hugh and subsequently in his reconciliation with Robert, a by now reformed alcoholic making his way by driving a taxi. For Duncan Petrie, Robert's renunciation of drinking indicates the novel's broader engagement with the past on a national level, but for Jamie tackling his father's reformation represents a particular challenge as it involves acknowledging the block to fathering that he has placed in his own life (Petrie, 2004: 176). Only by coming to terms with his past, rather than simply rejecting it, can Jamie hope to return to England, and Karen, with the aim of living a life that is facing towards the future. Such too is O'Hagan's moral for Scotland: turning towards a vision of post-devolution nationhood with a blind optimism about its success would be to wilfully ignore the mistakes of the past, yet to dwell too long in the past brings about its own psychological bottle-necking. What is required instead is an analysis of Scottish history sufficiently dispassionate and self-critical to encompass the multitudinous positive and negative versions of itself.

History in *Our Fathers* is not a distant or closed process; it is one directly accessible, as in the scene where Hugh encourages Jamie to climb the bell tower of Alloway Kirk to read the inscription on the bell, but there is an acknowledgement that, though change is inevitable, it is also productive and desirable for it enables an evolutionary sidelining of some ideas and the foregrounding of others. 'You can't stop change from happening' is one of Jamie's favourite sentiments and it represents a curious dichotomy which goes to the heart of the novel's consideration of the identity, the family, and the nation: change will always occur to sweep away the ideals, monuments, and ambitions of one generation, but it will not change the fundamental nature of things for there is a solidity that comes from the sedimentation process of pressure and time (O'Hagan, 2000: 269). Hugh's ultimate failing is his refusal to accept the obsolescence of his dream. By doggedly defending the purity of the idea, he is unable to recognise that time and change have rendered his protestations irrelevant. His fate is to face the prospect of dying in a building that he commissioned which is so ill fit for purpose that its lift cannot accommodate his coffin. Stable selfhood and nationhood necessitate constant construction and demolition but the building blocks remain the same for, in the words of Hugh MacDiarmid that conclude the book: 'There are ruined buildings in the world [...] but no ruined stones' (O'Hagan, 2000: 282).

Personality (2003)

O'Hagan's second novel also deals with the difficulties of establishing and maintaining a consistent, coherent identity, but here the questions of selfhood are focalised through and refracted by the late twentieth and twenty-first centuries' fascination with the celebrity. The novel begins during the celebrations for the Queen's Silver Jubilee in 1977 (importantly often portrayed as a time of collective national togetherness) and details the rise and fall of Maria Tambini, a thirteen-year-old singing prodigy who is attracted away from her home in Rothesay on the Isle of Bute by the prospect of appearing on the popular TV talent contest *Opportunity Knocks*.[6] Structurally the novel is based around a polyphonic account of Maria's rise to stardom on winning the contest and subsequent struggle to maintain that fame whilst trying to deal with the eating disorder anorexia nervosa, told from the perspectives of family, friends, her eventual lover, and those she meets on her journey – most notably her agent, Marion, and Hughie Green, the presenter of *Opportunity Knocks*. Intercut with these testaments (which focus sometimes only peripherally on Maria's career) are external, third-person narrated chapters that contextualise her rise to stardom against the prevailing conditions of Britain between the 1970s and the 1990s.

Formally the novel is O'Hagan's most ambitious; its heteroglossic construction, which never allows one narratorial voice to dominate, feeds the central theme of how the raucous glitz of celebrity life disguises an internal emptiness. The narrative incorporates not just many competing voices but also a significant generic diversity employing letters, transcripts from newspapers, song lyrics, dramatic scripting, and interviews alongside the more conventional first- and third-person narrative accounts. This formal profusion with its noisy collision of styles, registers, and idioms gradually begins to highlight a crucial narrative lack, however: that is, the voice of Maria herself. Maria's path to celebrity is narrated by those around her but never by herself, and it is not until the final page that readers are provided with her own, brief and unmediated, thoughts. This central silence counterbalances the clamour of information and opinion about her and points towards the moral and symbolic vacuity that O'Hagan sees in the cult of celebrity fetishism. Maria is another of O'Hagan's missing, those who are in some way lost to the values and ideals of contemporary society and whose absence is noted despite their presence. Even though her movements amongst the glitterati of London's showbiz community might make her appear anomalous in O'Hagan's customary casts of low-key, self-deluding male characters, her dilemma is fundamentally similar: how to live a life of integrity and authentic identity in a time when those qualities are harder than ever to define.

O'Hagan has claimed that *Personality* is the final part of a trilogy that includes both *The Missing* and *Our Fathers*: 'The three are stories that try to shine a sidelight into unexpected corners of UK society and dreams and distractions. [...] They say something about the way we live now and at the same time about my own life and consciousness' (in MacLaren, 2003: 14). One can certainly see connections with his previous work in, for instance, the psychological and moral impacts on the individual of place and belonging; the theme of being in exile either from one's community or from one's self; and the wide range of reference to popular culture. O'Hagan sees the three books as tied by the theme of idealism and believes that the idealistic social programmes he represented in *Our Fathers* are 'not unrelated to what individuals do when they are interested in performance and celebrity. They want to form a better and larger world for themselves' (in MacLaren, 2003: 14). It is Rosa Tambini's idealism that drives Maria towards a public audience. Trapped in an unfulfilling job working in the family café, with an unreliable quondam boyfriend and an over-critical mother making her life difficult, Rosa desperately wants her daughter to make of herself the kind of success of which she has been unable. There is a tension in the novel between the intensity of the narrow world of Rothesay and the expansive vista of possibility offered by London, and counterbalancing the successful relocation of Maria to the metropolis are the pinched and disappointed lives of those who have been unable to get away.

Rothesay is a vortex of secrets and lies that holds its inhabitants in place, making it difficult for them to escape the pull of the past and the ghosts of lost opportunities that haunt it. Rosa is a portrait of frustration and depression whilst her mother, Lucia, mournfully looks back on the time, during the Second World War, when she tried to elope to Canada with her lover, only for their flight to end in disaster with the death of both the lover and Lucia's eldest daughter. Throughout his fiction, O'Hagan writes frequently of the desire for escape: often what is being escaped is the family or events of the past, but the act of escape involves an unmaking of the self and a disentanglement from the past that is always problematic. As we have already seen in *Our Fathers*, the residues of place and history are carried with his protagonists, but, unlike Jamie Bawn, Maria manages to break with her home, and at the novel's conclusion we see her about to embark on a trip to Italy with her childhood friend and lover, Michael Aigas. Maria has effected her escape but only by deconstructing, pound by pound, the person she was and reinventing herself in the image of her audience's desire. There is hope at the end, but it is the hope of leave-taking, not arrival; given all her struggles for selfhood, Maria is finally caught between subjectivities.

In his 'Afterword' to the 2003 edition of *The Missing*, O'Hagan makes some useful comments on the politics of watching and being watched that are relevant to *Personality*. With the rapid introduction of CCTV cameras in many of its municipal and residential public spaces, Britain, he asserts, has become the most observed nation in the world. The principle of public security that underpins the implementation of this technology nevertheless has serious implications not only for the civil rights of the citizens of a liberal democracy but also for the psychological well-being of those citizens. Culture in its broadest sense is being infused with a voyeuristic instinct that has outstripped the claim to be preserving social order and is more centrally situated as a prurient and punishing super-egoism. Reality television – with its promise of a mainline to celebrity – and shows that rely heavily on CCTV instil a dynamic of passive observation, but, more than that, they suggest that 'selfhood is something [...] you construct in the echo-chamber of the watchful' (O'Hagan, 2004a: 259–260) and that validation of the self comes through being watched. If culture at large is indoctrinated with the assumptions of culture in the narrower sense of entertainment, then, O'Hagan argues, the implications for the formation of subjectivity are unsettling. The dramatic rise in visibility of celebrity culture since the 1990s has perpetuated the idea that the self can be formed and reformed at the whim of the camera, that identities can be changed as easily as parts of the body, but ultimately such superficiality masks only personal nothingness, an absence of being that merely reflects back the illusion of presence, or, as he argues in 'The Degenerate Heart of Reality TV', 'Fame comes at a price, and the price is often a removal of selfhood, a subtraction of dignity' (O'Hagan, 2005).

Clearly O'Hagan's thinking here informs *Personality*. Maria conducts herself throughout as if she is being observed; from the mock performances as a child in front of the mirror with a hairbrush microphone to the fantasies of her *This is Your Life* moment, she prepares herself for the public gaze. For her, life is a show, reality a performance with the 'best' self put forwards for judgement. The kind of celebrity that is created under the spotlight of observation is Warholian in its ephemerality, but it is one in which both viewer and viewed are complicit in creating. Of the *Big Brother* generation O'Hagan comments: 'we lap up their emptiness, considering it somehow an enlargement of our own mentalities, and we repay them by voting them into further fame, the glory of somebodyhood' (O'Hagan, 2005: 3). Though more idealistically constituted, the mantra of the novel's starmaker, Hughie Green, is not totally divorced from this acerbic sentiment, particularly in the acceptance that showbusiness requires not simply those who wish to become famous but also others who wish to make them so. Green is given two monologues in the novel and in these he expounds a philosophy of celebrity that regards it not as narcissistic and shallow but as altruistic and productive: 'Showbusiness is glory in the afternoon and sunshine after dark. [...] Showbusiness is tearing life down and putting it all back together again, funnier, larger, shinier, more harmonious, Goddamit, purer, more special' (O'Hagan, 2004b: 113).

Green is an ambiguous figure in the text, part showbiz shark, part guardian to Maria's fragile precociousness; he is characterised by his oleaginous familiarity and the use of pat phrases such as 'I mean that most sincerely, folks' (O'Hagan, 2004b: 114), which are clearly intended to be read as automatic, if not entirely insincere, nods to a knowing audience. Green's account of his life and struggle for a career in showbusiness against the wishes of a judgemental and rigid father suggests the hardened outer casing that he has developed to protect himself, and his celebratory attitude towards talent reflects an underlying fear of the emptiness of life. Talent makes life liveable, he asserts, not only by providing purpose but also by metaphorically oxygenating the banal, used-up atmosphere: 'I see them making the decade fit to move in and the air fit to breathe' (O'Hagan, 2004b: 114). Everybody needs the sparkle of fame, he suggests, and those who take to the stage do so as servants of an audience that requires the romance of talent to leaven their daily lives.

As 'the heart's bid for freedom' (O'Hagan, 2004b: 114), talent is of course not co-terminous with celebrity, and what Green's monologues indicate is the ironic process of anonymisation that follows the transformation of the former into the latter. Spoken as if to camera, even though we assume them to be internal soliloquies, Green's words veer between private reflections and performative gestures towards an ever-present audience. The only inner life ascribed to this character is one mapped onto his public persona, hence the continuation of on-screen catchphrases in the privacy of his consciousness. Green performs constantly not because he cannot distinguish between on- and off-screen but because both are the same to him; he inhabits the personality that he has constructed for himself and speaks through its confines in both public and private modes. As he says tellingly at one point: 'Talent is a demonstration of the fact that there are people in the world [...] who really believe they are what they pretend to be' (O'Hagan, 2004b: 114). Celebrity is a calcification of the abstract notion of 'personality' into the shape of a persona from which the performer cannot, or is not allowed by the public to, escape.

One notable thing about the novel is, as John Mullan has pointed out, that the famous figures that we encounter (Les Dawson, Liberace, Johnny Carson amongst others) conduct themselves off-stage exactly as they do on (Mullan, 2005). O'Hagan has not tried, in portraying real individuals, to conjure complex inner lives at odds with their public fronts, but has used our comfort at their familiarity in a disconcerting way: they are effectively defamiliarised by their very familiarity and become nothing more than the personality that they have been instrumental in creating for themselves. It is here that we have Maria's central dilemma as a character and as a narrative device. The more she throws herself into the public guise of Maria Tambini, the popular singing sensation, the less she is fully able to inhabit the psychological or bodily space of Maria Tambini, the vulnerable, thirteen-year-old girl from a Scottish island. To become a 'personality' involves losing grip on her existing personality and turning herself into an objectified and exilic being. Maria is able to function less and less as an emotionally and psychologically coherent individual the more she becomes the product of her mother, her agent, and the expectant public. By performing, she becomes real for her audience and a stranger to herself. Her ability not only to control, but even to know, what she becomes is diminished to such an extent that she ultimately falls into the narrative emptiness that defines her and the anorexia that nearly kills her.

O'Hagan's central point in this novel – that 'personality' devours personality – is not in itself particularly original, but what thickens this idea in thematic terms is the longer perspective that he assumes. He avoids directly critiquing the excesses of contemporary celebrity culture even though that is the central focus of his concern. Instead he examines the pre-history of this public self-abasement to the lure of fame, locating in *Opportunity Knocks* an early precursor of the kind of TV programming that draws its principal cast from the general public. The novel's initial setting in the 1970s usefully distances the narrative from the present whilst situating the birth of that culture in a period of significant socio-political change. Whilst never overtly as political as his earlier work, *Personality* nevertheless provides a snapshot of British social life in the latter decades of the twentieth century. The emergence of Thatcherism is an undercurrent in the novel, as is a growing Scottish antagonism towards the Union, but those political strains are displaced into the framework of popular cultural transformation that affects the currency of Maria's talent. From her impressive debut as the seven-time winner of the show to the pinnacle of her career, performing at the London Palladium alongside all the celebrated acts of her day, she retains an ingenuousness and vulnerability that encourage identification with and from the audience. The lustre of her innocence is gradually diminished both by changing popular taste and by her much publicised struggles with her weight and self-image, and, though she retains a popular appeal, her engagements become increasingly workaday (seaside and end-of-the-pier shows, opening supermarkets, seasons at Butlins and children's television). The descent from the glitzy to the tawdry reflects a popular cultural trajectory that has resulted in what Robert Macfarlane describes as a 'pop narcosis which now tranquillizes our culture', whilst one could see Maria's wasting disease as a metaphor for the leaching of all meaningful talent away from the contemporary culture industry in many of its manifestations (Macfarlane, 2003: 5). Emptiness and silence are at the core of contemporary celebrity in O'Hagan's opinion, and that nothingness somehow speaks to a loss in contemporary society. In the subjectivising circle in which anybody can become somebody before rapidly achieving the status of nobody, anything like an authentic identity is traded for a momentary experience of notoriety. For those who seek fame and those who vote them into it, the end result is the same: an intellectual and political fall into an inertia of being.

Be Near Me (2006)

For all its stylistic panache and strident social critique, *Personality* is a structurally problematic novel: too many of its sub-plots are under-developed and tend to distract attention from Maria's tragedy without sustaining their own narrative drive. The loss that dominates Lucia's story is strangely unintegrated with the main plot line, as is Michael Aigas' involvement with a group of blind war veterans. As Macfarlane has commented, this structural tension might well be a by-product of focusing the primary narrative on a character who for so much of the novel is both literally and metaphorically insubstantial (Macfarlane, 2003: 5). It was a problem that O'Hagan was not to repeat in *Be Near Me*, a novel where the resounding presence of the principal character is guaranteed by his erudite, weighty, and resonant first-person narration.

The novel is a moving examination of self-delusion, missed opportunities, and cruelly curtailed lives. It is also a contemplation of the uncoverable distance between human beings, the space that cannot be bridged by empathy. The losses that are outlined here are physical (loss of loved ones, of treasured objects, of the vitality of youth) and emotional (the collapse of ideals, the potentiality of reciprocally enlivening contact, the possibility of life), but what seems to underlie the novel is a deep sense of sadness at the indescribability of the human experience. O'Hagan's principal character longs to share something of himself with another human being but has erected such unbreachable walls of self-protection in the form of an introverted and aesthetically cultivated lifestyle that he cannot reach out to express the need for closeness and the meaning that comes from 'nearness'.

The novel sees O'Hagan returning to some transtextual concerns: the nature of community and its conflictual relationship with individuality; the divisive character of Scottish working-class self-regard; and the compromises to idealism that practical life necessitates. It also sees O'Hagan re-examining the part that religion plays in contemporary Scottish life. Religion has been a consistent theme in his early fictional work and a number of critics have commented on the impact of O'Hagan's Catholic inheritance on his work, particularly in the context of the strong Protestant tradition in Scottish writing (Linklater 2003). *Our Fathers* – whose religious intonations are as evident as its familial ones – offers a bleak and degraded vision of Catholic upbringing with Jamie being sexually initiated by his priest, Father Timothy, a man so pathetically conscious of his own weakness that Jamie finds himself acquiescing in his own abuse out of pitiful sympathy for the self-disgusted cleric. The Catholicism of Lucia in *Personality* is characterised by a bitter acceptance that all life brings is loss and hardship, which must be endured as an expression of faith. *Be Near Me* depicts the complex interiority of a Catholic priest caught between faith and love, unable to communicate either sentiment to those under his pastoral care and convinced of the ritualism of the religious life only as a welcome barrier to self-knowledge.

The plot is simply summarised: David Anderton, a middle-aged Catholic priest who is English by birth though with a Scottish mother, is sent to the fiercely Protestant, working-class diocese of Dalgarnock on Scotland's west coast. An outsider because of his nationality, religion, and cultivated tastes in music, wine, and food, he is treated with a suspicion by the local community that ranges from gentle mockery to full-blown hostility. Befriending two bored and disaffected teenagers, Anderton grows increasingly attached to a boy, Mark McNulty, resulting in a drunken and drugged attempt to kiss him, an attempt that is gently rebuffed only to lead to a full-scale witch-hunt when news of the incident leaks out. Brought before an unsympathetic magistrate, the priest's attempts to justify the purity of his motives only reinforce his outsider status. He is found guilty of sexual assault and removed from his position, and ends the novel in a state of dreamy directionlessness searching for faith and for a meaningful connection to the world around him. Such a bald recounting of the plot should indicate that *Be Near Me* is driven less by action than by O'Hagan's delicate dissection of his main character's wayward spirituality and myopic inability to recognise the destructive consequences of his actions.

Claire Messud has described Anderton as 'Neither Scottish nor English, neither wholeheartedly aesthete nor ethicist, essentially unbelonging and uncertain', and it is this equivocation, this Prufrockian timidity in the face of life's closed doors, that characterises his narration (Messud, 2007: 10). He is educated and cultured, articulate and aesthetically sensitive, but, at the same time, unsure of himself, naïve, and with the sort of ignorance about life that only a good education can provide. His measured eloquence is both an indicator of his lonely detachment from the rough readiness of the local community and a sign of his aspiration towards higher, more refined things. He already possesses many fine things; his rectory, a bastion of safety in a confusingly unpredictable world, reflects his taste for sophisticated music, literature, and good wine and, when the rectory is torched by vengeful locals in the wake of his exposure, it is the loss of these symbols of reliability and integrity that he mourns far more than his reputation or position. Even with all this material ballast, Anderton expresses the familiar O'Hagan protagonist's sense of dislocation, claiming at one point that he suffers from 'a kind of homelessness which has followed me everywhere' (O'Hagan, 2007: 5), and, at another, that his life has been dogged by a homesickness, 'a sense of existing in exile from a place where you might belong' (O'Hagan, 2007: 141).

This rootlessness is important to his character for it indicates a central lack that is not compensated for by the cultivation of his lifestyle. That lack is expressed most strongly as an emotional impassiveness, an inability to connect with other people in a meaningful way; the nearness that is alluded to in the novel's title eludes him both as an emotional salve and as a physical commonplace, as he comments at one point: 'A life is a long time not to think of oneself undressing for another person' (O'Hagan, 2007: 92). Anderton has lived his life in such a state of emotional reclusion that not only can he not reach out to others' suffering but also, for much of the novel, he cannot even understand his own actions in befriending and later propositioning a young man. Despite its privileged focalisation through Anderton's consciousness, the narratorial position does not readily disclose his motives either to the reader or, so we are led to suspect, to Anderton himself. He never explicitly analyses his actions or feelings towards McNulty, never acknowledges the danger to his position that such an inappropriate liaison might represent and, apart from an admission that he is excited by the hedonism of the youth's destructiveness (or 'desolation' as his existentialist gloss would have it [O'Hagan, 2007: 67]), never openly explores the nature of his attraction. It is a narrative lacuna that perfectly matches his psychological distance from what is going on around him and renders his actions not only self-destructively foolish but also meaningless.

Employing a priest as a narrator should ensure that the spiritual life remains at the forefront of the narrative, but, throughout the text, David Anderton does very little to evidence his vocation: the reader is never conscious of his conviction and rarely witnesses him performing ceremonies intrinsic to his profession, and, on the occasions when he does make pastoral visits, he seems hopelessly lost and inadequate to the task of counselling his parishioners. When told of her diagnosis of incurable cancer by his housekeeper, Mrs Poole – the only member of the Dalgarnock community who shows him any kindness or understanding – his only response is the trite platitude that he regards as the universal salve of his position:

'They are trying things' said Mrs Poole, 'but these drugs don't do anything.'

'You'll need peace and quiet,' I said.

She seemed puzzled and seemed to struggle for a moment to find her bearings at the foot of the stairs.

'Give it time,' I said. I knew then it meant nothing to say such things, but the right words escaped me. (O'Hagan, 2007: 74)

His limp efforts to conjure a consolatory form of words, notwithstanding Mrs Poole's evident faith in his position, points towards Anderton's deliberate self-abstraction and need to escape from a situation that demands anything more than the most formulaic sympathy. His emotional reflex is channelled into an insipid automatic reaction as he rapidly distances himself from engagement with someone else's interior life. Such empathetic indifference is characteristic of a man who is warned by his mother against making connections with others: 'In this life, it's the people you know who let you down' (O'Hagan, 2007: 1), she tells him, and his life appears to have been, apart from one notable episode, testimony to that cynicism.

Anderton's failure is not as a priest but as a human being, and, if the crux of the novel were to be seen as a crisis of faith, it would not be a faith in God that was in question but a faith in the ability of human beings to understand each other. This is played out in the privacy of Anderton's psyche, but also in the collision between sectarian worldviews that he encounters in the local community. By focalising the narrative through the eyes of a self-preoccupied, emotionally damaged outsider, the depiction of Dalgarnock becomes partial and one-dimensional. There is no subtlety to Anderton's appraisal of the predominantly working-class community, defiantly Protestant by persuasion and bigoted by instinct. He sees them as brute, uncultured and tattooed, driven by historical allegiances and hatreds, and umbilically tied to tribal practices such as supporting Rangers or Celtic football teams, depending on one's religious affiliations. He sees his parishioners as 'the people', a dismissive term he uses to describe their mob-like tendencies even before they turn on him; the people are characterised by their lumpen and unresponsive nature and represent a collective mass that the individualist Anderton finds unappealing and intimidating. In return the people of Dalgarnock treat Anderton with hostility that, though initially only verbal, quickly descends to physical violence once the tenor of his relationship with McNulty becomes known. This leads to several set-pieces where the community bonds together in its hatred of him, a hatred which clearly stems as much from his Catholicism, his Englishness, and his middle-classness as from the community's disgust at his conduct.

The scenes at the fair when he is attacked and knocked to the ground, and at the besieging of his rectory, where he has to be rescued by the police, represent for O'Hagan a bitter reminder that Scottish community solidarity operates most smoothly in the face of a common enemy. As he has argued in a number of essays, most notably 'Scotland's Fine Mess', the quality of Scottish unity is most remarkable for its contrariness: 'Behind many an apparent Scottish unity, within each togetherness I can think of, runs a bickering stream of segregationalist delight. Scotland is not a fellow-feeling country, though it likes to believe it is' (O'Hagan, 1994: 24). O'Hagan goes on to describe a scene at his local, Ayrshire fair – a scene he later uses as the basis of that in *Be Near Me* – where initial bonhomie turned rapidly and inexorably to enmity and division. Scottish community life he suggests is founded upon hatred (of self, outsiders, perceived enemies, or anyone believed to have done Scotland down) smoothed over with the merest veneer of social unity. Crucially, hatred is more unifying and cohering than commonality and a certain Scottish mentality depends upon this aggressive and destructive dynamic born of historically embedded segregations.

Mr Nolan best expresses these views in the novel. He is a stock type of O'Hagan's writing: the self-centred, bitter Scot in denial of his own country's history. This character turns away from the troubles of his own country in a desire to blame anyone else (but preferably the English) for the state of the nation. For O'Hagan this introversion is a blighting renunciation of responsibility for the conditions of the nation and wilfully ignores all that has been gained for Scotland by the relationship with the outside world. Nolan detests the twee touristification of the nation, its transformation into a series of clichés, but his bitterness ignores the money brought into the economy by the tourist industry. Anderton punctures his self-pitying diatribe against the English by pointing out the masochism of his position: 'I'd bet you anything he enjoyed the spectacle of his life in that town, the constant drama of his dislikes, his role as a man coming down hard on strangers and phoniness, all the while I suspect, more strange and phoney to himself than he ever thought possible' (O'Hagan, 2007: 63).

Implicit in Nolan's morbid dismissal of Scotland's present is, as Anderton realises, a nostalgia for a lost cultural authenticity that he locates in the past. It is a nostalgia that Anderton feels painfully with regard to himself and which he expresses through contrasting his youth with that of Mark McNulty and Lisa Nolan. Coming to young adulthood in the late 1960s, he experienced the social conflicts of the student revolution from the remove of his Oxford college but sensed that they represented a political utopianism that was founded upon the belief that collective action could bring about social change. His, he argues, was a generation of idealists where 'the future was a dream', in stark contrast to the nihilism of Mark and Lisa's generation, 'the great present: maybe the saddest place of all' (O'Hagan, 2007: 49). Whilst his was an education of aesthetic sensitivity based on high cultural exempla, theirs is a mid-Atlantic hybridisation of Scottish pop culture and MTV cliché that has its own humour and energy but lacks the ballast of history and tradition. Despite his cynicism, Anderton is drawn to the disaffection of the teenagers, misguidedly believing their boredom to be a way of transcending the present. In fact their destructiveness is whimsical and not tied to any greater idea of change, something that the priest fails to accept due in part to his conflation of their youth with that of the one true love of his life: Conor Docherty.

Docherty, a politically engaged, militant student peer and a man very much of the present, is the antithesis of Anderton's anachronistic and highly aestheticised apolitical philosophy, which looks to the past for solidity and meaning. Smitten by Docherty, Anderton comes as close as he possibly can to engaging with another person and the world around him in a meaningfully committed manner, only for Docherty's death to rob him of his desire for emotional openness. Devastated by loss and by the loss of the self that loving has caused him, Anderton retreats to the solace of the clerical life to submerge his sorrows in the consolatory rituals and order of the church. It is here that the appositeness of the nearness expressed in the epigraph taken from Tennyson's 'In Memoriam A.H.H.' becomes apparent, for, not only does Docherty's death curtail the only intimacy that Anderton has been able to achieve but it also sparks the crisis of spiritual faith that leads him away from human contact and ironically into the arms of the church, not as a way to find answers but as a way to avoid questions. In momentarily recuperating Docherty in the figure of Mark McNulty, Anderton expresses his need for closeness, but does so injudiciously and dangerously given his position in the community. 'A man cannot choose whom to love. He can choose how to live and can honour the truth of himself where he may. But he cannot choose whom to love' (O'Hagan, 2007: 263) explains Anderton as a way of justifying the waywardness of his choice. In truth, though, Anderton's narrative does not intimate love for McNulty; rather it reveals his thrall to the mystery of belonging that has forever eluded him, a thrall that is pitiful and pathetic in all senses. Love is a connection, human in scale, which speaks to a grander affiliation with truth, authenticity, and above all rootedness; without it, Anderton is as lost to his spirit as he is to the bleak material world he inhabits.

In the novel's final pages, Anderton passes Christmas Day with the widowed Mr Poole, both men counting their losses and both struggling with the painful knowledge that having is merely another form of losing: 'I've always been living the single life', philosophises Mr Poole, 'Maybe everybody does' (O'Hagan, 2007: 275). More portentously, Anderton reflects:

> The radicals believed only in idealism and the glorious emancipation of the future, until the struggle for those too became a romantic thing of the past. The Church gave me every reason to expect a bridge between the two, it gave me hope. Our journey will sustain many falsehoods to sustain that one truth: we wanted love, and without it only the broad universe would do, with its solid, perfumed dark. (O'Hagan, 2007: 272)

There is something here of the defeated recognition that, although idealism in essence will never change, the subjects of that idealism will eventually fade into a romantic nostalgia for the past. In that event all that seems to be left is love, and love, the message of the novel seems to suggest, cannot be controlled or directed. Anderton has lived a life of emotional reclusion for want of a more robustly trustworthy ethic. The evidence of his life has proved to him that love cannot be contained and that it does not live up to its sentimental myth, turning ultimately only to loss. Given this trajectory, his only recourse is to renounce love and feeling and replace it with a less demanding, more nameless devotion. In this of course he abjures his very palpable human need for intimacy and endures the tragedy of wanting.

The Life and Opinions of Maf the Dog, and of His Friend Marilyn Monroe (2010)

In a series of interviews and opinion pieces promoting the publication of his fourth novel, O'Hagan gave an insight into the beginnings of his fascination with celebrity, and in particular with the figure of Marilyn Monroe. When his father brought home a copy of Fred Lawrence Guiles' biography of Monroe, the 11-year-old O'Hagan fell upon it as if 'it had been sent to us by the god of laughter' (O'Hagan, 2010b). For a youth of the 1970s raised on sectarian football tribalism and inflexible givens of masculinity in an inwards-facing society, a fascination with the flashbulb glamour of Hollywood was a subversive, and not entirely healthy, pastime, but for O'Hagan the lure seems always to have been about escaping the social mean; reconfiguring the shape of his self beyond the strict parallels of 'what it takes for men to be men and for women to be women' (O'Hagan, 2010b: 15). In Monroe he found an exemplary model of self-reinvention. This woman, 'so unearthly, so classic' (O'Hagan, 2010b: 14), was to his eyes 'a perfect instigator of the imagination. It never occurred to me that her world wasn't my world: it was always my world, Kilmarnock or California, and she seemed, among all that rain and all that depression and all those samey houses, to be a complete ally in the fight for something less ordinary' (O'Hagan, 2010b: 14).

Where Lena Zavaroni had been a thinly disguised emblem of the stultification of Scottish ambition in *Personality*, Monroe was to become a hallmark of the possibilities of escaping the morose introspectiveness of O'Hagan's early surroundings. He details a compulsive, completist desire to find Marilyn, firstly through her performances and latterly through the incidental traces of her real life, and what emerges is a sense of both fulfilment and melancholy emptiness. And it is this paradox that in O'Hagan's various writings on Marilyn he grows to see as a manifestation of the uncanniness of modern celebrity selfhood:

> For me, growing up in Scotland, living my life as I have, the centrality of celebrity is so stark, so unavoidable, that it has become one of the great subjects of our time. It's become one of the ways that we understand selfhood. I wanted to know what the hunger to be present and public in a larger way to a human imagination does to a life. (in Randall, 2010)

This desire to *know* the celebrity, to inhabit her/his skin, is, O'Hagan argues in his essay 'Saint Marilyn', a feature of contemporary commodification in which the 'authentic' essence of an individual is packaged as if it were not only attainable but also transmissible. The essay focuses on the sale in 1999 by Christie's auction house of Monroe's personal effects, an event that, for O'Hagan, blurs the boundaries between high and low culture, momentarily reconciling the two in a marriage of spectacle and money:

> The old superstition about High Art, 'Rembrandt actually touched this canvas', can now be applied to the personal belongings of the century's most famous woman – this object actually touched Marilyn – and thus our era's tangled worries with the meaning of fine art are for a moment resolved. Pop culture became its opposite number: the ordinary minutiae of the extraordinary life came to seem as formally expressive as *Guernica*. (O'Hagan, 2008: 67)

The astonishing prices paid for ephemera-turned-art – $167,500 for a cardigan, $1.26 million for the dress in which Monroe sang 'Happy Birthday' to President Kennedy in May 1962 – reflect a crisis of authenticity because they valorise and monetise the performative guise of Monroe, buying into the inauthenticity of the glamour as if it were, in itself, a marker of her true being, rather than the trappings of a consciously invented persona. And yet, for O'Hagan, the purchasers are also knowingly buying into the misery of Norma Jeane Mortenson's life, not wholly for the fetishistic prurience that it brings but also to remind themselves that failure, suffering, and despair have increasingly become the currency of success in the paradoxical world of celebrity. It is as if Monroe's tragedy is emblematic of something self-renewing about America's schizophrenia: success and fragility go hand in hand, disproving the bullish notion narrativised in the American dream that success is the product of hard work and adaptation, and instead installing an unsettling postmodern paradigm that contemporary success is understood foremostly in terms of loss and absence. It is another instance of perhaps the most common thread in O'Hagan's work: a sense of self is predicated on buying into the illusion of the world, but an illusion which we nevertheless knowingly generate and are eventually trapped by.

Amongst the items sold at the auction were six Polaroid photos of Monroe's dog, Maf – short for Mafia – and, not unlike his mistress, the Maltese terrier finds a tragi-comic afterlife as the hero of O'Hagan's novel. *The Life and Opinions of Maf the Dog, and of His Friend Marilyn Monroe* is both familiar and unusual to readers of O'Hagan's work. It reprises the key theme of *Personality* – the self-destructive glamour of a life lived publically – but it treads new ground in being set beyond the geographical and psychological confines of Scotland. It narrates, from the perspective of Maf, the final three years of Monroe's life, though the dog concludes decorously before the dénouement. As its title suggests, there is a strong debt to Laurence Sterne's *The Life and Opinions of Tristram Shandy* (1759–67), and to the eighteenth-century novel in general. Maf is a picaro, who is whelped in Scotland and travels to the English home of Vanessa Bell and Duncan Grant, before being purchased by the mother of Natalie Wood, to be given to Frank Sinatra, who makes him a present for Marilyn. The novel is thus picaresque in its concentration on the adventures of an outsider (though Maf is too effete to be a rogue) who intersects with the high and low of society, maintaining an ironic detachment frequently manifested as a comic diablerie, and thereby exposing the pretensions and follies of those around him. There are moments of satirical bite in which Maf's Trotskyite idealism clashes with the Cold War pragmatism of the early 1960s, but cynicism is not the dominating tone of his account, just as it is not a quality of O'Hagan's other writing on Monroe. 'Saint Marilyn' is a breathless eulogy to a subject for whom O'Hagan shows genuine affection, and Maf's account is equally adoring of his 'fated companion' (O'Hagan, 2010a: 104). He follows her to sassy nightclubs, to her classes at the Actors' Studio, to unbearably pretentious gatherings of critics, and onto the sets of increasingly dysfunctional films. But he also observes her private struggles to come to terms with 'The Girl' persona that she has created: futile psychoanalysis sessions; her craving to be regarded as a serious actress; her attempts to forget the father who abandoned her; and her growing reliance on drugs to function.[7]

All this Maf narrates in a voice that is comically ill-fitting to his surroundings. Hugely erudite and intellectually catholic, he draws on the history of

Western thought to situate the demise of his companion within the philosophical tradition of selfhood, elevating it from the tawdry to the exemplary with mock-heroic flourish. From Aristotle to Sartre by way of Plutarch, Machiavelli, Descartes, Marx, Schopenhauer, and Freud, he navigates the metaphysical terrain with aphoristic élan and nimble precision. O'Hagan gives him a literary frame of reference too (Zola, Flaubert, Carroll, Proust, Kafka, Mann), but Maf is first and foremost a philosopher and he scorns the poetic etherealism of cats, whose narcissism he cannot abide. Along with dyspeptic Jewish robins ('Poor Limey Schmucks' [O'Hagan, 2010a: 19]), argumentative Brooklyn rats ('Summa us got woik to do' [O'Hagan, 2010a: 69]), and easily pleased squirrels ('Peanut butter ... life is sweet' [O'Hagan, 2010a: 98]), Maf's realm parodies that of his owner, undercutting human neuroses and vanities with the immeasurable pleasures of an unexpected snack or well-placed tickle. In this regard, O'Hagan draws on a long history of anthropomorphic exemplars of which Virginia Woolf's *Flush* (1933) is the most well known, and he allows Maf to range across the gamut of animals in literature, coming to the conclusion that:

> That's what humans do. They talk to you. They talk nonsense. They talk to you and they talk for you. And so they create a personality which is defined by the way they act you out. Every minute they are with you they are constructing you out of what they want, a companion, a little man, a furry friend who can only love their owners for their mothering tongue. (O'Hagan, 2010a: 78–79)

Maf's reversal of this ventriloquial identification is played for comic effect, but the more serious undercurrent concerns the epistemological challenge that is offered by the dumb other. 'If only they could talk' might be a cliché but it reveals a super-ego anxiety about how the self is perceived and about what judgements are silently being reached by our companions. It also painfully reminds us of the commoditisation of the celebrity who is constructed, legitimated, controlled, and dispensed within the fantasy of the onlooker. Neither Maf nor Monroe have voices with which to present the truth of their thoughts, O'Hagan suggests; both bark without being understood.

That is not to say that Maf's bark lacks its own rotundity, nor metaphorical bite. His tone throughout is aloof, and, for all his leftist politics, he displays clear pride in the aristocratic lineage of his Maltese terrier ancestry, scions of which were owned by Mary, Queen of Scots and Marie Antoinette. He can be irascible and intellectually pompous, dismissive of learning when he sees it as fundamentally self-serving – as in the case of Monroe's psychoanalyst Marianne Kris – but these traits are in tune with the tradition of satirical anthropomorphism that employs the hyperbolic and the mock-heroic to lambast through exaggeration. A number of the novel's reviewers termed this characterisation whimsical, usually on the way to dismissing the novel for a lack of depth, but the text itself provides a more fruitful reading through the notion of camp.[8]

O'Hagan (2010b) makes clear that it was Monroe's quality of camp that he admired as a young man brought up in an austerely heteronormative family home. As a way of questioning the boundaries between the serious and the ridiculous, the banal and the extraordinary, the camp became for him a way of freeing himself from the rigidity of a gendered behaviour. Consequently, it is only slightly arch when, at a literary party to celebrate the *Partisan Review*, Maf encounters Susan Sontag, who outlines the ideas that would form the basis of her essay 'Notes on Camp', which would become her breakthrough piece of writing for the journal. Sontag identifies camp with an aesthetic mode of exaggerated, stylised artifice. It is 'to understand Being-as-Playing-a-Role. It is the farthest extension, in sensibility, of the metaphor of life as theatre' (Sontag, 1982: 280). Though the camp is apolitical and disengaged, it adores passion, especially where that is exaggerated, leading Sontag to the conclusion that camp is 'seriousness that fails' (Sontag, 1982: 283), but fails through naivety rather than pretension. Whimsy has none of camp's hard edges and thus describes less accurately the melancholy affection that O'Hagan invests in both Monroe and Maf. The division between the high cultural references of the philosophical tradition and the ridiculousness of them being mouthed by a dog falls along the fault-line of the camp in the same way that Monroe's desperate desire to be taken seriously competes with the desire of everyone else to regard her as a freakish novelty. In addition, O'Hagan's debt to camp underpins Maf's delicacy around his owner's death. For Sontag, there is seriousness in camp, and certainly pathos, but there is 'never, never tragedy' (Sontag, 1982: 287). Though her dog is believed to have been with Monroe at the time of her death, to dramatise that would have created a narrative clash with the tone of the rest of the text, and admitted a genuine tragedy, whereas, by focusing on her fall and by having Maf not admitting that he knows the future fate of his owner, O'Hagan can retain a sense of ingenuousness. There is true tragedy underpinning the narrative, but it is kept at bay by the *faux-naïf* disavowal of Maf and by the true naivety of the camp.

Camp also operates to question the boundaries between the novel's various levels of fantasy, particularly that between the hyperreal bubble of stardom and the tortured process of self-making. The key distinguishing difference between humans and animals, according to Maf, is that the latter 'have none of that fatal human weakness for making large distinctions between what is real and what is imagined' (O'Hagan, 2010a: 2). For animals the two states are more or less the same, but humans have been alienated, he suggests, forced to live 'in a place they invented with their own minds' (O'Hagan, 2010a: 2) and which consequently crushes them into shapes that accord with their own invention. Without the daring to live in the imagination, they are condemned into believing in themselves as qualitatively split between the constrictions of their reality and the freedoms of their fantasies, finding in the cinema the quintessence of the latter, which they are unable to inhabit for more than the running time of a feature. The problem is one of authenticity, stemming from the duality inherent in the Platonic ideal in which 'reality' is a poorer expression of the integrated, unfissured epitome. Maf stands amazed at this wilful blindness:

> 'To thine own self be true,' said the bard. Yet in all the animal kingdom, only humans consider integrity to be a thing worth worrying about. I grew up in the golden era of existentialism, so you'll forgive me for finding the whole idea of a self that one must be true to a little ridiculous. We are what we imagine we are: reality itself is the supreme fiction. Despite years of excellent evidence, humans cannot get the hang of this condition; they live like the people in Plato's cave, never quite believing their shadows are as true as they are. (O'Hagan, 2010a: 22)

Humans, he suggests, refuse to accept the imaginary as an indivisible part of reality and thus, like him with his limited spectrum of colour, only see the world within a specific band which is acceptable to them, and are forever craving something more. In America, Maf discovers a whole country engaged in a search for its own authentic singularity whilst simultaneously ignoring the multiplicities of fantasy that sustain its dynamism.

The country that Maf encounters in 1960 seems to be undergoing a collective self-reimagining, putting behind it the paranoia and insecurities of the 1950s and beginning to reach towards the liberalism that would be a feature of the new decade. The memory of the McCarthy investigations is still fresh for those like the *Partisan Review* critics or Monroe's recently divorced husband, Arthur Miller, who have felt its effects most keenly, but Maf experiences an America where amnesia is a necessary virtue. On the brink of significant social and political change, it is a country where reinvention is always better than coming to terms with the past, and where future prospects eclipse former realities. Significantly, Maf arrives when John F. Kennedy is president elect rather than president, suggesting the nascence of change rather than its completion – or indeed its failure in the scandal of the Bay of Pigs invasion and Kennedy's violent death in 1963. The convergence of Monroe and Kennedy towards the end of the book acts as an abrupt reminder that both would soon be tragically glamorous corpses and America would be entering a new phase of civil and international strife. At this particular moment though – at least in the worlds in which Monroe and Maf dwell – an exaggerated, childlike optimism dominates, as is evident when Monroe is shown some of Roy Lichtenstein's early canvases; their comic-book extravagance reflects a new aesthetic that the gallery owner breathlessly abbreviates to 'Wow is the new Why' (O'Hagan, 2010a: 88).

Such exuberance, such enraptured submission to the novel, captures a spirit of camp that O'Hagan identifies with America's devotion to style and affect. The cartoon quality of the Pop Art generation tallies with the outlandish sexuality of the Girl persona projected by Monroe; a hyper-inflated desire machine, she embodies not just the commoditisation of sex but also an underpinning absurdity that renders her consonant with the commercialism of Lichtenstein, or Warhol, whom she meets on exiting the gallery. Maf detects this perverse aesthetic early in his relationship with his owner: 'Marilyn was a strange and unhappy creature, but at the same time she had more natural comedy to her than anybody I would ever know. More comedy and more art. Not for her the stern refusal of life's absurdities: Marilyn had a sensitivity to jokes and moral drama that would have delighted the chiefs of psychoanalytic Vienna' (O'Hagan, 2010a: 62–63). Monroe is a fantasy of modernity, constructed and self-constructing through the codes of fragmented subjectivity that govern mediated reality, offering more than she can give but wryly aware that her fixity in the eyes of her fascinated beholder amounts to little more than clever puppetry.

For her admirers, the fantasy appears as unalloyed reality. Those drawn in to her ambit – without the desire to exploit or demean her – are star-struck by the ideal of femininity she represents, mistaking glamour for glory in an act of very willing disbelief. The coterie of Marilyn-watchers that dog her steps in New York are attracted to her as courtiers to some regal presence, and the passers-by she encounters are transported into frenzies of obeisance by her beauty and eroticism. For them she is real in a way that unproblematically rejects the boundary with fantasy; in the apparently effortless embodiment of style they perceive the authentic. Whether these onlookers distinguish real from fantasy is moot, and irrelevant for O'Hagan's point is that it is perfectly possible for the inauthentic to become authentic once one abandons the Platonic idea that they must be distinct. Maf's complaint that humans too strictly compartmentalise the real and imagined would therefore seem to be not wholly true, for the habit he discovers in America of mistaking the shadows on the cave wall for the truth of the world creates an ontological interstice in which both can not just co-exist; instead, they fuse.

For many of the characters with whom Maf comes into contact, the narrowness of the space between fantasy and reality is America's gift to the world, for it provides room for reinvention. He is brought to the country by Mrs Gurdin, a Russian émigré whose family has escaped the Bolshevik revolution and who has found in California 'a kind of paradise [...] a place where the bare truth was seldom sufficient and seldom reliable' (O'Hagan, 2010a: 23). Gurdin is also the mother of actress Natalie Wood, who is referred to during her short appearance in the narrative as 'Natalia, Mrs Wagner, Natasha, Natalie' (O'Hagan, 2010a: 27), indicating the multiplicity of roles she inhabits. Maf is passed through these offices to Frank Sinatra (the child of Italian immigrant parents) and then on to Monroe, who goes by three names – Norma Jean Baker, Norma Jeane Mortenson as well as Marilyn Monroe. The sound of America is thus:

> that of old Europe boiled down to its modern sap, the sons and daughters of immigrants claiming America's newness for themselves. Carson was Lula Carson Smith; Marilyn was Norma Jeane Baker; Mr Trilling was Lionel Mordecai, just as our friend Lee Strasberg was Israel Strasberg. They were like children in the little garden of America, alert to something new in themselves and excited to be in an environment that might readily shape itself in accordance with their wishes, each of them investing all the while in a quantity of forgetting. (O'Hagan, 2010a: 191–192)

Maf himself is the bearer of many names: Mafia Honey, Snowball (in homage to *Animal Farm*, Orwell's pig being a caricature of Trotsky), Dreamboy, Sizzle, and Maltese, each suggesting that he, like his human companions, is subject to a fluctuating identity, and one that is as much imposed as it is sought.

Alongside Monroe, Sinatra is the most fleshed out character in the text and is emblematic of both America's comfort with self-reinvention and the chasm between appearance and reality. He is a bully, a narcissist, and a bigot, and lacks any kind of fellow feeling. Obsessed with status, he coruscates those around him, including the president elect, for their failure to appreciate his true value, and cruelly lambasts Monroe and Peter Lawford for their deficiencies whilst masking his own behind a veil of public relations. Maf likens him to John Locke's notion of man in the absence of God: 'no law but his own will, no end but himself. He would be a god to himself, and the satisfaction of his own will the sole measure and end of all his actions' (O'Hagan, 2010a: 55), but he also acknowledges the effectiveness of his publicity machinery: 'He did what he wanted, good or bad. And yet, he appeared in our time to exude the kind of goodness that made people healthy' (O'Hagan, 2010a: 55). Sinatra gobbles up the trust and vulnerability of others and spews back only the bile of his own frustration at not constantly being the centre of attention. To an extent, he represents the worst characteristics of a society of consumption and individualism – he is frequently depicted drinking or eating – but his celebrity functions as a mediating screen whereby the nastiness of his hubris is converted into a salutary example of an immigrant making good in America.

Unlike those of Sinatra, Gurdin, Lee Strasberg, or Marianne Kris, Monroe's self-transformation is less firmly rooted in the belief that one is how one appears, and much of the pathos of the novel emerges from the tear in her psychology as she manages the public face of The Girl whilst desperately seeking the meaning and approval of herself. Despite orchestrating the self-conscious artifice of the Monroe character, she nevertheless continues to believe in the separation of private and public personae. Her private self, in flight from the abusive entanglements of her familial past, is rent with insecurity about her acting talent, her intellectual credentials, and her depth of personality generally. Her struggle to complete *The Brothers Karamazov*, or to embody the role of Anna Christie in Eugene O'Neill's play, are attempts at self-validation but they play to the desire of others – Arthur Miller, Lee Strasberg – to shape her meaning in ways which support their, rather than her, reality. She gravitates around a world of privilege that she does not fully understand and is often, despite her celebrity, the one who is outside the cordon of respectability. At the *Partisan Review* party, for instance, she is nothing more than a novelty, an adjunct to Miller's controversial career, and an example of a new phase of America's search to wriggle itself free from the influence of Europe. Effectively, she is the joke that the writers and critics are self-consciously making about themselves, without truly believing in their intellectual vulnerability.

Ultimately, her flaw lies in her conviction that beneath the artful façade there is an authentic core to identity which is immutable. She delves amongst the traumas of her past for the residue of a personality that is undamaged, consistent, and beyond the gaze of the public eye, but she finds only contradiction and exploitation. O'Hagan's America is less a place of self-recovery than self-discovery, a land of the manufactured, where the past is reshaped into newer and grander stories whose very exaggeration supports their credibility. Monroe's search for the missing element in herself that would collapse the distance between Norma Jean Baker and Marilyn Monroe, and ultimately make The Girl character redundant, reveals a faith in something about which her industry and her country are resolutely sceptical.

For Americans, Maf concludes, the authentic is best expressed through its production, as much evident in the public sincerity of Kennedy or the wholesome rags-to-riches story of Sinatra as it is in the mock Tuscan villas and French chateaux of Hollywood. He sees 'something beautifully real, something essential and human at the core of its inauthenticity' (O'Hagan, 2010a: 46) which nevertheless reflects a mental struggle, unfathomable to dogs he believes, to mark the dividing lines between what is real, what isn't real, and what seems real. Some humans, his owner included, do not sit totally comfortably in this imaginary but are forever drawn to the ideal of the real in all its hard specificity, whereas dogs are comfortable with onto-logical ambiguity. Once one accepts the veracity of the shadow on the cave wall, Maf contends, one does away with the need for a more metaphysical truth that is obscure, and probably unattainable. Fiction, he argues, is the truth of reality; the constructed is that which human beings desire but don't quite have sufficient faith to believe in fully, a point which reminds us of the novel's Rabelaisian epigraph, which states that 'Faith is the argument of non-evident truths'.

Humans have erected a world of fantasy with which they would like to replace reality, but, ironically, cannot fully believe in the truth of that fic-tion and are thus left searching for the roots of a real beneath the illusion that they have manufactured. This is ultimately what O'Hagan discerns in the sale of Monroe's effects in 1999. The artificiality of art requires more than its own inauthenticity to guarantee its affective value; it requires something in which its purveyors can have faith. When the designer Tommy Hilfiger pays a fortune for two pairs of jeans that Monroe wore on the set of *The Misfits*, he is doing so partly because they are the trap-pings of an immaterial fantasy and partly because he has genuine faith in their authenticity to her experience. He does not regard the transcend-ence of this ordinary art as irony but as something fundamentally insep-arable from the moment, and from Monroe's uniqueness. Like the person who paid $63,000 for Maf's tag and licence, he sincerely believes that these relics allow him to 'grasp the meaning of the twentieth century.' And who, asks O'Hagan, 'is to say that person is wrong?' (O'Hagan, 2010a: 69).

The Illuminations (2015)

After the Californian sun and comedic lightness of *Maf*, O'Hagan returned to his more familiarly Caledonian tonal palette for his fifth novel. *The Illuminations*, like *Be Near Me* before it, revolves around the often damaged lives, and always damaged dreams, of those on Scotland's Ayrshire coast, and confronts the reader again with characters struggling to reconcile their beliefs with the moral challenges that life has delivered them. In it, O'Hagan swaps one consistent set of themes – celebrity as a metaphor for the collapse of private into public life – for another: the prohibitions of family life and in particular the limiting consequences of the stories that people tell about themselves. The principal cast of *The Illuminations* is held in the disabling grip of a kind of narrative regret – disappointed, and to varying degrees bitter, that the stories of themselves in which they have invested are unable to sustain them in times of crisis. The two sets of themes are not, in fact, distinct, for much in the novel speaks to the construction of public narratives of identity that in time come to infect the private subject with a sense of dislocation and self-alienation. The conflict between the stories his characters would like to believe about themselves and those that they are increasingly forced to accept is a persistent thread across O'Hagan's writing, but here it is given additional traction by moving between the micro-conflicts of daily life to the actual wars which have kept the twenty-first century constant company.

O'Hagan's direct connection with the Afghan conflict – around which half of *The Illuminations* is based – comes from his work as an ambassador for UNICEF, which led him to visit the country in 2013 and to witness 'a country caught in the middle of some insane politics' and a war that 'we not only appeared to be losing, but that we didn't understand' (Wood, 2015). He subsequently described his experience meeting child jihadis in an article for the *London Review of Books* (O'Hagan, 2013), and felt 'overpowered by the need to get involved in the conflict and write about it' (Wood, 2015: 4). O'Hagan describes the post-2003 Afghan war as 'our Vietnam' (Wood, 2015: 4), and *The Illuminations* conveys well a comparable sense of hopeless entrapment and ever-decreasing moral justification for an unwinnable war. It is a conflict of attritional gains prosecuted in the face of widespread public opposition by teenage soldiers on behalf of politicians with dubious motivations and ill-considered strategies.

Caught in the middle of this geopolitical mess, Captain Luke Campbell, Major Charles Scullion, and the men of A Section, Royal Western Fusiliers ferry around a hostile and forbidding country, clueless about their overarching mission but finding in each other's companionship an antidote to the oppressive heat and trepidation that are their lot. In the novel's central dramatic scenes, the Section is involved in Operation Eagle's Summit, supporting the transportation of an electricity turbine to the Kajaki Dam power station in Helmand Province, southern Afghanistan, a centrepiece mission of the Allies' 'hearts-and-minds' campaign in the summer of 2008. As O'Hagan presents it, the operation is haunted by doom-laden presentiments as the men veer between being stoned, bored, and terrified whilst their commanding officer experiences a wholesale nervous breakdown leading to a massacre of civilians and his own maiming in a firefight. Luke, through whom much of the narrative is focalised, kills a group of young boys in a panicky over-reaction to their perceived threat, and, in the aftermath of the operation, is court-martialed out of the army. The massacre is the consequence of an accumulation of excessive stress, but it is also a failure of responsibility on a personal level and on the part of governments, resulting from the latter's wilful masochism in hubristically continuing a war with very little prospect of victory. O'Hagan does not absolve the soldiers of their guilt, but it is clear that he regards those fighting in the Iraqi and Afghan wars as 'victims of bad politics' (Wood, 2015: 4). The failure is personal and institutional, a collapse of democratic principle into a Conradian colonialist nightmare, but, through it, O'Hagan dramatises a contemporary anxiety about the obscurity of clear principles in an age of moral, political, geographical, technological, and ontological relativism. This focus on the world's confusion draws Luke's narrative into the same frame as that of his grandmother, Anne Quirk, for whom confusion is painfully literal.

Anne, a talented and aspiring documentary photographer in her youth, is, in her old age, confined to an assisted living community in Saltcoats on Scotland's west coast. There, she is falling gradually into confusion brought on by Alzheimer's, her memory flitting between the present and a past that was dominated by her relationship with Harry Blake, a photographer and lecturer by whom she was made pregnant with twins and subsequently abandoned. Her unstinting devotion to the mythologisation of Harry as a committed, caring, and loyal lover unbearably aggravates Alice, the only surviving child and Luke's mother, who is sidelined to the point of invisibility by Anne's deluded faithfulness to the memory of Harry as a good man. In an echo of *Our Fathers* and *Personality*, the damage done to one generation is visited on its successors, and Alice has alienated Luke with her wounded self-justifications, failing to recognise his sensitivity and resenting his creative affiliation with Anne. Just as Anne's emotional life is given over to the preservation of Harry, so Alice's is devoted to nursing her own sense of injustice, leaving little room for a positive encouragement of Luke's interests in literature and art. Instead he turns to his grandmother for visits to galleries and discussions about books, and Anne takes a pointed pleasure in nurturing a spirit so unlike her daughter's. Her increasing otherworldliness leads her to confuse Luke with Harry, running them together in a way that turns the past and present into a singular continuum.

There is irony in Anne's misapprehension, given her commitment as a photographer to documentary realism, to the telling of the world as it is. Her reputation – growing in visibility as she fades from view – rests on her ability to frame the world in ways that reveal disregarded beauties and ordinary truths. As a young woman she took as subjects the nightlife of Blackpool in the 1960s and the artefacts of mundane domesticity – 'a kitchen sink with old taps and a pair of breakfast bowls waiting to be washed and a milk bottle filled with soapy water' (O'Hagan, 2015: 29) – and transformed them in such a way that their artlessness became the very basis of their aesthetic edge. This capturing of a time-bound social reality reveals her conviction in a world of appreciable things, bodies, and objects that dwell outwith the realm of abstractions and that can only be understood through direct, physical engagement. 'The task', she advises Luke, 'is to see' (O'Hagan, 2015: 65), but her methodology emphasises that seeing goes beyond passive perception to embrace artful creation. 'The colour red', she attests 'only exists as an idea in your head. Always remember that. You create it yourself when your imagination meets the light' (O'Hagan, 2015: 65). Maureen, Anne's neighbour in the retirement complex, marvels at how the contents of the sink photograph 'shone like nothing on earth' (O'Hagan, 2015: 29), painting the world with a luminescence that sits somewhere between nature and art. It is one instance of illumination in a novel that struggles to find paths through the confusions of grief, self-loss, the fog of war, and the benighting impact of preconceptions and bias.

For Anne, and increasingly for her protégé Luke, the world is made real by the light we throw upon it. Truth is illuminated not by the tearing away of illusion but rather by the careful direction of the light that picks it out. Such is the artistic effect described by Anne in one of her reveries: '*Masking is a technique whereby you hold back some of the light from one or two areas by placing a mask on the printing paper itself. It will affect the image you see and the reality you observe*' (O'Hagan, 2015: 229, italics in original). This deliberate manipulation of the observed belies its neutrality, making clear the novel's premise that the hard objectivity of the phenomenal world depends for its authenticity on the way it is presented. Truth, O'Hagan contends, is about faith more than it is about empiricism, and, caught in situations of existential uncertainty, his characters happily supplant what they fear to be true with more comforting verisimilitudes. For all her hearty imprecations of seeing as the gateway to understanding, Anne has spent her life blinkered against the unpalatable truth of Harry's betrayal, displacing her catastrophic loss into a narrative web that romanticises everything about him and their liaison. His phoney war as a film processor in a chemist's shop becomes a heroic career flying spy planes; a night school photography course becomes a glittering bohemian reputation at the centre of a post-war art movement. Everything must be done to preserve the 'Extraordinary Life of Harry Blake' (O'Hagan, 2015: 96). The unpalatable truth of his rejection of her and their children must remain as unacknowledged as the death of her son in a road accident, a combined loss that can only be metonymically represented through her maternal concern for a ceramic rabbit. Anne's memory, like her craft, necessitates the masking of specific, unphotogenic areas to favour the remainder with light; her narrative of Harry, of their life together in Blackpool, and of their avant-gardist commitment to reality must be illuminated at the expense of its darker penumbra.

However belligerent Anne's denial of history might be, it is fundamentally enabling, a coping strategy that defuses the emotional turmoil of her life. In the case of Maureen and, to a lesser extent, Anne's daughter Alice, the narratives through which they offset the truth appear barbed and life-denying in a deliberately masochistic way. As the youngest member of the assisted living community, Maureen has sought early refuge from life, and there she finds in herself a supportive and caring persona completely at odds with the experience of her own familial network. Her three children are a trial to her, their independent lives and divergent values little more than a rejection of all the selfless effort she expended on them. She resents their freedom from guilt with a passion and dreads the time she has to spend with them, time that she would rather spend with her audiobooks and memories of her father, for whom she was the centre of the world. For all this, Maureen considers herself a happy person, but one who cannot convey the pleasures of caring for others 'for fear they might stop pitying her' (O'Hagan, 2015: 169). Hers is a life of small and carefully measured pleasures underpinned by a reservoir of bitterness towards those who have moved beyond her reach and whom she can no longer influence. She detests her daughter's middle-class persuasions (pasta with fresh parmesan) even more than her job as a therapist, and never fails to drive any wedge she can between her children and their remarried father. Just as Anne creates a cordon around herself by reimagining Harry, so Maureen engineers a narrative of ingratitude in order to disguise her failings as a mother and wife. Projecting onto her children the causes of her own failure, she is able two-facedly to proclaim her pride in her family to the other residents. She excels at passive aggression, but the rope she gives her children to hang themselves is her own ligature, blighting her life as she tries to force others to care about her.

Such self-defeating narcissism is a familiar trope in O'Hagan's writing and it encapsulates that particular strain of Scottish self-excusing that he finds so exasperating and cripplingly introspective. Through Alice he displays how a willingness to manufacture and internalise self-justifying narratives can operate on a national as well as an individual scale. More so than Maureen, Alice has reasons for the resentment she feels towards her family. Her mother's adoration of Harry and grief over her lost son has left little room for Alice, and Anne's grandmaternal love for Luke further negates her. But, when she meets the traumatised Luke on his return to Glasgow, she illustrates not only her inability to express love towards her son but also a failure to value the lessons about the world that he has learnt. The scene is a painful one for it opposes Luke's hard-won cynicism about self-justifying narratives with her platitudes on the noble causes of conflict. Pride, patriotic sacrifice, and heroism are the virtues to which she defaults, understandable sentiments perhaps, but nothing more than abstract ideals to Luke, for whom war means only chaos, guilt, and the cleansing of others' dirty consciences. Alice's insistence that he has fought for his country, a country no less that appears to be moving towards self-determination, brings about the angry riposte: 'Dump the flags and the drums and the pipes. They're for the museum. Like all the junk of all the nations' (O'Hagan, 2015: 178). For Luke, the simplicity of a reassuringly uncomplicated nationalism is more than disingenuous; it is an ideological blindness to the effects of an increasingly fractious globalisation that has called into question the very notion of the nation state:

> There's no nation, Mum. There's only people surfing the Net. People like your husband sending cod in parsley sauce to people in France. And the money pouring into your life via PayPal. And every person imagining the world as he wants to see it, just like the guy in the turban behind the wall with an explosive vest who thinks he's going to Allah. He thinks he loves his country, too. And he thinks his country is being exploited. And he thinks his pals are a nation. (O'Hagan, 2015: 178)

The damp-eyed sentimentality of home has been burnt off for Luke in Afghanistan and replaced by a conviction in the irrelevance of the nation in the borderless age of digital capitalism and neoliberal imperialism. Wars are no longer fought for principles, he believes, but to protect the free flow of resources and to maintain the global balance of power, their protagonists mere puppets of political expediency. His mother's idealism is an expression of the sentimental blight afflicting the nation, Luke and O'Hagan believe. Scotland may be the sum of 'its hills and its inventions' but it is also the sum of 'its sense of injury' and 'its sentimental dream that there's nobody like us' (O'Hagan, 2015: 178), faults of exceptionalism that, when expressed through Maureen or Alice, reveal a spirit that is introverted, self-defeating, and delusional. 'I don't know what convinced you', Luke rants at Alice, 'that building walls would make you better inside' (O'Hagan, 2015: 178). Small-minded nationalism is a failing in O'Hagan's view because it breeds a casual, comforting idealism that ignores the world as it is, but at the same time he acknowledges the need for the kind of narrative shaping of the world on a large scale that mimics his characters' private reimaginings of their lives. It represents an attempt to cleave simplicity from chaos, meaning from confusion, and, for all his condemnations, Luke's experiences in Afghanistan have taught him that such narrative illumination is dangerously seductive.

The Allied mission in Afghanistan is replete with interlocking narratives of order designed to make sense of a war that has increasingly come to resemble an unwinnable conflict of attrition between irreconcilable worldviews. From the macro-narrative of the liberal West freeing the Afghans from theocratic despotism to the daily battle between inertia and peril afflicting the soldiers, the story of the war is constructed in numerous ways to justify the seeming zero-sum game into which it has resolved. For the young men of Luke's Section, raised on *Call of Duty* video games, the uncomplicated truths they have learnt about war in front of their screens are infinitely more appealing and exciting than the real thing. In their downtime between missions they take turns on the Xbox, being dragged away reluctantly to write their short final letters home – 'just in case' (O'Hagan, 2015: 42). Death is just the 'next level', a material analogue to a pixelated fantasy, and for men who had 'run important missions with their best mate from school and called in air support, over their headsets, from some kid in Pasadena they'd never met, some kid like them in a box-room. [...] beaten the Russian mafia with the help of club-kids from Reykjavik and bodyboarders from Magnetic Island. [...] obliterated the *A-rabs*' (O'Hagan, 2015: 71–72), the boredom of military life is a poor substitute. Luke knows that 'graphics, screens, solid cover and fuck-off guns you could swap' is 'part of their understanding' (O'Hagan, 2015: 71) of the world, and, where his combat co-ordinates are literary – Hardy's *The Trumpet Major* and *Far From the Madding Crowd* are referenced – those of his men are more interactive.

That contemporary culture mashes virtual and actual, to the point where neither virtual nor actual are distinct ontologies, creates a parallel with the novel's destabilisation of the national–global divide, and ultimately with the them–us paradigm currently fuelling the tensions between Islamist ideologues and the West. Everyone, Luke argues using Anne's maxim, creates the world as s/he would like to imagine it, 'just like the guy in the turban behind the wall with an explosive vest who thinks he's going to Allah' (O'Hagan, 2015: 178). The stories told of nation, faith, ideology, morality, and all the other abstract absolutes of the twentieth century have become hopelessly confused, requiring newer narratives of illumination that provide simple explanations. The world has become a horribly complicated place, suggests O'Hagan, and what has emerged to resolve this are usable, if compromised, truths. It is these we see in operation in the novel's central scenes in Bad Kichan. As high on marijuana as on the black–white moral decisions of *Call of Duty*, the Section is unable to judge whether the actions of the Afghan National Army turncoat captain are part of a wider ambush masquerading as a wedding party. The massacre that ensues when one of their own is killed (O'Hagan, 2013) is the outcome of a lack of illumination, the result of a willingness to create the world without the ability to see clearly.[9] Murder is thus the consequence of the same self-protecting narrative system that in less visceral forms underpins Anne's, Maureen's, and Alice's self-denials. For Luke, and particularly for Scullion, the failure of vision at Bad Kichan ensures that the truths by which they themselves go are exposed to the harshest of lights.

Scullion is a career soldier whose experiences in Northern Ireland, Sierra Leone, the Balkans, and Iraq have shaped a consciousness that is as far from the toy soldiers of Section A as can be: 'don't give me points', he declares in relation to their Xbox games; 'give me a body count any day' (O'Hagan, 2015: 71). He believes unequivocally in the necessity for aggressively suppressing opposition, not as a means to an end but as the end itself. Though he is prepared to try the more emollient hearts-and-minds strategy that the Kajaki Dam irrigation project represents, he argues that this is ultimately a means towards the same end of returning the world to an order which sees the West in charge through military force. His philosophy may be uncompromising, but it is also underpinned by an understanding of his role that harks directly back to the nineteenth century. He keeps a copy of Matthew Arnold's poems by his side and yearns for the romance of the Great Game – an ironic counterpoint to *Call of Duty*. Whilst his mission is not overtly civilising, he is nostalgic for a time when he had 'imagined the world could be put right and made whole' (O'Hagan, 2015: 150) He has his own version of simple truths and his own ways of masking the bloodier episodes of his life 'so that now he only saw Kipling's vistas of white carnations' (O'Hagan, 2015: 44). However, Scullion's bellicose convictions are brought low by his inability to cope with the continuous prosecution of wars that the geopolitical dominance of the West demands. His frayed nerves incapacitate him in a firefight, and his poor leadership and bad judgement lead to the Bad Kichan massacre. When he is eventually invalided out of the war, it is through a suicidal one-man assault that leaves his men without their commanding officer. In hospital and aware of his catastrophic failure, he veers between despair and an unbending loyalty to the mission, declaring: 'We brought light to those people' (O'Hagan, 2015: 210). The extent to which he believes this is questionable, but it and his desire to retire to India to read Kipling under a banyan tree affirm the judgement that Luke also passes on his mother: 'You're from another age' (O'Hagan, 2015: 212).

The narrative of the white man's burden that echoes through the novel resounds with all the other strains of the past that are repeated in the present. As Anne's and Alice's disconnection attests, the destructive legacy of events is felt through time, resurrected and rearmoured with each fresh iteration. One generation damages the vision of the next, inflicting on them the debt of lies and half-truths that they have used to create their own life narratives. 'You've got to live a life proportionate to your nature' (O'Hagan, 2015: 97) is one of Anne's axioms, but it might just as easily be recast as a life proportionate to your lies, for all the major characters are in thrall to the stories they would like to believe about themselves. In the novel's final sections, Luke chooses to indulge his grandmother's truth and takes her to Blackpool in search of illumination both literal and figurative. The trip is redemptive for him as, by granting Anne the truth of her illusion, he begins to discern a way in which he might be able to reclaim his own narrative of himself as a good, decent man. Ultimately, *The Illuminations* revels in a broad sentimentality that suggests acceptance and the possibility of the renewal of torn familial fabric; Luke sees a way to reconcile with his mother, and, in helping to organise the exhibition of Anne's work, hopes to return Anne to the self that preceded Harry. But the novel cannot be said to resolve unproblematically, for, as much as O'Hagan acknowledges that the lies we tell to sustain ourselves are not pernicious, he is equally sure that, for all the areas that we illuminate, the ones masked and occluded never fully disappear.

Coda

O'Hagan's fondness for the wraith-like presence, fading before the hungry eyes of the observer, presents his initial willingness to ghostwrite the Assange autobiography as an understandable move both in terms of the imaginative challenge it would offer and the continuity it would represent with his fictional concerns to date. Indeed, the project would have consummated the twin interests in the nature of contemporary celebrity and the importance of the often deluded narratives of self-subjectivisation that have insistently recurred throughout his prose writings. The technological developments that allowed Internet 2.0 to become truly interactive and dialogic have created platforms on which the self can be projected in an unlimited variety of skins and poses, but, for O'Hagan, this democratisation has only exacerbated the insubstantiality that attends the society of the spectacle. 'Isn't Wikipedia entirely ghosted?' he asks, 'Isn't half of Facebook? Isn't the World Wide Web a new ether, in which we are all haunted by ghostwriters?' (O'Hagan, 2014). The possibilities for anonymity that have shaped the infrastructure of the Internet bring the question of the separation of public and private realms into sharp focus, but those possibilities are only the newest instantiations in the everyday of forces that have underpinned culture for decades – forces that reduce the individual to transparency. The invisibility that is a paradoxical consequence of a society of obsessive scopophilia can only be remedied by the narrative backfilling and self-mythologisation that constitute contemporary subjectivity. The layering of anonymity, revelation, and fabulation that surrounded Assange's confused rise to celebrity collapses together all of O'Hagan's anxieties about the status of embodied individualism in an immaterial and intrusive age. The illumination that Assange's and Wikileaks' disclosures offer may appear to throw light into dark corners but must be read, O'Hagan reminds us, in the context of those areas that have been masked from view, areas that increasingly suppose the indivisibility of the private and public and the penetrability of the individual.

Notes

1 See for instance Scurr, 2006; Taylor, 2003.

2 See for instance Nick Hornby's comments in Robson, 2003; Turner, 1995.

3 *Maf* is the obvious exception here, being focused largely on America in the early 1960s, but O'Hagan has asserted that he believes it to be his 'most Scottish book, because the form of that book is entirely Scottish' (in Mansfield, 2011).

4 In the febrile and often vitriolic atmosphere that surrounded the independence debate, O'Hagan largely kept his own counsel regarding his views on separation. This did not prevent his previously expressed opinions being co-opted, and largely turned against him, by those with strongly partisan sentiment in both camps. In 2011, Pat Kane quoted O'Hagan's 2007 description of the Scottish National Party as a 'parcel of rogues' (Kane, 2011), whilst Tim Lott (2011) recalls a literary argument in which O'Hagan denounced English arrogance. Broadly, O'Hagan's politics seem to have been in favour of continuing the Union, and a comment about the idealistic vision of the 1707 Union would seem to support this: 'The very idea of erecting a non-ethnic-based society is a very modern idea of a state, and the United Kingdom exhibits that in a way many so-called liberal states could only dream of doing' (Nicoll, 2007). One of his few public statements during the campaign was to co-sign a letter with eleven Scottish academics protesting at what they perceived to be the restriction of pro-Union speech by Shona Robison, the Scottish National Party's Cabinet Secretary for Health, Wellbeing and Sport (Mcfadyen, 2013).

5 See also O'Hagan, 1994, 1999b.

6 Though denying that he specifically based Maria's story on that of the 1970s TV starlet Lena Zavaroni, O'Hagan has fulsomely acknowledged that he employed her as an exemplum. Criticised by some reviewers (and Zavaroni's family) for the factual similarities, O'Hagan has defended his position by arguing that Zavaroni symbolised a significant cultural shift in British life; she was 'the last gasp of the entertainment world that existed before global corporate sponsorship and MTV' (Andrew O'Hagan, 'On Celebrity Memoirs', in O'Hagan, 2008: 166). For an overview of the debates on O'Hagan's 'appropriation' of Zavaroni, see Goring, 2003; MacLaren, 2003.

7 'The Girl', says O'Hagan in 'Saint Marilyn', 'would at first seem to release her from the bad things of her childhood, but which later became like one of her childish ghouls, leaning over her, making her all sex, and suffocating her' (O'Hagan, 2008: 69).

8 See Akbar, 2010; Churchwell, 2010; Kemp, 2010; Mueller 2011.

9 The dead soldier is Mark McNulty, the object of Father David's ill-starred approach in *Be Near Me*.

3

Tom McCarthy

For a writer who, by his own admission, has 'nothing to say' (McCarthy, 2012: 8), Tom McCarthy has a great deal to say about nothing. The absent, the cryptic, the negative, the uncategorisable are such recurrent tropes in his writing and conceptual installations that it is not unreasonable to describe McCarthy as the contemporary author most interested in nothing. In a riposte to the hysterical realist trend for recent fiction to be explicitly and declaratively 'about' something, McCarthy pursues an artistic agenda wedded to intangibility and dispersed phenomenal affect. His fiction is indubitably not about chronicling the kind of social reality to which Wood has directed writers; rather he enthusiastically inscribes non-human spaces into a cartography of the immaterial and invisible (Wood, 2001b). But then saying something about nothing is what McCarthy believes all serious writers do; 'If you've got something to say', he says in his essay *Transmission and the Individual Remix: How Literature Works*, 'you're not a writer' (McCarthy, 2012: 8). By this he intends to advocate not the total self-effacement of the writer but the necessity for a quietness that will enable to writer to tune in to 'a set of signals that have been repeating, pulsing, modulating in the airspace of the novel, poem, play – in their lines, between them and around them – since each of these forms began' (McCarthy, 2012: 9). Literature demands an exigent listening to the diffuse and non-continuous signals that are commonly termed 'tradition' but that in fact penetrate cultural praxis in non-linear, indirect, and unprogrammatic flows. These signals can accumulate in any expressive form but are heard most insistently and viscerally in the avant-garde, where their repeaters are most acutely attuned.

McCarthy's line here clearly leads back to the modernists' imperative for artistic impersonality, and in every pore of his writerly self one detects the influences of Conrad, Eliot, Kafka, Mann, Woolf, and particularly Joyce and Beckett. Behind them are equally important but less insistent strains of Aeschylus, Ovid, Dante, Cervantes, Baudelaire, Mallarmé, Rilke, Musil, and the more recent influences of Burroughs, Perec, and Pynchon. Though he is an unapologetic believer in the value of the highbrow, McCarthy discerns incisiveness and philosophical relevance in a range of cultural products but, as Matthew Hart, Aaron Jaffe, and Jonathan Eburne comment, he is 'highbrow even in his popular cultural choices. (Hergé's *Tintin*, not René Goscinny's *Asterix*; Lewis Carroll, not Charles Kingsley; Kraftwerk, not Jean Michel Jarre)' (Hart, Jaffe, and Eburne, 2013: 660). In his 2006 work *Tintin and the Secret of Literature*, he mixes Hergé with Derrida, De Man, and Blanchot to produce a piece of deconstructionist criticism that takes its own comic intentions seriously without ever losing its lightness of touch. Such celebration of popular culture within the context of high art might (twenty years ago) have been regarded as an exercise in postmodern irony, but, for all its knowingness, McCarthy's incorporation of the popular is far from opportunistic. Instead it references a fundamental comic absurdity at the core of human being that is as present in Hergé as it is in Beckett and Bergson. For Bergson, laughter is an anxious reaction to the force of repetition, which, through duplication, destroys the uniqueness of life. Throughout his fiction, McCarthy's protagonists struggle and strive to escape this bathos of repetition, to realise themselves as singular ideals rather than shabby coalescences of rehearsed interpellations, but the resistance to individuation of a universe of comic cruelty always thwarts them. Their gravest intentions of authenticity are continually undercut by the obduracy of the material realm that repeatedly pulls them back towards to the worldly, thwarting their hopes of overcoming themselves and the conditions that have shaped their worlds. Whether it's the narrator of *Remainder* (2005) fretting over the nonchalance of his gait; the luckless cosmonaut caught in space whilst politics reshapes his homeland in *Men in Space* (2007); Serge Carrefax dying of an infected insect bite as he orchestrates the signals of the universe in *C* (2010); or the corporate anthropologist narrator of *Satin Island* (2015), who analyses the creases in jeans through abstract Deleuzian tropes, McCarthy's fictional worlds are underpinned by the dark irony of matter. Much to his characters' frustration, there is no prospect of slipping the chains of the physical world because the metaphysical is always beyond both grasp and comprehension. McCarthy's is therefore a universe of things, geometries, patterns, inscriptions, and networks, but it is never a place of transcendence.

In the writers, artists, film-makers, and theorists whom he admires, McCarthy finds a common interest in grappling with this problem of transcendence, a problem he believes to be at the heart of how literature works. The art work, he suggests, is always seeking to be more than itself, searching for ways to break free of form and function to dwell (in a Heideggerian sense of having a place) in outsideness. But it is always stymied by what McCarthy has called the 'mattering of matter' (McCarthy and Critchley, 2012), the reassertion of the law of the symbolic, and the negation of metamorphosis. In *Men in Space* this is very appositely illustrated in the iconic image of a saint whose ascension is barred not by any divine proscription but by the frame of the painting in which he is portrayed. As he has reached the limit of his rise, his halo has become compacted by the painting's edge, converting it into an ellipse. This failure of transcendence is repeated (with Bergsonian comic anxiety) again and again in McCarthy, revealing not just the unwillingness of matter to overcome itself but also the systemic inability of art to effect that transformation in symbolic terms. As he acknowledges to Frederic Tuten, the form he has predominantly employed is trapped by its own limitations: 'I think the novel is and always has been dead, and this is the very precondition of its perpetual regeneration. *Don Quixote* is a novel about how novels don't work [...] about a fundamental, systematic dysfunction written right into the medium's core. And that's more or less the first major novel!' (in Tuten, 2015). Like the enframed saint, creative expression is bound by the medium in which it is envisioned, preventing the possibility of being other than itself, and this formal self-parasitism ultimately prescribes the shape of the content. The novel is, to use McCarthy's term, a 'zombie art form' that 'stumbles onwards, ineluctably, gorging and disgorging its own death, its own deadness' (in Tuten, 2015).

The serious novelist perpetually faces the punishing absurdity of this dilemma: how to articulate the possibility of transcendence through a form that, in its very artistic legitimacy, disavows that possibility. The contemporary novel has addressed this problem, in McCarthy's view, by largely shedding seriousness. He has been a consistent and vocal critic of the rise of the middlebrow novel with pretentions to literariness – what Jim Collins has termed 'Lit-lit' (Collins, 2010: 246) and what McCarthy scathingly refers to as 'Oprah Literature' (McCarthy, 2014a: 21–22). This genre is as undead as the highbrow literary novel but 'ambles along happily' (Tuten, 2015), believing in the durability of uncritical realism and seemingly untroubled by its own structural contradictions. This clearly gets under McCarthy's skin; the conventions of realism are as knowingly artificial as any avant-garde metafiction and provide 'no more purchase on the *real* than anything else' (Hart, Jaffe, and Eburne, 2013: 679). Burying one's head in a naïve realism and ignoring the legacies of modernist and postmodernist experimentation is culturally ingenuous and would be the equivalent of 'ignoring Darwin' (Purdon, 2010). At the same time, McCarthy is wary of construing the literary landscape as a 'Scylla and Charybdis' (in Hart, Jaffe, and Eburne,

2013: 679) of avant-garde experimentalism and middlebrow realism between which the independently-minded author steers a middle way:

> I'm not really interested in middle ways. The task, as I see it, is to be genuinely radical. It means pushing experience right up against language, and against the fact of its embedding within language, and affirming the primacy of desire, and putting desire and the Law on collision courses, again and again and again, and affirming the death drive. (McCarthy in Hart, Jaffe, and Eburne, 2013: 680)

Contemporary publishing houses are reluctant to risk serious capital on serious writing, McCarthy suggests, preferring the security of predictable middlebrow returns and the kind of uncontentious content that such business strategy promotes – McCarthy even wryly suggests that his own inclusion on the Man Booker Prize's shortlist in 2010 must have come about because 'someone must have read it [*C*] as a kind of historical novel' (in Hart, Jaffe, and Eburne, 2013: 680). This cultural divide between formally conventional and adventurous fiction was an issue highlighted, though in less boldly pejorative terms, by Zadie Smith in her *New York Review of Books* essay 'Two Paths for the Novel', a text partly responsible for McCarthy's growing profile and the source of the gleefully marketable quote that *Remainder* was 'one of the great English novels of the past ten years'.[1] Smith's essay has frequently been referenced in recent debates about the healthiness of the contemporary novel, and it already feels clichéd to refer to it in introducing McCarthy, but it does throw a light on the extent to which the realist and avant-garde traditions are portrayed by the literary establishment as rivals in the effort to depict a contemporary real – an artificial opposition with which McCarthy would disagree.[2]

Smith argues that 'in healthy times', the novel cuts 'multiple roads, allowing for the possibility of a Jean Genet as surely as a Graham Greene' (Smith, 2009: 71). These are not, in her view, healthy times, and the stark contrast she draws between *Remainder* and Joseph O'Neill's *Netherland* (2008) suggests that they are not getting any healthier. The latter she describes as sitting 'at an anxiety crossroads where a community in recent crisis – the Anglo-American liberal middle class – meets a literary form in long term crisis, the nineteenth-century lyrical realism of Balzac and Flaubert' (Smith, 2009: 72). Yet the kind of avant-garde novel represented by McCarthy has 'been relegated to a safe corner of literary history, to be studied in postmodernity modules, and dismissed by our most prominent public critics, as a fascinating failure, intellectual brinkmanship that lacked heart' (Smith, 2009: 73). The dig at James Wood – a long champion of the Flaubertian tradition, and of *Netherland* – is subtle but pointed, and, at times, Smith's essay comes across as a bristling rejection of the kind of liberal humanism that

Wood's criticism advocates.[3] Her broader point, though, is that McCarthy's fiction, with its 'brutal excision of psychology', was seeking to 'shake the novel out of its present complacency' (Smith, 2009: 93) and represented a direction of travel into the future, rather than the past. For McCarthy, the issue is not really about realism or anti-realism as a formal mode but about the extent to which any act of inscription can approximate the real that outmanoeuvres the symbolic. Serious literature – whether realist or avant-garde – addresses this same problem of absence at the heart of language's desire:

> Dickens is meant to be the apogee of realist, character-filled writing, but the first passages of *Great Expectations* are totally deconstructionist. Pip is in this Bataillean, murky mud-plane kneeling in front of a tombstone running his finger along the incisions, the carvings in its surface – names which are his family's – and meditating on the identity of things and looking at the horizon. It's completely conceptual, modernist, structural writing. [...]
>
> With the really good stuff, it's not like there's deconstruction-compatible writing and humanist-compatible writing. It's always already deconstructed in itself. We just don't know how to read it properly. (Hart, Jaffe, and Eburne, 2013: 681)

McCarthy's abiding interest in the cryptographical, the secret, the unchartable is, at heart, a concern to discover new ways to read the illegibility of the outside of symbolism, and, as he has demonstrated with his visual art works and performances, the literary is not the only way to parse that outsideness. Since 1999, he has been involved with what is always referred to as a 'semi-fictitious' art collective, the International Necronautical Society (INS), in which he acts as the General Secretary alongside the Chief Philosopher, Simon Critchley. McCarthy situates the origins of the INS in the crossover between his literary, artistic, and philosophical interests:

> I was interested in how the art manifesto might play out now. It seems like nowadays you could only have an inauthentic or an ironic version. So I wrote this pastiche-manifesto, which the art world picked up quite quickly, and that led to exhibitions, residencies and the like. I appointed INS committees and subcommittees. The INS became a structure. I call it a 'fiction' – not that it isn't real, but because it's a construct that not only references but also cannibalises a whole bunch of other cultural moments. (Armesto, 2011)

Channelling a Soviet-style bureaucracy with mock trials, official bulletins, and occasional purges, the INS has fronted a philosophical and artistic ambition to 'map, enter, colonise and, eventually, inhabit' the space of death (International Necronautical Society, 1999). The desire to explore death's spatial parameters is fundamentally a desire to overcome its resistance to the symbolic order, and is thus in total consonance with McCarthy's aim in his fiction to plot the shape of language's exteriority. Through installations at institutions such as DasArts Foundation in Amsterdam, the Moderna Museet in Stockholm, the Kunst-Werke Institute for Contemporary Art in Berlin, and the Institute of Contemporary Arts in London, the INS, and McCarthy independently, has taken the necronautical transmission into the arena of visual and conceptual art, and, in the process, resituated the debate about the limits of language's law across a number of media platforms (International Necronautical Society, 2001, 2004; Kunst-Werke Institute for Contemporary Art, 2008; Moderna Museet, 2008). In all these endeavours, one detects seriousness cut with humour, commitment with an acute awareness of absurdity, and it is not unreasonable to suggest that this is McCarthy's defining contribution to the contemporary cultural scene. The avant-garde has always had an element of pantomime about it, and McCarthy's writings and performances bring this licence into the twenty-first century, where the currency (in all forms) of the middlebrow seems to have become serious business.

Remainder (2005)

McCarthy's first published novel – though not the first he wrote – might be described as a novel about how the not-known becomes known. It details the process of coming-into-being that transforms the inchoate into the symbolic, giving body to the shapeless and solidifying the current that links imagination with memory. It also displays McCarthy's interest in inscription as a process that continuously flows around and through what we customarily understand as 'meaning' without ever being able to provide complete and satisfying access to any transcending core. This interest is manifest in McCarthy's conviction that 'everything must leave some kind of mark' (McCarthy, 2007: 94); a belief that the world is constructed by and understood through intersecting symbolic exchange networks. Into these networks the individual fits her/himself 'like a gramophone needle into a groove', reproducing through conscious and unconscious re-enactment the looped and coded information that each network contains (Kastner *et al.*, 2009). Such envelopment within inscribed practice positions the subject as a reader – and frequently a misreader – of signs, but rarely their author.

The schools of poststructuralist thinking that dominated the European philosophical scene in the latter decades of the twentieth century invalidated a belief in the author as an originating speaker, but they also highlighted the problematic status of the 'auth-' prefix after the linguistic turn.

Etymologically rooted in concepts of originality, genuineness, self-awareness, and agency, the 'auth-' of author, authority, and authenticity has indicated, in the prevailing intellectual context of the academy, the kind of faith in a Romantic transcendence associated with metaphysical epistemologies. The idea of an 'author' of a work or event suggests a conscious intentionality that has been increasingly decentred in literary critical (and literary fictional) circles since the 1960s in favour of the writer as a 'receiver, modulator, retransmitter: a remixer' (McCarthy, 2012: 28). For McCarthy to write a novel about a man seeking to author himself is thus an intriguing intervention in contemporary debates about anti-humanist fiction.

Remainder details the post-trauma re-engineering of a self by an unnamed narrator, recompensed to the tune of £8.5 million after a freak accident in which he has been struck by falling 'Technology. Parts, bits' (McCarthy, 2007: 5) and, as a consequence, has been temporarily disabled and robbed of all but the most functional memories. This unfortunate incident is McCarthy's way of hollowing out his narrator, withdrawing from him any canny sense of the phenomenal world as a place of semiotic connectedness or consistency. Denying him a name does not invoke everyman status; quite the contrary in fact, for, just as the coincidence of being in the wrong place at the wrong time singles him out for back luck, so the narrator is a special case in an imaginative sense, an exemplary character only skeletally fleshed out, functioning more as a combination of external effects than psychological nuance. He is a figure that will become familiar in McCarthy's fiction – a characterless character that sits somewhere between the subjective and the objective, channelling a philosophical *Zeitgeist* without ever being connected to it or able to describe its parameters. Like Serge Carrefax in *C* and U in *Satin Island*, the narrator of *Remainder* is an embodied renunciation of what McCarthy regards as the naïve humanism of the realist artistic tradition, for he serves no socially or morally representative function, achieves no self-consciousness, and rewards no psychological analysis (McCarthy 2012: 21–22). His role is not to slot comfortably into the prescribed dimensions of a fictional universe as a recognisable textual function but to remind us that reality is the product of fictional creation, and, as such, needs to be continuously inscribed.

Using his windfall, the narrator sets out to do exactly that: to reconstruct his life in as faithful an homage as he can to the remnants of his memory. His objective is not verisimilitude, nor is it simulacrum, but the realisation in the material realm of a Platonic ideal with which he can wholly and seamlessly converge. This goes beyond nostalgic imitation to a craving to enter the past, not through memory – with all its attendant half-truths – but through transcendent and total inhabitation. He identifies this as an unimpaired coalescence with himself that feels unequivocally authentic: 'to be real – to become fluent, natural, to cut out the detour that sweeps us around what's fundamental to events, preventing us from touching their core: the detour that makes us all second-hand and second-rate' (McCarthy, 2007: 244). The pathos he describes here echoes an imaginary transcendence, but he is determined to actualise his ideal and he uses his compensation to create – literally, to create – his unique reality. Every element of his vision – from the specific block of apartments to the cats on the roof opposite his window; from the tang of frying liver wafting from the flat downstairs to the exact contours of a bin-bag as it strikes the perfectly recreated tiles – is painstakingly attuned to his hyper-discriminating sensibility. By perfecting his physical surroundings, which swiftly extend beyond his dwelling, the narrator trusts that the malleability of the object world and the sympathetic tailoring of others' actions might return his disarranged consciousness to comprehensible order and familiarity. The model of authenticity that the narrator fetishises therefore involves not just an internal re-mapping but also a correspondence with a version of the outside as an extension of his ego, relating solely to his experience of consciousness. Through this, others become merely objective material for the implementation of his fantasy, and consequently tend to be drawn only in the barest of outlines. Greg, his friend; Catherine, his potential girlfriend; and Naz, the enabler who facilitates his schemes, are presented as narrative furniture to be moved around the text just as the narrator moves models around the miniature stage sets that he constructs to map his personal vision.

The accident, which set him adrift in a realm of self-unknowing, has destroyed a contiguity between his inner and outer landscapes that had allowed him to connect to the world in a way that he understood as unforced. Before the accident:

> all my movements had been fluent and unforced. Not awkward, acquired, second-hand, but natural. Opening my fridge's door, lighting a cigarette, even lifting a carrot to my mouth: these gestures had been seamless, perfect. I'd merged with them, run through them and let them run through me until there'd been no space between us. They'd been real; I'd been real – been without first understanding how to try to be. (McCarthy, 2007: 62)

Authenticity lies, for him, in this intuitive flow from inner to outer, but the accident has disrupted that, turning complex and overwhelming all that had been fluent and unconsidered, and thrusting him from an experience of flow to one of juddering disarticulation. Instead of a whole, he has become a collection of conjoined bodily and mental prostheses that fulfil tasks automatically without reference to a commanding purpose. Hospitalised, he describes the usurpation of his body by 'all sorts of tubes and wires pumping one thing into my body and sucking another out' (McCarthy, 2007: 6) and details the mechanistic process of re-learning to eat and walk through meticulously considered stages. The experience of living in the world is thus reduced to the combination of a sequential performance of tiny, disarticulated codes, each routine and singularly meaningless but, when accelerated and considered as a whole, that mimic the dramatic semblance of normality. This discrete mechanical enactment of the human's being has a deindividualising effect and renders agency more a function of programming than instinct, for it suggests that the consciousness of selfhood can be broken down in a manner similar to the way in which the narrator employs a motorbike enthusiast whose sole task is to take apart and rebuild his bike, or the pianist who is required to methodically practise passages of music, decoupling their musical motifs from their wider context before reassembling them into a whole. Such exercises in orderliness represent the narrator's initial attempts to manufacture an authentic sensibility, but they involve forcing things into meaning by understanding the tiniest parts of their being. It is an attempt to understand the whole by examining it with a microscope and does not provide the satisfying feeling of naturalness for which he searches.

The narrator makes the assumption that the authentic is a consummation of external naturalness in space with a form of internal perceptive flow that circumvents contemplation by accessing a state of pure being. The easy, unselfconscious swing of the refrigerator door, or the nonchalant command when lighting a cigarette, speak of an order of veracity and predictability for which he is continually striving as a confirmation of his validity in the material world. Frustratingly for him, there are moments when he believes he has captured this; micro-moments of perfect convergence when his nagging discomfort falls away and he is left in a condition of messianic transportation:

> Remembering it [the accident] sent a tingling from the top of my legs to my shoulders and right up into my neck. It lasted for just a moment – but while it did I felt not-neutral. I felt different, intense: both intense and serene at the same time. I remember feeling this way very well: standing there, passive, with my palms turned outwards, feeling intense and serene. (McCarthy, 2007: 11)

The image that he projects of himself here – static, accepting, with palms turned outwards – suggests both openness to the connectivity of the moment and a Christ-like gesture of entreaty. It is a sensation that he describes elsewhere as a 'calm contentedness' (McCarthy, 2007: 138), and it is in these rare moments of transcendent being, when he feels instrumental to the moment, that he comes closest to achieving a form of authenticity as an experience of immanence.

Craving this sense of fulfilment on a permanent basis, the narrator expands the scope of his project to include the world beyond the controllable domain of his apartment building. With Naz's ever-obliging assistance, he recreates in painstaking detail a motor mechanic's workshop, and, as his mental condition deteriorates and his need to inhabit an affective space takes a darker turn, the re-enactment of a gangland killing, which eventually leads to the performance of a bank robbery that rapidly crosses the line between simulation and crime, leading in turn to the death of one of his actors. What drives his obsessiveness is the attractive possibility of total immersion in an authentic experience, an immersion that would leave no libidinal excess but would map desire absolutely onto outcome. Such a contrivance would represent a perfect transcendence because it would leave nothing behind – no trace, no residue, no remainder. It would, in effect, be a completely closed and efficient correspondence between the material and immaterial realms that would negate the requirement of any symbolic compensation.

The increasingly extreme re-enactments he demands are attempts to fix this ideal into concrete, reproducible shape. In the case of the mechanic's shop, for instance, the mundane task of replenishing his car's washer fluid becomes a moment of material commutation when the liquid decanted into the reservoir seems to magically disappear. The narrator's transport of delight at this apparent dematerialisation centres on the momentary uncoupling of stuff from the laws of matter; the solid seems through a process of transubstantiation to have become immaterial, leaving no remainder. Unfortunately the subsequent gushing of the fluid from the dashboard reveals the fault in the vehicle's plumbing system and repudiates this miracle, throwing the narrator back into the state of worldly imperfection that he associates with inauthenticity.

The example of the gangland killing takes this need for coalescence a step further and reveals his increasing inability to distinguish between enactment and re-enactment as he choreographs life's final moments in an attempt to achieve a form of authentic being-towards-death. By re-enacting the movements of the murder victim in the final seconds before his demise, the narrator hopes for a form of spatial coincidence of living and dead matter:

> in dying besides the bollards on the tarmac he'd done what I wanted to do: merged with the space around him, sunk and flowed into it until there was no distance between it and him – and merged too, with his actions, merged to the extent of having no more consciousness of them. He'd stopped being separate, removed, imperfect. [...] Then both mind and actions had resolved themselves into pure stasis. The spot that this had happened on was the ground zero of perfection – all perfection. (McCarthy, 2007: 184–185)

If one understands the narrator's authenticity as a pathos of coalescence, such experiments in re-enactment are attempts to access the authentic through the profoundly inauthentic process of endless recreation, robbing the moment of its spontaneity through forensic aestheticisation and examination. Analysing an experience of being in such minute detail profoundly dehumanises and denaturalises the event, reducing it to its signifying constituents but decontextualising them from any broader structure of meaning. However, it is only in this disarticulation that the narrator is able to identify any transubstantiation between the material and the immaterial. Lying on the ground, imagining the world from the perspective of another, enables his sensation of connectedness, not only to the consciousness of another person but also to the sub-strata of the material world. The realness for which he strives can be perceived through the slow-motion deconstruction of events, but its quality is fundamentally scenographic and the authenticity attained is always troubled by the taint of a residual inauthenticity.

McCarthy's work with the INS, has focused on this residual inauthenticity as an indicator of the failure of artistic creation to achieve transcendence. At the heart of McCarthy's interest in the idea of authenticity as it relates to the concerns of the INS is the idea that death is a space beyond the human and yet inextricably underlies the experience of subjectivity and the relationship to representation. The failing of art is its inability to transcend either death or itself. The traumatised repetition that is involved in the creative process, and in the re-enactment in which the narrator of *Remainder* indulges, is circumscribed by the materiality of matter and its attachment to the world of concrete phenomena. The narrator is engaged in a vain attempt to master his self, to be individual rather than dividual, to cohere singularly rather than recognise the continuous process of splitting and reformation that constitutes post-deconstructive subjectivity. His attempts to reconstruct unreliable memories and re-enact the coalescence of the sublime moment of individuation are all doomed to fail in the face of the obdurate materiality of matter. There is always 'a remainder that remains: a shard, a leftover, a trace, a residual' and this remainder is the 'mark of inauthenticity' (Schwenger, 2008). The narrator expresses his desire for a totalising, mystical unification in moments such as those discussed above, a perfect coincidence of self with un-self, yet, in each case, the transcendence is denied – experience is inauthentic because it remains within the phenomenal. From the necronautical perspective, this failure to transcend becomes the motivating imperative for rejecting singularity and embracing the constant splitting of self into matter. Matter, and its valorisation, becomes the focus, and the emphasis on its imperfection the means to articulate the subject's stable or singluar belonging.

The remainder – that which foils transcendence and cannot be assimilated into the authentic – is encapsulated in the motif of the figure of eight and its symbolic correlate to infinity: ∞. This pattern features prominently in the £8.5 million sum that the narrator receives in compensation for the accident, and is repeated in various guises throughout the novel. The integrity of the unbroken loop of infinity strongly suggests the perfection of the authenticity that the narrator seeks, a closed circuit that refers to nothing outside itself and yet sustains its own energy. However, the simplicity of the figure of eight is complicated by the 0.5 supplement that attaches itself not only to the narrator's bank account but also to his psychological make-up: 'The eight was perfect, neat: a curved figure infinitely turning back into itself. But then the half. Why had they added the half? It seemed to me so messy, this half: a leftover fragment, a shard of detritus' (McCarthy, 2007: 9). The financial 'Settlement' is supposed to be the thing that 'would make me better, whole, complete (McCarthy, 2007: 6), some kind of complement to counterbalance the erasure of the past, and yet the narrator is constantly troubled by the 'remainder' – the 0.5 surplus matter that stubbornly will not resolve itself into something whole. As the novel draws to its close, the figure is iterated once again as the aeroplane that the narrator and Naz have charted to flee the re-enacted-heist-turned-real adopts a pattern of back and forth looping as the narrative rests inconclusively between escape and retribution. This final image of wholeness is undercut, as is every other example in the text, with the failure of transcendence and a pained scepticism towards the possibility of authenticity as anything other than a momentary epiphany of self-coherence. Consequently, McCarthy leaves his reader with a disconcerting sense that authenticity is simultaneously plausible and implausible; a guarantor of presence and a marker of its flight; both a space of rooted belonging and a horizon of desire.

McCarthy's reflections on the status of individual authenticity need to be read within the context of his understanding of the self's relation to the things, effects, and others across which subjectivity operates. As previously suggested, *Remainder* is dominated by a tone of objectivity, in which character development is subordinated to the relative positions in space of the dramatis personae. This has become a recurring feature of work in which McCarthy has explored the technological and human networks that hold his protagonists in relationship. *Remainder* portrays a world laced by the hidden lines of interconnection that link people to places, to events, and to things in grids of symbolic dependence. One such grid is the sports field to which the narrator gravitates as a comforting reminder of order:

It was tucked into a maze of back streets and fenced in by knitted green wire. Inside the first fence another one caged in a beautiful green asphalt pitch. The pitch was multi-purpose. All sorts of markings cut and sliced across it: semicircles, circles, boxes, arcs – in yellow, red and white. It was beautiful for me, but to anyone else it would just have looked shoddy and run-down. (McCarthy, 2007: 98)

As he sets about his ambitious world-building, he divides space into manageable blocks, moving his employees amongst them in orderly patterns and establishing cycles of communication which channel information across that space in invisible networks. By mobile phone and walkie-talkies, the narrator communicates his instructions to Naz, who dutifully passes them on to the next node in the informational chain, creating an effective feedback loop that transforms desire into a form of reality. It is the efficiency of this infinity loop that underpins the narrator's sense of security not just within the knowledge system but also within the order of signification from which he has been roughly excluded by the accident. He seeks an informational guarantee from the object world, and his pleasure in form and structure derives from the illusion that shape can contain a totality which, in turn, can be understood by the sum of the symbolic exchanges that take place in that space. Thus the novel's preoccupation with connectivity and the networks of communicative transmission that underpin our existence gestures towards the narrator's need for coincidence with something that is beyond him and that ties him not only to the space he inhabits but also to an ineffable context of being.

McCarthy repeatedly returns to the idea of how space is inscribed, re-inscribed and over-inscribed in his writing. For him, this inscription, or 'encryption' – to use the term he commonly adopts – marks the ground zero of humanity's struggle to match the indefinite nature of expression to the experience of world; inscription, he says, 'opens up the possibility of literature, politics [...] history – the lot' (in Kastner *et al.*, 2009). Yet inscription is not confined to the mechanics of language or visual representation. In *Tintin and the Secret of Literature, Men in Space, C*, and *Satin Island*, McCarthy shows how technology has increasingly filled the immaterial space of the air with signals, codes, crackles, static, whirring, humming, pops, and buzzing. Such inscriptive manifestations remove meaning and intentionality from the prisons of the page and the alphabet and send them out to propagate and miscegenate as pure signals in the ether to be heard and decoded, or to remain unreceived by any interpreting ear. The radical attempts by *Remainder*'s narrator to locate himself in a world of familiar material and immaterial codes become in McCarthy's subsequent fictions a questioning of the parameters of the code itself, and, in his next book, an investigation into what the code protects and masks.

Tintin and the Secret of Literature (2006)

Despite its seemingly whimsical title, *Tintin and the Secret of Literature* is a serious critical consideration which identifies in the works of Hergé textual tropes and narrative mechanisms common to sophisticated literary writing. The study reveals McCarthy's intellectual debts to the continental philosophical tradition of Maurice Blanchot and Jacques Derrida and the history of psychoanalysis, and is a useful indicator of the concerns with the elusiveness of meaning and the cultural circuitry of inscription that have informed McCarthy's fiction, visual installations, and performance work with the INS. The book addresses the interrelationship of the world and writing in a way which emphasises its complex metaphorical interdependence but also stresses the resonances and signals that emerge from apparent silence, absence, and dissonance. McCarthy sees in Tintin what he sees in literature in general: the encoding of patterns by which we understand and, importantly, misunderstand the world around us. One of his key interests here – as everywhere else in his writing to date – is the outside of interpretation and how the reliability of any interpretational structure is dependent upon the codes by which we read the real. For him, reading is commonly about misreading, or, at least, reading without full comprehension; however, rather than representing a failure of attention or perspicacity, these misreadings can liberate alternative readings or posit new angles from which to interpret (and profitably misinterpret) the codes we encounter. McCarthy observes in Hergé's *Tintin* books the frequent need to correct readings, to re-read clues, codes, situations, and utterances in the light of information that emerges tangentially and post hoc. He also notes how (mis)readings often overlap to produce different, and potentially revelatory, readings, such as in the maps that Tintin has to overlay in order to find the co-ordinates for hidden treasure in *Red Rackham's Treasure* (1944). Codes and interpretations therefore mingle and cross-pollinate to produce a complex web of signification, but definitive meaning is always deferred through a process of sequential encryption:

> If Hergé's *oeuvre* contains cryptic mechanisms, this does not mean that it simply hides something so that it can be discovered, but rather that it keeps forming crypts. If Tintin busts one gang, finds one transmitter, the crypt just relocates and starts transmitting elsewhere [...] through a fantastically dynamic set of overlayings and cross-encodings, it pulses out sequences that resonate at levels far beyond that of any individual, re-encrypting themselves even as they speak. The crypt underwrites a creative process, not an analytical one. It is on the side of the pathology, not the cure. (McCarthy, 2006)

This anti-hermeneuticism in which meaning always recedes beyond the horizon of language locks into McCarthy's consistent interest in how the beyond, or that which is outside, manifests itself in the arena of the known. This seems to be at stake in his writing on the crypt, which represents a way in which the unknown encrypts itself into the world of living perception, but not necessarily through significatory practices such as writing. Instead, codes and signals stand alone as information ready to be variously decoded before being re-encoded in different ways. What we might think of as meaning thus becomes simply a continuous cycle of re-encryption within different hermeneutic codes – as McCarthy says, it is 'on the side of the pathology, not the cure'. Much of the material in *Tintin and the Secret of Literature* has commonalities with the INS objective of charting the space of death and there is a sense that what McCarthy sees as the 'secret' of literature, and at the heart of Tintin's engagement with the crypt and the hidden, is the negotiation of the unchartable territory outside symbolisation. His subsequent fiction also displays a continuing engagement with the elusive beyondness of the real that exceeds reality, and the frustration of being doomed never to gain access to the mystery of death and life.

Men in Space (2007)

Men in Space was McCarthy's second published novel but its writing pre-dates *Remainder* and it addresses a similar constellation of ideas. Like its forebear, the novel is concerned with the relationship of the individual to the space s/he moves within, the nature of the experience of authenticity, and the relation between meaning and non-meaning at the outer limits of signification. Most insistently though, *Men in Space* readdresses the failure of both physical and metaphysical processes to achieve transcendence, to unbind themselves from the logic of their rationales in order to assume the status of unquestionable truth. Yet, where *Remainder*'s narrator is concerned with reinforcing purely his own sense of authentic belonging through obsessive, perfectionist re-enactment, the narrative of *Men in Space* broadens out the notion of failed transcendence to encompass historical, political, aesthetic, and geographical dimensions.

Set primarily in Prague during the period surrounding the political division of Czechoslovakia on 1 January 1993, the novel consists of five intersecting narratives that revolve around the lives of a group of bohemian artists, a criminal gang of Bulgarian exiles, and an operative of the Secret Police. At the heart of the story is a puzzlingly individual icon stolen by the Bulgarians, copied by one of the artists, and tracked by the Secret Police. The painting remains a mystery throughout the novel for it fails to conform to the rigid codes of iconic art and offers instead a series of tantalisingly oblique metaphors which remain unsolved even at novel's end. The painting functions diegetically – it is surreptitiously triplicated by artist Ivan Maňásek, accidentally transported to Holland, and tracked by both Secret Police and criminals – but more importantly it operates as a nodal point for contradictory significations. It appears to represent part of a tradition, a continuity of artistic practice that is historically located and locatable. However, the meaning of the painting is never established with any sense of certainty: its symbolic code does not resonate with tradition, its inscription seems not to correspond to any standard religious text, and the meaning of the elliptical halo is tantalisingly always beyond grasp. Like so much else in this novel, the painting seems to offer access to a form of authenticity that guarantees something to different people – money to the Bulgarian underworld; tradition and meaning to the artists; order and ownership to the Secret Police. Yet it always exceeds these meanings, outreaching the frames of each interpretation and remaining narratively ambiguous: both over- and under-determined.

This ambiguity is crucial to a novel that concerns itself with the flux and indeterminacy of hermeneutic practices, whether they be on the level of the individual or the global. By setting his novel at a moment of historical transition, framed within the broader shift in ideological change that overtook the late twentieth century, McCarthy has drawn attention to the unrooted quality of meaning-making on the level of broad, overarching structures. The narrative of history, as represented in *Men in Space*, is temporarily in abeyance as the domineering logic of Soviet Communism is superseded by the licence of proto-capitalistic free enterprise. The novel begins by detailing the entrepreneurial spirit of the city's immigrant community, which is profiteering from the sudden lapse in authoritarian control, and continues to detail a space of business, artistic, sexual, creative, and intellectual freedom. Prague, like much of Eastern Europe, is in a condition of transition, but with the licence that this releases comes the problem of knowing which boundaries are real and which are imagined. As much as McCarthy sees in this historical moment a criss-crossing of forces and lines of flight that speak of possibility for new orientations and meanings, he is equally preoccupied by fear of the failure of transcendence; that this newness will reveal itself to be only a different kind of meaninglessness. 'Everything falls back [...] eventually' (McCarthy, 2008: 53), complains Ivan in just one of the host of images of falling that the novel contains, and it is in this context that we must interpret the potential for exuberant reinvention offered by change. One very clear example of this instability lies in the handing over of the governmental machinery of Czechoslovakia to members of the artistic

community led by Václav Havel. This is important because it brings to the
fore a historical dialecticism in which the flows of history and authoritarianism are forced into congruence with the idealism and utopianism of art.
Art and government are thus brought together into one historical vector,
and drawn within the same field of signification. One does not instinctively
associate art and government as consanguineous practices – the former generally offering resistance to the latter – so their alliance in the same space
here is not only interesting but also semiotically problematic. Art, as is clear
from McCarthy's statements elsewhere, is fundamentally concerned with
the transmutation of the ordinary into the aesthetic; its role is to enable the
transcendence of the material frameworks of history, economics, and politics through elevation to the symbolic realm. But, in the co-option of government by the agents of art, the aesthetic is framed by material realities; it
cannot transcend because it has become part of the process of history and is
determined by its competing forces.

Elsewhere in the novel the potential for art to be more than itself, and
to refer to more than its own internal logic, is challenged. Art is reduced
to the status of commodity (the elusive icon) or to the level of pastiche (in
the film-montages and collages produced by Prague's art set). Art cannot
transcend the material here, always falling back to the level of the ordinary.
The closest approach to transmutation comes through Maňásek's studied,
meticulous preparations for copying the icon. In the complex mathematics and mechanics required to produce a credible simulacrum, his skilled
actions effect a form of spiritual transformation, but what must be remembered is that they are in the interests of reproduction only – expression is
bounded by an already existent frame. Maňásek's artistic transcendence is
counterpointed therefore by a descendant materiality that becomes fatally
evident when he is murdered by being thrown from his studio window. The
inability of art and the artist to break through to the metaphysical is continually reiterated by the representational problems of the icon itself.

The painting's most compelling element is the red-robed figure of a saint
ascending above a landscape but so trapped by the frame of the painting that
his gold halo has been flattened into the shape of an ellipse. The meaning of
this curious figuration escapes the novel's characters, but they recognise that
the value (in both aesthetic and exchange terms) of the icon derives from its
unique code, which is at once meaningful and meaningless. That is to say
that the meaning of the painting lies not in its fixity within the symbolic
order but its relevance to the particular codes of interpretation which people
apply to it. The painting represents a dizzyingly complex history of aesthetic
and religious practices that dictate (and yet also disturb) its formation, and,
yet, at its heart is the lack of certainty about what value that history bestows.

For the Bulgarian gang, its value lies in its rarity and is purely economic, whereas for the artistic community its value lies in its aesthetically unique play with the codes that determine iconic meaning. All are searching for the 'Golden Section' where 'the divine mystery resides' (McCarthy, 2008: 120), but McCarthy's attention is directed towards the space of interpretation that exists around the solution. In *Tintin and the Secret of Literature* he writes, quoting Derrida, of how the secret is 'eternally unreadable, absolutely indecipherable, even refusing itself to any promise of deciphering or hermeneutic' (McCarthy, 2006: 146). Codes merely allow access to other codes of interpretation. Even when Helena tracks down the key to the code as a mirror reflection, it does not solve the problem because she is left with the problem of how the three words that appear on the icon – 'Love', 'Understanding', and 'Solitude' – relate to each other. Thus there is never the resolution that the viewer might require of the 'Golden Section'; any explanatory coherence is denied and instead we are thrown into the infinite recess of codes.

In *Men in Space* McCarthy creates a framework of intersecting epistemological forces which continuously criss-cross and cross-fertilise with dynamic vibrancy, but the vectors do not produce anything that might come close to meaning. The novel's numerous misreadings of codes has a particularly pertinent political dimension given its setting at a liminal historical moment in which Europe is being split into new geographical and ideological formations, with the forces of communism and capitalism exchanging territory and influence. Codes of behaviour and interpretation are being redrawn in a time and space of flux. McCarthy's Prague is a city filled with immigrants (American, Bulgarian, Dutch, English, Greek) and a plethora of languages, intersecting and cross-pollinating with an unregulated promiscuity. There is a figurative and literal intermingling of people, objects, and words in space leading to the clashing of codes and hermeneutic processes.

McCarthy's emphasis on space as anti-specific, anti-hierarchical, and anti-political draws attention to the provisionality of physical and imaginary zones before they are inscribed within the domain of place. The clearest example of this is the dissection of a land-space called Europe into various geographical and national concepts; the land mass remains the same whilst the internal boundaries of the countries shift with huge historical and political significance. The split that takes place between the Czech Republic and Slovakia on 1 January 1993 is thus a completely arbitrary redrawing of the borders between imaginary states in a purely inscriptive sense, but, in a politico-historical sense, it is invested with enormous emotional freight. Space is cut by wires, grids, frames, shapes, and perspectives, all of which contain it in (often) artful but arbitrary ways. It is shaped into structures where no such structures exist. Various kinds of space-relations might be said to be going on, not least of which is the kind of overlaying (or redrawing) that we see in the relationship between art and government that was suggested above.

The number of images of grids and co-ordinates is overwhelming, and objects are often described in relation to others within an organising system. For instance, Anton, an ex-football referee, describes the constantly shifting scene of the pitch as expressing a contained order: 'the trick was to see all the near-identical shirts, repeated runs, sudden departures, switches and loop-backs as one single movement, parts of a modulating system which one had to watch as though from outside, or above or somewhere else' (McCarthy, 2008: 3). However, this enframing, which displays its own internal consistency and meaning, needs to be set alongside a parallel reduction of distinct spaces to a singular perspectival plane. The novel's fictional epigraph stresses this, describing how the murals of Bačkovo Ossuary use 'inverted perspective and multiple points of view' to 'represent several moments of a story on a single panel' (McCarthy, 2008: 1). What is presented, therefore, is a constant sliding of frames around, over, and under each other, suggesting that the overlaying grids of history, politics, and art are being brought into a kind of perspectiveless synchronicity. The effect of this palimpsest of encoded spaces is destabilising, for each exists within its own frame of meaning but is subject to change and liable to be misread by others. There is a vertiginous delirium in the freedom of this unlicensed interspace, a temporary lack of belonging within a recognisably familiar context. But this freedom is double-edged for the novel's Soviet cosmonaut, trapped in orbit because the country from which he blasted off no longer exists and no one is prepared to lay claim to him. Adrift and homeless, he is a perfect metaphor for the novel's concern with a lack of fixed determination. He is a significatory outlier, lacking perspective on, and unrelated to, the world and its events, but also elliptically circling it and able to see everything as flat.

This flattening of perspective brings the novel's characters and historical events into a single plane and generates such a confusion of signification that it is difficult for all to distinguish the meaningful from the meaningless, and to understand which signals are important and which are merely noise. This is a subject to which McCarthy was to return in much greater detail in *C*, but, in the narrative of the Secret Police operative we have a crystallisation of his interests in encryption, reinscription, transmission, and reception. The operative's role in the narrative is to be a surreptitious party to all of the aural traffic that surrounds Anton's and Ivan Maňásek's lives, but crucially he is required to listen indiscriminately. His job is to provide a summary of all that takes place, which is then passed on for analysis and more acute, informed hearing. His primary role is thus as a receiver, not as an interpreter, which reduces him in the process to an animate version of the machinery of surveillance that he employs in his work:

> They have a holding signal on the whole conspiracy. This gives them enormous power. [...] I feel it rushing through the air around me – and feel that I, too, am held by it, or rather within it: neither its origin nor destination but one of its relays, its repeaters. I am satisfied with this: satisfied with my place within the overall field of transmission. (McCarthy, 2008: 97)

Always presented as alone, he is nameless, and he becomes increasingly identified with the equipment that he uses – equipment that, in the final analysis, dehumanises him as it renders him deaf and cuts him off both from work and his fellow human beings. He is McCarthy's vision of a human being as a node within the extensive system of informational exchange, but, as the authoritarian smack of Soviet government gives way to the multitudinous interchange of democratic freedoms, the operative is increasingly overwhelmed and disabled by the number of signals that seem to pass through and around him. In the final section of the novel, which is devoted to his narrative of increasingly scattered and indiscriminate observation, he is portrayed as living in a shipyard and sleeping amongst girders and wires. He has become part of the equipment of 'noise' but is unable any longer to identify the world as a place of meaning.

How one distinguishes the signal from the static, the meaningful from the meaningless, the authentic from the simulacrum, and one series of coded deferrals from another depends, in McCarthy's terms, upon the frameworks of interpretation that are open to one. We are surrounded by processes which bombard us with data, much of which we do not understand and cannot relate to the praxis of our lives, but the hermeneutic systems through which we read this coded information allow us to make sense, however partial, of some of that flow. We, therefore, like the characters in *Men in Space*, are the receivers, repeaters, and transmitters of our own codes, parts of a circuit which loops endlessly back on itself. What validates those hermeneutic systems is more problematic, for, as we see, without the authenticating heft of something fixed, each of the characters and artefacts is in a continual process of movement and redrawing. History, politics, national identity, and language do not, it seems, authenticate the individual and do not provide the ground from which one might take off, or transcend. Instead they provide a constantly shifting realm which disrupts any point of belonging. The question with which McCarthy concludes *Men in Space* is whether modernity's scepticism towards the metaphysical has robbed us of the possibility of being more than the material from which we are moulded. Like the stranded cosmonaut or the nameless saint of the icon, are we merely destined to push hopelessly at the extremities of our frames?

*   *   *

What might exist outside the boundaries of the known or operate outwith the logic of rational materiality is one of the chief concerns of the INS. The INS represents not just an interesting and provocative project in its own right but also a productive context in which to understand McCarthy's writing, for it allows him to develop his interest in space, inscription, and death in visual as well as literary forms. The collective, which is heavily influenced in method and self-publicisation by modernist avant-gardes, has functioned through mainstream publication (its founding manifesto was published on the front page of *The Times*), Soviet-style mock purges 'reported' online, and live events. For McCarthy, the fusion of the visual, conceptual, sonic, and literary arts offer opportunities to cross-pollinate ideas beyond the very conservative corporatism of the contemporary publishing scene: 'I still find the art world tends to be the type of place where lots of literary ideas get played out in a much more uncensored way because curators, unlike publishers, are not so concerned about the bottom line' (in Slenske, 2010). Certainly McCarthy's work with the INS enabled him to promote his ideas and artistic vision during the difficult process of finding a publisher for *Remainder*, and his written output has been faithful to the principles outlined in the initial manifesto and reiterated in subsequent 'Declarations'.

The first of these principles is that 'death is a type of space, which we intend to map, enter, colonise and, eventually, inhabit' (INS, 1999: 1). Death, as it is understood by the necronauts, is not only fundamental to the experience of humanness but also underlies all representation, for it is always the frame which art seeks to establish and describe. The unknowability of death, its resistance to the symbolic order, renders it the emptiness that representation strives to map, but without ever fully being able to enter the space that it occupies. Death is not a negative space for McCarthy, but it does articulate abject fears and unsettle the notion of the subject's security within the material world. Its codes are mysterious and its limits undetermined, but it underpins human self-expression and challenges the imagination in a profoundly disturbing way. The Necronautical ambition to colonise and inhabit death is thus grand, but it acknowledges its own provisionality – how can art which stands as an attempt to defer the inexpressibility of the beyond ever escape its own frames of representation to map the unmappable?

As we have seen, *Remainder* and *Men in Space* articulate the failure of art to transcend itself, or rather the failure of the materiality of art to enable its human originator to transcend the unknowability of experience and enter the 'golden triangle' of complete coherence and understanding. The narrator of *Remainder* is engaged in a vain attempt to master his self, to cohere singularly rather than recognise the constant process of unmaking that constitutes subjectivity. His attempts to reconstruct unreliable memories and re-enact the coalescence of the sublime moment of individuation all fail in the face of the materiality of matter. *Men in Space*'s icon represents a similar frustration. Framed by its own self-reflexive codes, it cannot represent more than it is, and the disconnect between its encrypted information and the artists who reproduce it without understanding its secrets emphasises the failure of art to be anything other than a 'repetitive mechanism' (INS, 1999: 1) that functions through theft, forgery, copying, and embedding. Representation may be a means of trying to reconcile the transcendent authentic with the knowledge of its impalpability, but the failing of art is its inability to transcend either death or itself to offer any mystical cohesion. Art is thus reduced to the practice of continuous but fruitless reproduction, effectively creating a cycle of traumatised repetition because it is always an unresolved – and unresolvable – search for formal means to transcend inauthenticity. From the Necronautical perspective, this failure to transcend becomes the motivating imperative for rejecting singularity and embracing the constant splitting of self. The Necronaut's self has no core and no touchstone of identity to which s/he can refer. Instead the Necronautical perspective offers a vision of subjectivity as continuously fracturing and increasingly dehumanised. But this dehumanisation does not necessarily need to be viewed as a diminishment. Instead, as we see in McCarthy's next novel, the rejection of core authenticity can bring about new formations and horizons of becoming which reduce the subject's humanness to a hindrance to the constitution of selfhood.

C (2010)

McCarthy's commitment to the mapping of the formless territory of death and the asymbolic beyondness of the 'outside' is revealed in its fullest expression in his 2010 novel *C*, a work which, through the form of a *Bildungsroman*, addresses the convergence of technology and death in the early twentieth century. *C* incorporates many of the concerns that arise in McCarthy's previous writing and work with the INS, cross-fertilising considerations of the signal–noise dichotomy with the cryptographical, and the technological uncanny with the history of Freudian psychoanalysis. All are circumscribed by the inaccessibility of death, with each of the novel's four sections exploring an aspect of the relationship between the experience of living and that which exists beyond it. As a result, *C* builds to be an ambitious reflection on the human need to decode not only the quality of material existence but also the penumbra of indecipherability that informs and structures it.

The narrative describes the life of Serge Carrefax, born at the dawn of the twentieth century and shaped by its technological, epistemological, and socio-political currents. Based loosely on the early life of Sergei Pankejeff – whose pathological trials form the subject matter of Freud's 'Wolf Man' case history – Serge is associated with the kind of literal electrical surge that propelled the rapid acceleration of technological experimentation and implementation in the early decades of the century. McCarthy positions Serge in locations pertinent to the development of ways of thinking about the subject in a culture of machinic modernity. Serge is never portrayed as the typical protagonist of a *Bildungsroman*, and *C* is a novel interested in the idea of humanist character only in its broadest terms, and certainly not with the 'fully-rounded, self-sufficient character [...] as he travels through a naturalistic world, emoting, developing and so on' (Robson, 2010). Serge is an active protagonist only inasmuch as his presence enables a historically specific experience to be described; the impact on him of that experience is always minimal. Rather, and unlike the modernist forebears to which this novel writes back, McCarthy's objective is never to psychologise Serge. Like the narrator of *Remainder*, or the Secret Police operative of *Men in Space*, he is primarily an outsider; detached and awkward, he coincides with the world around him and is acted upon rather than forging his own path.

From childhood, it is made clear that Serge lacks any ability to perceive perspective – his childhood painting exercises are characterised by their lack of depth – so the world appears to him as a flat, single plane, whose co-ordinates he can plot but which he can only partially understand. As a central character, he is therefore a strangely blank space, written but somehow always under-inscribed. He is identified less with other human beings than with the radio transmitters with which he enthusiastically experiments. Effectively he becomes a physical receiver of signals – in the first section he is always portrayed as listening in on other people's transmissions rather than sending his own – and, like a receiver open to all frequencies, he simply channels the signals with which he comes into contact, intersecting with codes that he does not understand. His is not a portrayal of moral or psychological nuance but rather of the human as a wireless shell primed for technological conduction.

Serge's shaping in this regard begins early. He grows to maturity at a peda-gogically radical school for the deaf and dumb run by his father, whose phys-ically interventionist methods for dealing with muteness render his pupils little more than machines. Convinced by theories of mechanical voice pro-duction, Carrefax senior trains his pupils in the dynamics of sound:

> The human body [...] is a mechanism. When its engine-room, the thorax, a bone-girt vault for heart and lungs whose very floor and walls are constantly in motion – when this chamber exerts pressure sufficient to force open the trap-door set into its ceil-ing and send air rushing outwards through the windpipe, sound ensues. It's as simple as that. (McCarthy, 2010a: 15)

By this logic, Carrefax reduces the human body to a machinic assemblage in which communication becomes merely a facet of applied pressure. There is nothing natural or mystical about the individual's process of communicating; rather, it is the result of violent extraction: 'speech is not a given: it must be wrung from him, wrenched out' (McCarthy, 2010a: 16). Vocalisation as part of a mechanical process points to a neo-Victorian, industrial fetishisation of aligned moving parts; it emerges solely from the empiricism of a manufactory mindset that attends to the malleability of the material world. There is noth-ing in this production line of communication that speaks of spirit or inte-riority, and yet Carrefax is able to programme his charges to memorise and automatically recite passages of hyperbolic poetry. At a comically disorderly pageant (heavily indebted to Virginia Woolf's *Between the Acts* [1941]), children are 'played-back' as if they were embodied recording-machines channelling pre-programmed vocal traffic: 'His words [...] seem to issue not from him but rather to divert through him – as though his mouth, once it formed and held the correct shape for long enough, received a sound spir-ited in from another spot' (McCarthy, 2010a: 19). In effect, the bodies of the children become fleshy radios, transmitting signals without in any way being their originators or editors. Medium and message are entirely separate realms without any hermeneutic bridge; immanence is replaced by storage capacity. This metaphor of the body as receiver–transmitter is an important one for it illustrates McCarthy's determinist model of subjectivity under the spell of technology.[4]

The narrative is filled with the innovations that defined the technological network of the early twentieth century. From the wireless set to Marconi's transatlantic transmissions, the nascent cathode tube to the war plane, *C* prof-fers an inventory of creativity that recalibrates the relationship between the human and the machine and between the known world and the unknown. Sitting late into the night as a young man, Serge explores the possibilities of this new technical episteme by listening to the wireless traffic that navigates the space both around and through him. He is immersed in an invisible flow of distant noises and fragmentary information – even the gurglings of his own digestive system are described as 'odour-messages from distant, unseen bowels' (McCarthy, 2010a: 66). From the static emanating from his wireless set he gradually learns to discern something approximating signal, a recognition that suggests to him the omnipresence of the communicational traffic that floods the telegraphic unconscious – he imagines his home as assailed by a 'vast sea of transmission roaring all around it' (McCarthy, 2010a: 64). He is surrounded and immersed in a global exchange of signal that, step by step, he is able to encode into a system that he can understand and utilise. From the insistent crackle of static, Serge begins a process of selection and rarefaction which initially colours the noise with an emotional tone – 'angry, plaintive, sad' – and subsequently resolves it into Morse code which, when transcribed, becomes 'curling letters' (McCarthy, 2010a: 63). What is thereby mimicked is a hermeneutic processing in which the passage of ethereal 'thought' becomes writing. Machine and human, material and immaterial are brought into congruence and a system of encryption is applied to create semantic cohesion. That orderliness is, however, contingent upon the mode of interpretation employed to decode the noise, and provisional, since it represents only a fraction of the total traffic. How to distinguish signal from noise thus becomes Serge's lifelong motivating driver.

This is, of course, a question that haunts McCarthy's earlier fiction, which repeatedly asks what distinctions between the real/fake, the original/copy, the meaningful/meaningless might actually signify in non-hierarchical networks of semiotic coding. Here he addresses similar questions through the relationships between the organic/inorganic and between life/death. In the opening section of the novel, there are numerous instances where those conditions are confused; where the signal from one becomes confused with that from the other, leading to the kinds of code misreading that punctuated *Men in Space*. On visiting the Carrefax house at Versoie, for instance, Dr Learmont is puzzled to hear what he believes to be a quiet electrical buzzing but which turns out to be originating from bee hives. When Serge happens across a copulating couple, there is a similar fusion of the organic and the inorganic: the sound of sex is described as 'a squeak like the noise of an unopened gate being opened and closed repeatedly' (McCarthy, 2010a: 60), and, seeing only the silhouettes of the lovers, he guesses 'It's some kind of moving thing made of articulated parts' (McCarthy, 2010a: 60). What these hybridisations suggest is the beginning of a conceptual shift towards a technological posthumanism in which the metaphors for human praxis merge the mechanical and corporeal, creating modernity's body–machine subject.

Any essentialist dichotomy between the natural and man-made is troubled by this fusion because it suggests that the natural is always a product of *techne* and vice versa; the two states become manifestations of a singular state of being which is neither wholly organic/inorganic nor alive/dead.

In keeping with INS philosophy, *C* is a novel about death that is paradoxically crammed with life. The central motif of the wireless signal that features in each section of the novel evokes an omnipresent, immersive, and global vibrancy that is counterpointed by a sobering morbidity. Surfing his radio dial, Serge becomes conscious of spectral bodies 'hovering just beyond the threshold of the visible, and corresponding signals not quite separable from the noise around them – important ones, their recalcitrance all the more frustrating for that reason' (McCarthy, 2010a: 68). He ponders the boundary that separates death from life when he sees his sister Sophie animating a dead cat's leg with electricity, wondering whether 'the morbid and hypnotic sequences being executed by the dead cat's limb contain some kind of information – "contain" in the sense of enclosing, locking in, repeating in a code for which no key's available, at least not to him' (McCarthy, 2010a: 62). And he experiences it again when he listens to the unsettling recorded vocal drills of the school's alumni on a gramophone:

> The voices [...] manifest varying degrees of distortedness and atonality; the letters warp and morph as they progress. They gather certain rhythms, patterns of repetition or half-repetition, then just when it seems that there's a logic to their sequences, break and relinquish them again. (McCarthy, 2010a: 43)

As in *Remainder* and *Men in Space*, language slips away from the orderliness of sense; there is always a teetering on the brink of nonsense, a rising of cohesion only to collapse. For Serge, looking into the horn of the machine, the noises that emanate from it suggest the claustrophobia of interment: 'entrances to caves and wells, of worm- and foxholes, rabbits' burrows, and all things that lead into the earth' (McCarthy, 2010a: 44). In operation is an explicit linkage of words/sounds/noise with something primal, unconscious, and subterranean and, as becomes increasingly insistent as the novel progresses, with the death of Serge's sister.

Though Sophie's presence in the novel is relatively brief – her death is revealed on page seventy-five – her absence haunts the text as an unresolved puzzle. Intellectually, she is allied to her father's materialist practice, understanding the world through processes of empirical taxonomy and scientific discipline, and, as such, completely contrasts with Serge's belief in the world as a melée of primitive and unstructured impulses emerging from the complex criss-crossings of conscious and unconscious signals. The deterioration

of her mental health as she becomes increasingly obsessed with her biological experiments and her early death through accidental self-poisoning
do little to suggest the impact that she will have on Serge's life. Hers is a
signal that resonates long after her disappearance from the text, and the mystery of her demise proves stubbornly resistant to the kinds of reading that
Serge is capable of applying. Through psychoanalytical decoding, the reader
is invited to explore one possible avenue for Serge's libidinal remainder, for
the text implies nascent incestuous desires between the siblings. When they
are children, Sophie playfully taps out a Morse-coded message on her brother's penis (McCarthy, 2010a: 22) and, at her interment, Serge experiences
an erection that in part gestures back to this precursive sexual encounter
but also seems to be generated by the gentle hum of electricity emanating
from the machinery used to transport her coffin to the family mausoleum –
a combination that would seem to link an unconscious incestuous desire for
Sophie with a post-mortem technophilia. He is also distracted during the
funeral service by the movements of a beetle in the grass, which anagram-
matically suggests an elision of 'insect' and 'incest' (McCarthy, 2010a: 80).

Whatever its origin, the dispersal of Sophie's 'signal' impacts the novel as a
site of traumatic dislocation destined to be repeated as both a corporeal and
a technological imperative. Such proves to be the case in the section where
Serge travels to the German spa resort of Klodĕbrady to take the cure for his
chronic constipation – caused, in part at least, by the uncathected trauma of
Sophie's demise. Her death and the melancholy it has released in him combine as Serge identifies the darkness in himself with the archaic and historical darkness of the world around him; the water of the spa 'bubbled up from
earth so black that no blessing could ever lighten it [...] filtered through the
charcoaled wrecks of boats and tumour-ridden bones of murdered ancestors, through stool-archives and other sedimented layers of morbid matter' (McCarthy, 2010a: 106). This inner tumult, repeatedly described by its
sufferer in metaphors of darkness, morbidity, and decay, is, so his clinician
advises him, the product of self-intoxication; he has become accustomed and
addicted to the poisoning that his organs inflict upon themselves. Consistent
with the self-feeding information loop that he believes to be immanent in
the material world, Serge's metabolic dysfunction is envisioned as another
kind of contained circuit, feeding back on itself to maintain a continuity of
(self-destructive) information. His doctor describes passage in one direction
as a natural 'process' and 'rhythm' (McCarthy, 2010a: 104), but for Serge
there is only 'repetition' (McCarthy, 2010a: 105). The signal, whether technological or corporeal, is thus firmly associated with death.

Information as enclosed and encoded within the dead or inanimate object,
and information as a metaphor for death, become, in the 'Chute' section of

the novel, information as literal death. Following Serge during his experiences as an RAF artillery target-setter in the First World War, this section displays a relationship between the human and the machine inspired by the Futurist celebration of the dynamic and violent potential of the man-made to remake the world. In the opening paragraphs of the section we see Serge considering the machine network's destructive capability but regarding it with an exhilaration emerging from the mad logic of self-annihilation. 'The sheer insistence of machinery breaking its bonds as it comes into its own' (McCarthy, 2010a: 119) speaks of a violence of the machine through a glorious and liberating parturition. This celebration of the machine in the context of the war's industrialisation of violence obviously lends a dramatic irony to the notion of technological progress, but, for the airborne Serge, the fusion of man and machine represents an overwhelming consonance with the unconstrained dimension of the signal. Whereas on the ground Serge is bound by the physical geometry of the material, in the air, the curves, banks, and rotations that he is able to perform render the landscape flat and perspective irrelevant. It is the perfect consummation of Serge's blankness as an observer and as a character. The dynamics of flight through uncluttered space position the pilot as controller of all that surrounds him; it is the movements of the machine in tune with his movements that determine his relationship with the world and make the purely physical world subordinate to that of the pilot–machine hybrid: 'as though no independent movement were permitted of the landscape anymore: all displacement and acceleration, all shifts and realignments *must* process from the machine' (McCarthy, 2010a: 124).

From the plane the world below presents itself as a complex of information that needs to be read and interpreted – the pilots are referred to as 'grand interpreters' (McCarthy, 2010a: 133). Villages and hamlets pop up 'to punctuate the strip like news reports or stock-price fluctuations' (McCarthy, 2010a: 138), and, as the plane soars upwards, 'the landscapes shakes beneath them and becomes illegible' (McCarthy, 2010a: 138). The glorious wonder of the machine is that is provides an aspect on the material world that is completely different from the labyrinthine gardens and buildings that so confuse Serge at Versoie. Everything here is about relative geometry, and the legibility that comes from that intersection of dimensional planes thrills him into an ecstasy of momentary comprehension:

> Serge feels an almost scared tingling, as though he himself had become godlike, elevated by machinery and signal code to a higher post within the overall structure of things, a vantage point from which the vectors and control lines linking earth and heaven, the hermetic language of the invocations, its very lettering and script, have become visible, tangible even, all concentrated at a spot just underneath the index finger of his right hand which is tapping out, right now, the sequence *C3E MX12 G*. (McCarthy, 2010a: 141)

The orgasmic exhilaration that Serge experiences whilst airborne is closely tied to the indisputable precision of his readings; that which was imprecise and impossible to parse on the ground becomes accurate and meaningful in the air. The relative perspectiveless panorama gives up its encryption key with a satisfying readiness, but, given McCarthy's warning in *Tintin and the Secret of Literature* that codes are merely displacements of other codes that revolve around some form of secretive quintessence without unlocking its meaning, Serge's transport of delight should not be mistaken for an unlocking of the 'golden triangle' that will resolve his affective inhibition. Rather, the decoding of one level of crypto-pathological complexity moves him only one further step towards grasping the 'secret' that underlies his neuroticism, a secret that increasingly reveals itself as a need to fully inhabit the asymbolia of death.

C's unification of man and machine is never a fearful resistance to hybridity but rather a celebration of the anti-humanism that can be brought about by technology. The human as machine contains the potential to transcend death through the logic of a self-perpetuating mechanism that can endlessly reproduce the same action or effect without any entropic loss of energy. Though traumatic repetition may be an instance of the death drive, it gives expression and form to the possibility of a circularity of death without chaos and non-being, an outcome entirely in sympathy with the aspirations of the INS. This transcendence of death through the channelling of human energy into a perpetually self-feeding circuit is a utopian aspiration, but, as a delirious Serge lies dying of an infected wound in his cabin on a Nile riverboat, the narrative draws towards such a conclusion. Fevered, hallucinating, and incapable of clear articulation, Serge envisions himself in an Kafka-esque projection of his techno-necrophilial desire:

> His gangly, mutinous limbs have grown into long feelers that jab and scrape at the air. What's more, the air presents back to these feelers surfaces with which contact is to be made, ones that *solicit* contact: plates, sockets, holes. As parts of him alight on and plug into these, space itself starts to jolt and crackle into action, and Serge finds himself connected to everywhere, to all imaginable places. (McCarthy, 2010a: 300)

He has become a 'giant, tentacular wireless set' (McCarthy, 2010a: 301), a grotesque fusion of organic and inorganic. As he slips closer to death, he becomes increasingly identified with the noise and signals of the transmitter 'making a repeated clicking sound, a set of quick fire *c-c-c-c's*' (McCarthy, 2010a: 310). At this stage Serge has become the signal, but, as the novel has established, signals are ubiquitous and timeless and the static into which he sinks 'contains all messages ever sent, and all words ever spoken' (McCarthy, 2010: 308). Death becomes not a culmination but an extenuation, a reaching out into the void of the unknowable space of the outside in a positive and liberating renunciation of the materiality of matter. Within it, through it, and around it, Serge dwells as a corporeal, electro-mechanical intensity, discarding the body as a site of belonging and embracing the formless ahistorical pulse of the necronaut.

Satin Island (2015)

To date, all McCarthy's novels have featured acts of falling as an imagistic trope and a figurative device to indicate the collapse of *logos* in the face of death. The narrator's accident in *Remainder* is brought about by an unfortunate coincidence with a falling object; Maňásek is defenestrated in suspicious circumstances in *Men in Space*; and, in *C*, Serge's comrade forgets to strap himself into his plane and falls to his death, inscribing a 'Bewsick-shaped mark' in the grass (McCarthy, 2010a: 129). In *Satin Island* the fall re-emerges in the stories of the elongated plummet towards death experienced by several parachutists whose canopies have failed to deploy. These stories are collated and filed by U, the novel's obsessive narrator, with a growing conviction that the spate of similar deaths across the globe cannot be unrelated. Whether they occurred by accident or through the nefarious interference of a third party, the incidents represent for U a contemporary meme whose reiterations must point towards a bigger, broader, deeper, and incontrovertible fact about the present. Of course, they do, but it is not the fact that U desires. For, whilst he is building evidence to suggest that the phenomenon reveals an obscure pattern in human affairs, McCarthy is drawing the reader back to the necronautical fall into the exteriority of death and meaninglessness. Falling is consciousness of the outside in his fiction – the outside of agency, the outside of symbolisation, and the outside of authenticity; it corresponds to the remainder outside meaning, that which is cut free from the determined positions before and after the fall. Falling is, moreover, a process in which the certainties of departing and arriving are suspended and in which the omnipresent latency of death is revealed for contemplation. Falling is, above all, the precursor to a crash.

U's quest for a schema into which these deaths will neatly fit is foiled not necessarily because there is no structure of kinship between them but because he is too neatly enfolded within a worldview that regards patterns and networks as fundamental to human praxis to acknowledge the possibility that no connection exists between the accidents. As an anthropologist, U is trained to determine the cultural geometry of his field, isolating and adumbrating the rituals of social behaviour to provide a meta-analysis of the human condition. He constantly sees around him the matrices of connection, as in the novel's opening pages, where, stranded at Torino-Caselle airport, he observes the behaviours of his fellow passengers for signs of unconscious contiguity. He does not see the bored energy of two young boys running around the concourse, but instead sees the ellipse that their route describes and the point at which one of them repeatedly falls over. He does not regard the television screens variously showing a football match and the aftermath of a truck bombing in the Middle East as distinct, but rolls them together so that the Bayern Munich striker and the bloodied survivor are running towards the camera in a congruence of ecstatic triumph and tragedy. U extrapolates from the specific to the universal, seeking an untimely non-attachment that will enable him to determine shapes and vectors rather than bodies and emotions.[5] Yet that professional adherence to method also makes him curiously insensitive to the affective realm. Video-phoning his girlfriend, Madison, he continues to spool through page after page of Web data, granting her only a modicum of attention before her face is abruptly frozen in pixelated buffering with the prescient words 'I'm lacking...' (McCarthy, 2015: 9).

U is a typical McCarthy character in that he is barely a character at all. He is granted little psychological depth, is largely devoid of empathy, maintains a passive detachment from the empirical world, and finishes the novel as unresolved to action as he begins it. For McCarthy he squints 'at the world through an ever-more-pixelated veil', a representative of the age of digital consumerism (in Keane, 2015). Mention of the veil recalls the caul which envelops and insulates Serge Carrefax at birth, and U is very much a relation of Carrefax and the narrator of *Remainder* – otherworldy, obsessive, and a vehicle for data rather than human sentiment. He is also the distillation of McCarthy's reading. His self-introduction – 'Call me U' (McCarthy, 2015: 12) – suggests the presence of Herman Melville's Ishmael (*Moby Dick* [1851]) in his genealogy, alongside Franz Kafka's K (*The Castle* [1926]) and Thomas Pynchon's V (*V* [1963]). McCarthy has acknowledged the influence of Ulrich from Robert Musil's *The Man Without Qualities* (1930–1943), a man lacking psychological content but happy to be 'shaped by the outward circumstances of life', and, although U suffers more viscerally from an 'awkward sense of things being out of sync, out of whack' (McCarthy, 2015: 6), he similarly drifts in the flow of external events (Sturgeon, 2015). More obviously, U is a direct address to the reader, enfolding her/him within the ethnographic purview of the narrative whilst simultaneously maintaining a distance that allows U to disavow any responsibility as a narrator; on the subject of plot he makes his position clear: '*events!* If you want those, you'd better stop reading now' (McCarthy, 2015: 13). This is a novel in which the reader has a stake, he suggests, but can expect few of the comforting conventionalities of its formal tradition.

U is a corporate anthropologist whose skills in determining patterns of social behaviour are invested in the pursuit of profit and the generation of the disambiguated narratives of aspiration that it takes to sell jeans or breakfast cereal. Weaned on Foucault, Deleuze, and Badiou, he is the product of his discipline's increasing intellectual abstraction, which he puts to work in the interests of consumerism, folding the radicalism of the European theoretical left into a corporate machine that 'could swallow everything, incorporate it seamlessly, like a giant loom that re-weaves all fabric, no matter how recalcitrant and jarring its raw form, into what my hero would have called a master-pattern' (McCarthy, 2015: 31). The hero to whom U refers here is the anthropologist Claude Lévi-Strauss, whose pioneering fieldwork U hopes to emulate. However, ensconced within the corporate framework, his subjects of study are determined only by the profit potential of a creeping market-driven globalisation. His affection for Lévi-Strauss reflects a professional traditionalism, and, despite the conceptual intellection of his day job, he has a strain of nostalgia for the solidity of material culture – his cluttered desk has the leather surface and blotter of a Victorian administrator, and he craves the distinct terrains of 'field' and 'home' that governed classical anthropological study. His reputation – such as it is – has, however, been made by an unconventional monograph on clubbing culture in which he thoroughly elided the space between subject and observer, furiously partaking of the club scene that he was meant to be studying. It is this elision of inner and outer that has brought U to the attention of the Company and of his new paymaster, appropriately named Peyman.

Peyman is an ambiguous figure for U. Frequently out of reach on high-level trans-national business, and gnomic in his communication when present, he is known to U more for his sloganeering in industry periodicals than directive management. He talks in aphoristic bursts – 'any strategy of cultural production [... must] liberate things – objects, situations, systems – into uselessness' (McCarthy, 2015: 44) – things that dazzle their audience with implied profundity without ever being substantiated or challenged. Peyman sits somewhere between the slickest of management gurus and a fast-talking huckster selling the flimsiest of promises, but his crowning talent is to make others feel 'connected' by the mere fact of knowing him. Connected to what is rarely specified, but, for U and the Company's clients, Peyman represents an unquestioned link to something valuable:

> he connected us, both individually and severally, our scattered half-formed notions
> and intuitions, fields of research which would otherwise have lain fallow, found no

bite and purchase on the present moment – he connected all of these to a world of action and event, a world in which stuff might actually *happen*; connected us, that is, to our own age. (McCarthy, 2015: 41)

What Peyman embodies is the supremacy of the network as the means for channelling the inchoate forces of contemporary epistemology; finance, ideas, politics, and aspiration funnel through him and across a global superstructure, forging all within an architecture of connectivity made possible by the mental reshaping produced by Internet technologies. For McCarthy, it is this shift to a networked mindscape that represents the significant shift away from the material residues of modernity and towards a conceptualism he associates with the nebulous shape of the contemporary. Information is now ethereal – in the Company's offices ideas are written on glass – and problems are no longer material obstacles but failures of systemic knowledge – U's friend Petr, dying of thyroid cancer, is no longer a victim of cellular malignancy but of network breakdown: 'If we had a better database', he regrets, 'then I'd be out of danger' (McCarthy, 2015: 52).

Within this invisible matrix of money, information, and supra-national influence, U's anthropological training appears quaintly but ineffectually empirical. Reading the world around him for patterns becomes optimistically random for he has no logical start or end points, only evidence of inbetweenness. In the novel's opening sections at the airport, he learns that Torino-Caselle is a hub airport predominantly used for transfer rather than as a destination in itself: 'The webpage showed a diagram of a rimless wheel, with spokes of different lengths all leading to the centre, such that communion between any two spots on the wheel's surface area was possible despite no direct line connecting these' (McCarthy, 2015: 4–5). This rimless wheel is a useful metaphor for U's dilemma, for, though connection between all the different points of interest that engage him – dead parachutists, oil spills, consumer waste, rollerblades – is technically possible, there is no evident master pattern by which all can be united within a common symbolic system. The tantalising possibility of connection is what fascinates U, but the realisation of a schema is frustratingly elusive; breakthroughs such as his hypothesis that the parachutists' equipment has been sabotaged are quickly disproved, leaving him in a welter of confusion, faced only with the unfulfilled promise of connection and files filled with evidence of betweenness rather than destinations. Tangentially U comes to regard intermediacy as itself a profitable path for investigation; the free-falling parachutists are caught as much between life and death as between plane and ground, their parachutes, whether deployed or undeployed, relevant only to the moments between jumping and landing. 'Was I lying' about the seriousness of his reflections, he ponders; 'I didn't even know' (McCarthy, 2015: 81).

This indeterminacy is perfectly encapsulated in the Koob-Sassen project, onto which U is co-opted and for which he receives laudatory notices.[6] This project is characterised by a complete lack of definition, and, although it seems to be a key focus for the Company and many of its clients, is beyond the description of any of them. U knows little about it save its importance and secrecy, but is too wary of revealing his own ignorance to ascertain exactly what is required of him in its implementation. He is therefore surprised to be congratulated and fêted for his instrumental role. Clearly, McCarthy's point is satirical, a laying bare of the emperor's new clothes of consultancy project management in which the greatest acclamation is made for the most nebulous of actual achievements and in which each alienated party believes that someone else has oversight. However, the more specific point about Koob-Sassen is that it reflects the decentring imperative of network culture that renders U's distinction between field and home redundant, for there are no longer inside/outside, beginning/completion dichotomies that can locate the project or its outcomes in place, time, or individuals. Everyone is simultaneously involved in the project and divorced from it; it is everywhere and nowhere; it has a distinctly contemporary relevance and a timeless use-lessness; it has meaning and is a semiotic black hole. In order to conceptual-ise it, U can only invoke this contradictoriness:

> this black box in which Koob-Sassen had become embodied seemed to be lying on the shelf of some administrative building. More accurate, perhaps, to describe it as resting on a *plane*, rather than plain: one geometric shape that sat atop another. As to its size: this, too, was far from clear. It was hard, in these visions, to maintain a sense of scale. Sometimes it seemed enormous, like an emperor's mausoleum; at others it appeared no larger than a trunk, or coffin; at others still, the size of a child's toy – or music-box. The only constant or unchanging aspect of it was that it was black: black and inscrutable, opaque. (McCarthy, 2015: 75–76)

U's confusion with Koob-Sassen and with the network's lack of mate-rial referentiality in general is, for McCarthy, a symptom of modernity's asynchronous temporality manifest in a continuous jetlag as his con-sciousness of experiencing the world drops behind his actual experienc-ing of phenomena. This sense of not being co-terminous with one's own reality, of being both physically and mentally out of joint, is U's constant condition. He is always at a loss as his comprehension is outstripped by the mass of things he suspects are significant but which he cannot fully connect. Whether it involves the mystery of why Madison has been to Torino-Caselle airport, the disorientation caused by overlapping text messages arriving out of logical sequence, or the myriad suggestive coincidental occurrences that he tries to parse, the effect is an uncanny dislocation, a buffer preventing full concurrence with a consciousness of the now. And buffering as an effect of digital transfer is the metaphor he employs to explain this hermeneutic disruption. He likens the sensation to the space between downloaded information and watchable content on a streamed video: 'that bar that slowly fills itself in – twice: once in bold red and, at the same time, running ahead of that, in fainter grey; the fainter section, of course, has to remain in advance of the bold section' (McCarthy, 2015: 68). 'If the cursor and the red section catch up', he knows, 'then buffering sets in again' (McCarthy, 2015: 68), an acknowledgement that experience is always about separation and delay, 'the hiatus created by the passage of a command down a chain' (McCarthy, 2015: 56), rather than co-temporality.

At the heart of U's temporal lag is his desire to be fully present in the now, something that McCarthy sees as a feature of his writing: 'all of my books are about this kind of quest for the now, to close down the buffer zone of consciousness and self-awareness and irony or language or whatever. Just to close that down and occupy "the now" – which is an impossible or unrealizable fantasy' (in Sturgeon, 2015). Consciousness of experience is, by this token, always ironic for it can only ever articulate the phenomenal affect through retrospection and construction. U's frustration at the buffer is a correlative of the narrator of *Remainder*'s need to open the fridge door or walk down the street authentically, by which he means in spatio-temporal harmony with his imaginary self. The distance between actuality and intentionality cannot be unironic because the lag always creates an inarticulable otherness that U's friend Petr ruefully recognises can only be unsatisfactorily resolved in the space-time of death:

> I'm about to undergo the mother, the big motherfucker, of all episodes – and I won't be able to dine out on it! Even if there turns out to be a Heaven [...] I won't be able to, since everyone else there will have lived through the same episode, i.e. dying, and they'll all go: *So what? That's boring. We know all that shit.* (McCarthy, 2015: 128)

Death brings into consonance the imaginary and the symbolic but cannot be narrated, thus eliminating the space of irony – though only in a cruelly ironic way. U's project, and McCarthy's beyond it, is to shape within the material realm an answer to the problem of buffering, forging a consciousness of the present that can unite the experience with its story, but for that purpose language proves hopelessly inadequate.

In contrast to the vagaries of the Koob-Sassen project, Peyman's direction that U should produce the Great Report is comparatively specific; it is to be

'The First and Last Word on our age' (McCarthy, 2015: 56). Conceived of as anthropology in real time, the Report will break 'cover like some colourful, fantastic beast, a species never seen before, a brand-new genus, flashing, sparkling – *fulgurating* – high above the tree-line, there for all to see' (McCarthy, 2015: 57–58). U is to do no less than spear the nature of contemporary existence, the multifarious indeterminacies of the network age, and present them in a report. Effectively he must close the space between the participant and the observer, eliminating the untimely distance of the social scientist in order to bring consciousness and experience into the same frame. His initial aleatoric methodology – eclectically mining the Internet and his own curiosity for material – moves him no further towards the report that Peyman expects, though he does at points consider handing his boss the files of undigested data, an empty folder, or even the blotter from his desk on which he has written the words 'Satin Island' – the eponym that refers to his dream of an island constructed out of waste.

In his more fantastical moments, he conceives of a resistance movement of 'U-thnographers' who would practise a form of guerrilla 'Present-Tense Anthropology™' in the vein of the Situationist happening, political terrorism, or, indeed, the INS. But at each turn he encounters the problem of 'finding a shape' – the phrase with which he rebuffs any enquiries about his progress – eventually slumping to the conclusion that 'this Great Report was unplottable, unframeable, unrealizable: in short, and in whatever cross-bred form, whatever medium or media, *unwritable*. Not just by me, with my limited (if once celebrated) capabilities, but fundamentally, essentially, inherently unwritable' (McCarthy, 2015: 117). What U highlights here is that the problem is less emphatically one of shape than of language – how can the present be *written*? If, for the anthropologist as much as for the novelist, writing requires the distance of untimely reflection, and requires the imposition of a speculative framework of meaning, then present-tense anthropology and the contemporary novel are oxymorons. Writing can never be self-present; it is always, to use U's analogy, the red cursor following the grey buffering line, but never sufficiently swift to achieve synchronicity with the experience itself. McCarthy has clearly stated this in interview: 'Nothing is less contemporary than contemporary art or fiction. Than art that has something to say about the now. I think the whole point of the now is that it's precisely what we can't articulate' (in Sturgeon, 2015). By this token, U's Great Report and McCarthy's *Satin Island* are systemic failures, doomed attempts to create the 'book-beyond-the-book' (McCarthy, 2015: 117) that would resolve the paradox of art about the contemporary.

Both of them might be described as knowing failures, however, for, whilst McCarthy teases his reader with an anti-novel about the impossibility of

writing the novel of the now, he nevertheless produces a work that is resolutely topical in its contemplation of whether writing as the expression of
a social reality has reached an end-game in the network age. Similarly, in a
novel that lacks conclusion, U nevertheless finds a resting point between
meanings, caught in the flow between the transitory and the terminal.
In the queue for the Staten Island Ferry, he experiences a mini-crisis of
agency for he is unable to decide whether taking the ferry will bring him
the kind of resolution he craves, and, 'suspended between two types of
meaninglessness' (McCarthy, 2015: 170), he settles for indeterminacy.
This is not necessarily a moment of self-realisation, nor, as Ben Eastham
has inferred, a desire for a sentimental connection with the human world
around him, but a cognisance of a restless intermediacy as the perpetual
position of humanity in the contemporary information–capital–culture
matrix (Eastham, 2015). McCarthy imagines this as a form of triangular
correspondence, the points representing anthropology, capitalism, and literature, and, to mark the novel's publication, he hosted a discussion on the
triangle at the Institute of Contemporary Arts.[7] Like the closed circuits of
C, or the infinity symbol of *Remainder*, the triangle is a hermetic system,
continuously feeding a signal around the network loop with no prospect
of escape or completion. As U stands amongst the crowd waiting for the
ferry to arrive he is at one peak – literally, for the terminal funnels passengers towards the prow of the boat – but to board would only be to
begin a journey to another point of departure, one equally articulated to
the others. Instead he turns back towards the city – the other triangular
limb – dimly conscious of a failure of action but painfully aware of his lack
of alternative.

U's flaw – if such a narratological conceit is apposite for such an under-
determined character – is his faith that there is an outside to the network
that he can inhabit with sufficient detachment, but McCarthy condemns
this as a 'naïve conceptual position' (in Kachka, 2015). It is one born of
a theological mindset that even in the absence of God seeks patterns and
master-meanings in chaos, and, like Nietzsche, to whom there are a number
of references in the text, collapses in the face of the abjection that it openly
courts. Like Nietzsche, U falls, but as an intellectual parachutist who, believing that his canopy of research methods is infallible, has to face the possibility that his supports have been irrecuperably severed. His fall is into a
knowledge of meaninglessness, but it is only marginally less catastrophic
than the plunges of the parachutists, for its destination is equally terminal.
As he pushes back out of the New York crowd, he has come to recognise that
the only thing outside the triangle of silk and cables that have enclosed, sup-
ported, and inhibited him is death.

Coda

Thanks in part to Zadie Smith's public boost for his work, McCarthy is beginning to attract serious critical attention in the academic community, and, whilst his formal and stylistic experimentalism represents a challenge to popular taste, the fact that *C* was shortlisted for the Man Booker Prize in 2010 suggests that a broader audience may await.[8] In truth, *C* was always an outlier on the shortlist, and it lost out to Howard Jacobson's *The Finkler Question* (2010), displaying, as is evident from the winners in the surrounding years – Hilary Mantel's *Wolf* Hall (2009) and Julian Barnes' *The Sense of an Ending* (2011) – the conservative, humanist tendency of the prize's awarding committees. McCarthy's comment that his work must have been mistaken for a historical novel is arch but probably accurate. British fiction in the twenty-first century has been dominated by a historicising brand of realism circulating around ideas of loss, memory, and recuperation, and, though McCarthy's writing addresses these issues too, his narratives dispense with the frameworks of character, plot, and historical development that underpin much of his contemporaries' work. Instead, McCarthy's fiction is built on the unravelling of a philosophical anti-humanism that does not require the full architecture of realism to describe the emptied-out subject that is the product of the modern episteme. As Pieter Vermeulen argues, the history of the novel and the history of the modern subject are so inextricably entwined that the challenge to the subject in the post-deconstructive, post-postmodern moment is also a direct challenge to the value of the novel as an expressive medium (Vermeulen, 2015). McCarthy's response is to rethink the novel into a form of pathological intensity that addresses the contemporary condition as a dimensionless matrix of intersecting lines of technological and philosophical flight from singularity into the unchartable space of the real. If there is a subject piloting this flight, s/he is not seeking individuation in the manner of the realist protagonist but the kind of dispersed, boundary-less immersion of the necronaut. This might not recommend McCarthy to a wide readership beyond the literati, but it makes him one of the most interesting of Britain's practising writers.

Notes

1 Originally published as 'Two Paths for the Novel' in the *New York Review of Books* (Z. Smith, 2008), the essay was included as 'Two Directions for the Novel' in *Changing My Mind: Occasional Essays* (Z. Smith, 2009). The quotation about *Remainder* comes from the latter edition and appears on page 93.

2 McCarthy has praised Smith's essay as setting up a 'framework for thinking, and ultimately for disagreeing', asserting that 'this dichotomy of realistic stuff and avant-garde stuff simply doesn't hold' (in Kachka, 2015).

3 The niggling disagreement between Smith and Wood goes back to his critical review of her debut novel *White Teeth* (2000), in which he coined the term 'hysterical realism'. In this instance 'Wood responded to Smith with a modest shrug, remarking that perhaps *Netherland* is a little more radical than Smith suspects, *Remainder* a little more conservative' (Lewis-Kraus, 2015).

4 I have discussed this in greater depth in Lea, 2012b.

5 I use 'untimely' here in the anthropological sense of marking 'a critical distance from the present that seeks to establish a relationship to the present different from reigning opinion' (Rabinow *et al.*, 2008: 59).

6 Hilary Koob-Sassen, to whom this is most likely a reference, is a visual artist who works across a number of media including music, sculpture, and film. McCarthy worked with Koob-Sassen on a trans-media project at the Institute of Contemporary Arts in January 2015 (Institute of Contemporary Arts, 2015). See also Haglund, 2015.

7 Between 23 and 29 March 2015. See Institute of Contemporary Arts (2015). McCarthy also curated an exhibition at the Institute of Contemporary Arts recreating in concrete form the associative jumble of U's basement office at the Company (see Fig2, 2015).

8 If sales data are indicative of readership, the size of that audience may not be enormous: prior to the announcement of the 2010 prize winner, *C* had sold 2649 copies, the second fewest of the shortlist of six, and well behind the frontrunner Emma Donoghue's *Room* (2010), which had sold 33,923 (Stoddard, 2010).

4

Sarah Hall

Sarah Hall is a dirty writer but a good dirty writer. She writes about the messy urgencies of sex as the bodily culmination of needful affects in search of meaningful articulation. Her lovers are rarely other than manifestations of instinct, tearing into the being of another and consuming whole the body and brain as a buttress to their contradictory identities. There is nothing romantic and nothing romanticised; only uncivilised spirit. But Hall is also a good dirty writer because she captures the filth-under-the-fingernails nastiness of life. She is a writer of shit, piss, phlegm, semen, rot, mud, and death, who sees in the depths of the human body and the wildness of nature an obscene denominator which underpins all relationships, animate and inanimate. Her fiction is full of bitter quarrels between body and world where only the brutal indifference of the latter can be victorious. Frequently, Hall's dirtinesses intersect, either through sexual struggling in the forests and fells of Cumbria or in refined metropolitan surroundings where sex must be painful, hasty, or illicit to remind its participants of the sharpness of its spurs. The female clients of Eliot Riley who urge him to fuck them on the floor of his insalubrious tattoo parlour in *The Electric Michelangelo* (2004) are, like the desperate infidelities of the semi-incestuous Susan in *How to Paint a Dead Man* (2009), expressions of a libidinal drive rooted in every tenebrous fantasy of the human animal.

Hall would seem to write about exceptions; caricatures or grotesques drawn from the social and fictional margins placed in contexts of huge change, where the heightened emotional drama accentuates their exceptionality. Certainly many of her works rely structurally on the outsider encountering forms of closed community – a close-knit Lake District hamlet; Coney Island during its heyday; a radical feminist intentional community – and recognising both their difference from and kinship with the social fabrics they have ruffled. Yet, for all her interest in the potential of alienation,

Hall consistently writes about commonalities between her characters, all of whom are shaped from the same, continuous chaos of existence and struggle to order the world into a manageable state. The exceptionalities in character and setting that mark her world-creation are the points at which the skin between order and chaos is thinnest and most compromised. Whether it's the precariously maintained peace between the women in *The Carhullan Army* (2007), the stubbornly uncooperative landscape of the Cumbrian hills in *Haweswater* (2001), or the mutability of romantic love in *The Beautiful Indifference* (2011), security is clawed from uncertainty only with difficulty, and guaranteed only temporarily. The patina of respectability that attends life at its best in Hall's writing is never more than paper thin, and what lurks beneath is too readily imaginable to be comfortable.

Discomfort is a common theme and quality of Hall's fiction, but very rarely of her writing style, which is richly, organically rotund. She began her creative life as a poet, and it is not difficult to see the legacy of the lyric in her novels. Most manifestly this can be discerned in a style which is highly metaphorical, but there is also an attention to the density of language as a function of place which is striking. Each of her fictions to date has been located (at least in part) in Hall's native Cumbria, and she punctuates, and often punctures, passages of vivid description with dialect terms such as 'cruttered', 'spean', 'spelk', 'smooring', 'sool', and 'winnety', fixing onomatopoeically the relation between her characters' understanding of the world and the *parole* from which it emerges. Place gives forth language for Hall, and her vocabulary is firmly rooted in the quiddity of turf, water, and Cumbrian rock, emerging from it as smooth or jagged as if found. This placedness has become increasingly insistent in her mature work, which favours stylistic rawness over the effortful writerliness of *Haweswater* and *The Electric Michelangelo*. Recent fictions have been more tightly constructed, displaying skilful concision without the loss of such characteristically apposite metaphors as a baby's hands described as 'bumpy and curled like cabbage leaves' (Hall, 2010: 125) or a man's face 'like a daub of glass taken out of a furnace' (Hall, 2007a: 11).

Haweswater (2002)

Hall's first novel was written when she was living and working in the United States, and, in its soggy depiction of a Cumbrian landscape that is as much water as rock, there is a nostalgic longing for home and the predictability of an unpredictable climate. Water is the dominant motif of the novel – from the breaking of Ella Lightburn's waters in the opening scenes, through the ice that her son Isaac breaks to gaze on the underwater universe, to the snow drifts that envelop and suffocate unwary sheep, water in all its forms is the keynote. The novel's drama stems from the construction during the 1930s of the Haweswater dam to provide a reliable water supply for Manchester, which necessitated the flooding of the Mardale valley in the Lake District. The depopulation and destruction of the villages of the dale concentrates the human consequences of historical change into a narrative of dislocation and moral juxtaposition. Civic priorities sit uncomfortably together on national and local levels, just as industry rends the traditional relations of the valley with the noises of an unfamiliar – and unwelcome – modernity. Hall's novel is defiantly anti-pastoral; the landscape is never romanticised and its harshness never undersold. Those who earn their living from the unforgiving land do so by tearing out the means of bare subsistence, and the novel's descriptive passages are fulsomely muddy, bloody, and gutsy in their evocation of hill farming in the 1930s.

Structurally, *Haweswater* is a three-act tragedy which tells its story through a series of well-wrought parallelisms: city and country; art and industry; sex and violence; surface and depth; tradition and modernity; the authentic and the manufactured. The novel's plotting is slightly cumbersome and the balance between the characters not entirely harmonious, but what is striking about the novel is Hall's confidence with description, and her ability to evoke a landscape she knows well with compassionate clarity. Her talent for strikingly precise metaphor is here in abundance, such as in her description of someone's laugh as 'moderate, inclusive [...] like apples rolling down a gentle bank towards a harvester's basket' (Hall, 2003: 53). Life on the hills may not hold much mercy, but Hall conjures a rough beauty from it and, though she is occasionally undone by her own descriptive effulgence – as in her imagining the sky as 'a deep saturated yellow, dark, greyish blue' (Hall, 2003: 17) – there is an intensity to the detail of her work which sits somewhere between prose and poetry.

The physicality of Hall's prose is in contrast with the shape-shifting propensities of the water which dominate the novel's scene-setting from the beginning. In the prologue, Samuel Lightburn cajoles his horse and cart across a rutted landscape, through waist-deep floods which suck, sluice, and slosh with menacing sibilance. They are 'dangerous and slow and final'; 'eerie and unending' (Hall, 2003: x) and the cart is described as 'cutting' (Hall, 2003: ix) the liquid, a violence which suggests a weighty, bodily quality to water that has a 'tensile voice' that speaks as 'a continuance of text in a land of broken fluid, of forced rock' (Hall, 2003: ix). Everything appears to endow the water with a resentful energy, yet it also sings 'somatic music that fills in space and time' (Hall, 2003: x) and emits a 'soft-washing hum' (Hall,

2003: ix) which holds Sam within it. This eerie caprice adds to the defamiliarising effect of an element that is simultaneously beneficent and sinister, elemental and knowing.

This opening sets the tone for the novel's portrayal of water as a substance that transcends its own materiality, transforming itself back and forth across the human/non-human divide. The people of the valley are frequently identified not just with, but as water: the owner of the village shop is described as having 'a soaked neck' (Hall, 2003: 47); Janet is 'like light grown in water' (Hall, 2003: 118) and 'a statue of rain' (Hall, 2003: 136); the young Isaac is a 'briny-looking child' (Hall, 2003: 56) who has 'Too much watter in t'lad's heed' (Hall, 2003: 69). Yet the metamorphoses of flesh and water are two-way. 'Pools of meltwater' are as blood which has 'spilled out of the warmed veins of hills' (Hall, 2003: 87) and the 'high-altitude pools were vascular, open grey walls collapsing deep into the earth's core' (Hall, 2003: 185). Just as the climatic exigencies of hill and valley have seeped into the cells of its farmers, so the slow-beating blood of the villagers has found its way, as if by osmosis, into the valley's body.

This transference is illustrated well in Isaac's habit of submerging his face in freezing mountain brooks to observe life beneath the surface. There he discovers a universe careless of the observing eye, entire unto itself, but, though the separation between the worlds appears absolute, he intermediates, absorbing the chill of the water until it is no longer punishing. He becomes of the underwater world and experiences there 'the freedom to fly, weightless and sighted through the currents of the valley's water' (Hall, 2003: 77). Such consonance reoccurs in the novel's final moments when the adult Isaac, now a diver, is drowned in the reservoir:

> There is a voice in his head that is speaking to him, telling him that this is who they are, she [Janet] and he, people from this carnal realm of water and earth, full of the atoms of this old, dying, re-living place. The blood in his hands will tell him where he belongs, where it will be brightest. (Hall, 2003: 231)

His death is fittingly described as a reabsorption of atoms – 'The land suck[ing] back in what once it helped to produce' (Hall, 2003: 236). What makes him could equally have made the grass, the water, the rock, or the air, and Hall concludes with the commutation of soul and substance that suggests the people and the landscape of the dales are indivisible. Here, as everywhere in *Haweswater*, the locals are presented as extensions of their environment – 'People of kept stone' (Hall, 2003: 185) as the novel's artist Paul Levell describes them – who emerge from, and blend back into, the hard greys, duns, and greens of the landscape.

Hall's Mardale in 1936 is a community rooted within the cyclical pro-ductivity of the seasons yet on the brink of change that is dictated by ideas of progress and efficiency. As the agent of that change, Jack Liggett is asso-ciated with the hard pragmatism of industrial reason. His role within the Manchester City Waterworks, with all its material trappings (the mod-ern sports car and refined suits), demands a different kind of integration of people and landscape than that practised by the farmers of Mardale, to whom he comes to inform them that their land is to be sequestered for the Haweswater reservoir. His is a rationality based on national rather than local duty and on commitment to the greater good, and it is a rationality that elevates the beauty of industry above the poverty of agriculture. Liggett is a self-made man in every sense and his ambition for the community is equally transformative. Industrial efficiency, he argues, is the expression of a divine gift, the mastery of the vagaries of nature through the miracle of civil engineering. The dam will transform the 'slothful, idle' water in the valley bottom into a workable asset which would be 'sent roaring in pipes down to the city' (Hall, 2003: 50) with the energy of an unassailable modernity. Liggett works on the locals with a similar proselytising efficiency, moulding their 'sculpted, inorganic quality' (Hall, 2003: 53) into acquiescence with the same artistic flair that he applies to his own self-construction. He is a performer who knows how to modulate his emotional register between bull-ish optimism about the necessity of moving with the times and pathos for the loss of the known and loved, but he is also conscious of his position as an outsider and enemy of the people. His manufactured quality is picked up by Levell's thumbnail sketch in which Liggett's 'face [...] was made up of many layers, of paper and office objects, his cigarette a stack chimney, his thin smoke. In the man's hair were the bright wings of industry' (Hall, 2003: 45).

An amalgam of industry and bureaucracy, Liggett is not just differ-ent from the villagers; he is an undreamt-of alien. His vision of harness-ing the valley's resources on a grand scale rather than scraping a living is infused with a brutal beauty, but also with a casual arrogance that assumes the ultimate success of any scheme sufficiently ambitious. In this sense he is a harbinger of changes afoot beyond the Cumbrian hills, changes of which teacher Eliza Bowman learns on her regular journeys to Penrith to collect newspapers for the village school. Stories of society girls are intercut with the more sobering geopolitical events of the early 1930s; riots, hunger strikes, and murders sit alongside the discovery of Pluto and the flight of Amy Johnson. All is overshadowed by the growing threat of Nazi Germany and, as Bowman inks the new boundary lines to Europe's nations into her school atlas, she melancholically reflects that: 'In this world there is always the intrusion of one structure or another into the sacred, self-governing heart' (Hall, 2003: 21). Liggett is responsible for the structure that intrudes into the valley, but he is also responsible for seeking to dismantle the sense of interdependence and self-sufficiency which animates the self-governing hearts of its inhabitants. As such he represents a kind of imperial logic of modern utilitarianism which is monolithic, incontestable, and all-inclusive in the way that it draws all into centralised planning for a national, rather than a local, identity.

Liggett's nemesis is Janet Lightburn, although in many senses neither opposes the other. Unlike her mother, Janet is not driven by absolutes but rather by a hybridity that places her between man/woman, tradition/modernity, superstition/scepticism, human/animal, and fire/water. In physical appearance she is a blend; to Liggett, her hair appears to have 'an almost blue sheen' but that gives way to a 'dark yellow' (Hall, 2003: 81). Unlike the fiery redness of her father's hair, or the amphibian pallor of Isaac, Janet is a combination of both the blue of the water and the yellow of the sun. In temperament too she repudiates the accepted mores of the valley – swearing alongside the other men in the pub, defying her mother's admonitions against seeking out Jack – leading her father to judge that 'there are no absolutes to be found in the blood on her wrists, and under her nails. She has feral qualities not belonging to either sex' (Hall, 2003: 73). Her commitment to the valley (particularly to the maintenance of the school) is more rigid than any other, and yet the affair that she begins with Liggett is passionately contrary to her desire to rid the valley of him and his ambitions. Their lovemaking is consequently quarrelsome in the extreme:

> There were always injuries. Bruises as she struggled to leave him, again and again, a ring of blue fingers round her wrist, her ankles. Pieces of her hair torn out when she demanded he leave, feigning indifference, pushing him back. He grasped her anywhere he could, a handful of hair. She would scream, demand her release. (Hall, 2003: 120)

Each tears at the other's body as they tear at each other's values, seeking to eviscerate self and other in a sexual cataclysm. Their struggles are less to destroy that in the other which opposes them than to eradicate the appeal of the other's worldview that they cannot deny in themselves. Slowly, Jack's feeling for the unreconstructed asceticism of the hills and valleys grows to challenge his faith in the miracle of engineering. His dangerous night ascents of the mountains release in him an ecstatic otherworldliness generated by the 'blind murder of landscape' (Hall, 2003: 128), a *mano a mano* mastery of his surroundings far removed from the victory of industrial processes. Significantly, he describes his elation as 'pure, fluid exhilaration' (Hall, 2003: 128), a watery indicator of his *volte face*.

His *peripeteia* – for *Haweswater* is a tragedy in a quite traditional sense – occurs when the frivolous bet he has made with a local poacher to capture and kill a golden eagle comes to fruition. Initially mooted in a moment of hubris, this blind murder floods him with shame, causing him to seek an – at least symbolic – redress by returning the bird to its nest. His death in the process is poetic but lacks a fully cathartic impact for, with a quarter of the novel still to be played out, the emphasis shifts to Janet's suicidal attempt to destroy the dam. Her grief at Jack's death is all-consuming. Wild, self-flagellating despair mirrors the violence of their lovemaking, but with none of the ambivalence; it is as if Janet is possessed by a feral energy which, no longer contained by the moderation of an opponent's quarrel, is released from its restraints. It is a grief that is primeval and has absorbed the benthic darkness of the depths, surging from the unknown below into an unmanageable hysteria. Janet's grief is of such incandescence that it is fitting that her death comes from fire. Seeking to undermine the foundations of the dam, she inserts quantities of dynamite and is torn apart in the ensuing blast. Her end comes not with the cataract of water for which she hoped, as the dam is barely damaged by her actions; but she nevertheless experiences her final moments as a form of drowning in a 'sea of red darkness, swallowing air' (Hall, 2003: 238). Her eviscerated remains are a suitably watery epitaph to her place within the valley: 'Ticking bubbles of liquid leave her chest, but it is simply the spirit-levelling of fluids in her body. She is dead' (Hall, 2003: 241).

Of course, Janet is not entirely dead as her remains are buried beneath the Janet Tree, which is rumoured to be involved in more than its fair share of accidents on the winding hill roads. And this resilient residue of superstition gains symbolic weight in the final evaluative pages, which regard the action of the novel from the distance of half a century and the kind of accustomed modernity that Liggett predicted. This archaic superstition speaks of the same mysterious depths that lie beneath the waters, in the primeval corners of the human–animal brain, in the consanguinity of man and landscape and in the elusive aesthetic of the natural world. These mysteries will sustain, argues Hall; they will not succumb entirely to the succession of physical and metaphysical structures that determines modernity's scepticism. Instead they remain just beyond the knowable, fluid rather than concrete, but nonetheless substantial for that. As, we shall see, Hall returns to these kinds of dualism insistently in later work, and never more theatrically than in her next novel.

The Electric Michelangelo (2004)

Hall's second novel went a significant way to establishing her as one of the most impressive new voices in British fiction, and built on the promise of *Haweswater* with a narrative greater in range, confidence, and technical aplomb than its forebear. The book was shortlisted for the 2004 Man Booker Prize and it is easy to see why, for *The Electric Michelangelo* contains all the elements that recent literary prize-giving has come to respect: historical scope, lavish detail, melancholy lyricism, and a consciousness of its own literariness. It is undeniably a 'Booker novel' in the sense that it rewards the reader with a certain middlebrow heft, but, whilst it may have gained a reputation as Hall's most substantial achievement to date, it also shows her on a stylistic path of luxuriant metaphorical ornamentation that she was to abandon in the stripped-down fictions that followed. *The Electric Michelangelo* is nothing if not value for money; Hall creates a *Bildungsroman* of baroque indulgence, amply peopled by Dickensian grotesques, wrapped in the carnivalesque trappings of seaside resorts on both sides of the Atlantic. Her tale of Cyril Parks, the son of a Morecambe hotelier, whose apprenticeship as a tattoo artist takes him to Coney Island in America, and back, over the first half of the twentieth century, is a glance at the underbelly of popular spectacle told in the shapeliest and most extravagant of descriptive adornments. There is a richness to the prose which often belies the tawdriness of the worlds Hall describes, but there is also a surfeit in the striving for perfect metaphors that slows the drama to the pedestrian, drawing attention to the luscious ripeness of the artifice. In a novel about the stories that art tells, the art of the story becomes overtly visible.

The Electric Michelangelo is a novel about suffering and about the ways that suffering gets turned into art. It opens by balancing two orders of suffering, one bodily, the other psychological. The seven-year-old Parks is required to service the hackings and desperate expectorations of the tubercular tourists who visit his mother's Morecambe hotel in the hope that the softness of the sea air will ease their symptoms. Queasily revolted by the basins of blood and phlegm that he removes from the dying clientele, he trains his eyes on the horizon and his mind on the elsewhere, knowing that he will nevertheless be tempted to glance at the putrefying fragments of lungs. He is disgusted by the messy deliquescence of the body but recognises in its disorders an affinity with the sea and with the cycle of loss and return that the waves promise. Having lost his father to a storm at sea the day before his own birth, Parks is attuned to the spasms of hope and despondency that follow the ebb and flow of the tide, the promise of restitution always damned by the certainty of recession. Like the waves, the holidaymakers and conva- lescents who patronise the Bayview Hotel return with dogged insistence, their desires fuelled by the restorative possibilities of freshness, diversion, and rebirth. As Parks swills the discharge from his basins, he discerns in the bloody mucus a vision of his father's boat with a man waving, and, in this moment, Hall suggests the key thematic frame that will drive her novel: the opposition between the transformative potential of beauty and the inescap- ability of human suffering.

Early in life Parks learns that pain is a constant of the human condition, and the loss of his father and the suffocating decline of the tubercular guests are mere pinpricks in the tapestry of suffering from which the world is woven. The import of the mysterious after-hours comings and goings of lachrymose young women to Reeda Parks' hotel is lost on her son, as is the full meaning of the mangled male bodies that return from northern Europe's first contin- ental war, but death and decline are everywhere present, even in the fading charms of the resort, which, by the novel's final pages, has slid indecorously into anachronism. Moreover, pain comes to determine the shape of Parks' life and brings him into contact with his manifest destiny in the form of the master tattooist Eliot Riley. In fact, the key turning points of his life are heralded by moments of destructive upheaval: his birth coincides with the death at sea of his father; he is apprenticed to Riley following his mother's death from cancer; his graduation from apprentice to practitioner occurs after Riley's hand is damaged beyond repair by his enemies; his emigration follows Riley's suicidal drinking; his love for Grace is thwarted by the violent intervention of her assailant; and the extreme retribution they exact forces his exile into the military and eventual return home. Pain and suffering are thus motivators – both narratively and morally – and, as an apprentice to Riley, Parks learns that this energy needs to be fixed into memorials which speak not only of the experience of pain but also of its overcoming.

Riley is a gothic monstrosity, a distillation of the seamier qualities of resort life who, with his 'dull black morning jacket, the woollen hat, the gloves with the finger ends cut out' (Hall, 2004: 98) gives off the musty redolence of a Victorian caricature. His grotesqueness is accentuated by his cruelty, by his pathological drinking, and by the squalid quarters he keeps, which have more of the lair about them than reputable offices for business. Yet, on first meet- ing him, Parks is aware of the counterbalancing virtues of black humour and 'soft-surprised cognition' (Hall, 2004: 63), which draw him to Riley 'like water [which] was already tunnelling past him. Some rip current had already taken him, and he was going without fighting' (Hall, 2004: 78). The watery metaphor is appropriate, for Riley has both the predictability and mutability of the sea, and, like Parks himself, is identified as standing somewhere between the solid and the liquid. He has the same effect on the boy as the quicksand holes on Morecambe beach with which Parks and his friends experiment somewhat injudiciously. Lowered into the sand, Parks is sucked down with by a remorseless, digestive peristalsis before managing to release himself at the final moment. Such is the compulsive effect on him of Riley. His chores at Bayview have prepared him for the grotesque things of life, and one of the chief attractions of his employer is that he is 'utterly unperturbed and unaffected by blood, gore, and odour' (Hall, 2004: 90), but it is in the shades of Riley's personality that Parks truly feels the draw. His darkness is not particular but rather a channelling of a more universal quarrelsome humanness, and to it Parks is lured with an appalled fascination because he sees in himself the same attraction to the odorous and visceral aspects of human failure. With Riley as a fatherly surrogate and wayward guide, Parks gradually lowers himself into the indeterminate space where pain and desire meet.

For Hall, there is something execrably dirty beneath the surface of human behaviour; it is constituted of both a literal filth and a moral darkness which is ever present but removed from the proximities of the higher functions. This darkness is a vortex of inexorable impulsion which contains all the instinctual, uninhibited, pleasure-in-pain contradictoriness of an abjected force. It rolls together sex and violence, transgression and chaos, suicidal and homicidal desires, all kinds of sin and deviancy, and fetishes for cataclysmic destruction on personal and worldly levels. Throughout her writing, Hall returns to this notion of a gangrenous hinterland to licit human desire which threatens to irrupt into the healthy respectability of the social and is barely kept at bay by orderliness. It underpins everything that Parks learns about the tattoo trade, for he quickly apprehends that, without the extremes of behaviour and the suffering that they cause, there would be no regular business. He muses on this fact after his arrival in America:

> There were the beatings, the cheatings, the welts from the buckles of belts on the hide of sanity, the ploughing of fists through faces, the avalanche of cocks against orifices, the rapes, the killings, the loss of loved ones from a blade, a gun, poison, lunatic voices in the head. There were gangrenous scars of the undead. What was he if not a conduit for the brutalized stories and the mending characters of a new country? His needle found out their suffering like a surgeon's scalpel. People were pricked and spilled their lives like pus. And one day he might go mad from it all. (Hall, 2004: 262)

The pain of having the needle pick out a particular form of suffering on one's body, he soon realises, is an expiation of a specific violence through the endurance of pain, but it is fundamentally a concentration and codification of the universal reality of human destructiveness.

The structure of above and below that I am using to explain Hall's dichotomy is not entirely true to the novel, for, though she does frequently use metaphors of surface and depth, and of the downward pull of the unknown, she also utilises parallel as a narrative device to stress the co-existence (and co-dependence) of her two worlds. They sit side by side, inhabiting the same space, and each relying on the other for credibility. The most obvious parallel in the novel is between Morecambe and Coney Island, but, in each instance, Hall makes clear that the interlacing of the scared and the profane is mutually beneficial. Both are places of entrepreneurial dynamism and energy where death and life, growth and decay, the entertaining and the grotesque are blended together. They enjoy seasonal bouts of wealth and frugality, and the citizens are able to turn their hand to money-making with a protean flexibility that situates them somewhere between respectability and criminality – as Reeda Parks' casual sideline as an abortionist well illustrates. Without the balance between the titillation of the transgressive and the safety of the crowds, neither would flourish, and it is within the frame of this co-dependency that we must read the status of the tattooist as somewhere between aberrant artisan and artist.

To Riley's mind the tattooist is a cultural bogeyman because he honestly and non-judgementally depicts the exhibitionist fantasies of his clients. The tattoo, he claims, is dismissed as a degraded art form because it is too democratic; it forcibly holds the mirror up to nature not for contemplation but as a challenge to the pretensions to empathy of the crowd. It is the more aggressive of a pair of twins, for, where high art protects and nurtures its mystique of transcendence, the tattoo loudly glories in its roots on the body and in the indelibility of its making, which suggests the impossibility of its transcendence into ethereality. In short, the tattoo is all body where 'art' is all mind and spirit. Yet as Parks learns his trade – learning that 'any solution could be used to dissolve and bind pigments – blood, spit, a woman's juice, semen, piss' (Hall, 2004: 136) – he grows to recognise a unique beauty in the worldliness of his practice. Riley, he sees, is a technician of extraordinary skill whose demons never impinge upon his professionalism and who is a true artist of the people in the sense that he draws his inspiration not from the ideal of what humans should be but from the given of what they are. Their profession involves permanently memorialising the body's organic temporality, fixing in images of potency the fecundity of the client's imago.

This is an artistic process not of wild imagination but of an eye that sees beneath the surface of the skin:

> He was a vessel through which these messages passed, for better or for worse. What he pulled out of people and drew on them was as varied and degenerate as it was

honourable and illuminating. On his walls were warrior signs and heads with swords clean through them, women on their knees bending naked towards men's cocks, next to Christ on his cross, the scales of justice and doves with olive branches. From all the world's distilled meanings, from the chaotic jumble, Riley located human totems and gifted them to their patrons. (Hall, 2004: 94)

The tattoo becomes in the tattooist's hands the gift to the individual of their own abstract desires, emotions which they cannot always articulate but which the artist brings into expression. The tattoos represent an art as individual and disorderly as its canvas for they do not abide by the logic of formal construction but rather collide together the fantastic, the supernatural, the fetishistic, and the taboo in an undiscriminating collage. Importantly, too, the tattoo is an art of compression rather than extrapolation. The design books from which the clients select contain symbolic distillations of common experiences and emotions, effective visual short-cuts to complex and inchoate interior lives. From these templates, Riley and Parks abbreviate the stories which are brought to them, giving shape to the pain, pride, or pomposity of those who seek them out. For many, the pain of having the needle pick out a particular form of suffering on one's body is an expiation through the endurance of temporary discomfort, and for Hall the individual motive/motif crystallises the simple realities of experience on a much wider scale:

The tattoo was a jump too far. It was implicit. It was explicit. It was utter intimacy, intimacy with the whole basic fucking, killing, loving world. These were the prime colours of the life, were they not, the original three, and human beings simply mixed them up into civilized hues from there. (Hall, 2004: 148)

Hall's *reductio ad absurdum* here is aptly tempered with a painterly metaphor, and it reminds us that in *The Electric Michelangelo* the aesthetic is closely linked to forms of violence. Beauty keeps company with destructiveness throughout, merging at times to form startling juxtapositions such as when Morecambe's western pier burns down during a snow storm producing a dazzlingly surreal dissonance of rising embers and falling flakes 'like thousands of migrating flaming birds across the sky, flocking, reforming, conflagrating' (Hall, 2004: 44). Destruction is wrought into a fine metaphorical passage here, one which is typical of a novel where poetry and prose blur. Hall's stylistic method could be regarded as well suited to her material for there is a conscious effort to render the everyday in language which transforms it into the artistic. Though the novel is heavily descriptive, it eschews naturalism, preferring in its Morecambe sections a blend of local myth and lore and in the American sections a hyperbolic carnivalesque. Both locations are endowed with a faintly unreal quality and Hall emphasises this with metaphorical abundance which heightens their symbolic resonance.

Often she layers metaphors, as we can see in the full passage describing the burning pier:

> The brilliant snow moved like thousands of migrating flaming birds across the sky, flocking, reforming, conflagrating. It was like meteors swarming and rushing on some swift and undisclosed passage, riding the rapids of the cosmos. Or like being spun with his eyes open in a circle on a clear night except that he was standing still and the sky was whirling of its own accord. It was like pieces of a mirror being smashed in the heavens, in a fury of narcissistic disappointment. [...] And the two boys stood watching the impossibility of the entire western portion of the sky alight with burning snowflakes. (Hall, 2004: 44)

Image is laid upon image, forcing the reader into a metaphor overload and yet somehow retaining the richness of the moment. Hall has a poet's aptitude for insightful metaphorisation, and this novel is full of moments of such crystalline precision, but, as we saw in *Haweswater*, there is a tendency to over-work material to the point of imagistic contusion, which, in the process, focuses the reader's attention more on Hall's self-conscious stylisation than on dramatic development. Interestingly it is a narrative problem which she addressed in subsequent fictions, and in her collection of short stories, *The Beautiful Indifference* (2011), the stripped-down formal constraints endow her lyricism with powerful clarity.

Whether or not one considers Hall's artistry overly stylised, one feature of it stands out in *The Electric Michelangelo*: the attention on visuality. The novel opens with the disgusted Parks' wish to see the world as other than it is – 'If the eyes could lie, his troubles might all be over' (Hall, 2004: 7) – and proceeds to explore the paradoxes of sight and blindness in depth. Seeing in these early sections is closely associated with knowing, and particularly with access to the mysteries of the adult world. Parks' mother's illicit trade as an abortionist is made apparent to him only when he peers through a keyhole, and his spying initiates him once again into the squelching, messy realities of life. This knowledge, the awareness that the human is little more than 'wet slop like pulled fish-gut when the gulls had flocked and pecked and ruined a catch' (Hall, 2004: 27), cannot be unseen or worked back into safety by stories of innocence. And seeing is also connected phonetically and thematically to the sea, and to that which has disappeared under its surface. Parks' dreamy stares over the Irish Sea long for his father's resurrection from the depths, and, as a result, sight tends to be associated with both loss and the caprice of water. Morecambe Bay is a perfectly apposite location in that regard, for the enormous bay is notoriously dangerous as in-rushing tides catch those on the sands unawares; as with so much else in this novel, what appears to be solid and reliable rapidly defaults to a soggy and undistinguished liquidity.

In America, sight is subject to the sensory overload of a culture devoted to excess and the insatiable consumption of the new. Coney Island represents a concentration of fantasy and carnival into a permanently impermanent carousel of the spectacular; it is Morecambe's 'richer, zany American relative. A fat, expensively dressed in-law with a wicked smile and the tendency, once caught up in the mood, to take things too far' (Hall, 2004: 182). In this place of kaleidoscopic hybridity where immigrants mix and circus freaks profit from the grotesqueness of their deformities, Parks learns that he can no longer trust his eyes because the real and the absurd are no longer clearly separate. He can, for instance, not make the connection between seeing and understanding when he witnesses the bizarre shadow-play of Grace and her horse sharing her apartment played out on the wall opposite her window. In every way, his expectations are assaulted by the dizzying hyperreality of his surroundings. America is a country – and Coney Island its quintessence – that cannot be fully taken in but that nevertheless depends for its appeal on the abandonment of rationality to the primacy of the senses:

> Voyeurism was key to the attraction, because Americans at leisure wanted to witness something to take away thought and replace it with emotion, they wanted beautiful smut, a punch in the gut. There was that pivotal ocular quality to anything on offer. The devouring eye. (Hall, 2004: 185)

Whilst the nation's relentless appetite for new sensations surprises Parks, he is unsurprised to discover that it feasts from the same menu of erotic fantasies, hubristic violence, and broken taboos which have underpinned the profitability of his profession. Coney Island is the dark imagining of Riley writ large with the sign of its own perversion proudly displayed. Thought is supplanted by sentiment, the beautiful by the imaginable, and, in the middle of it all, Parks plies his trade immune to fashion because, where the eye may be sated by passing sensation, the tattooed body represents a site of deeper and more primitive fascination: 'It was something that could be done to the watching, yawning, masses that included them, sensation actually felt by them. That was the very nucleus of its longevity – inclusion, involvement, connection' (Hall, 2004: 207).

In the American sections, we find the convergence of the themes of spectacle, beauty, and violence, and particularly so in Parks' relationship with Grace, where beauty becomes tied to the politics of seeing and the violence of appropriation. Grace, a bareback horse rider who lives in the same apartment block as Parks and who soon becomes the subject of his affections, hails from a mélange of central European heritages, but her precise derivation is never clear. Instead she represents the early twentieth-century mass migration of European peoples to America with the desire to build new lives. Like both Parks and Riley, she is first introduced to the reader by her eyes, which are 'solemn', 'territorial and displaced and dark' (Hall, 2004: 214), and the darkness speaks of a past of traumatic upheaval as a Jewish émigré, miraculously berthed in a new country whilst still a child, and abandoned to the kindness of other settlers. She announces herself dramatically with an extraordinarily vivid description of the horrors of war given to some of Parks' cocky soldier clients, but, he reflects, her experiences could equally be 'the stories of immigrant Poles and Russians and Czechs [...] told in sorrowful ritual and stitched into the patchwork quilt of the place' (Hall, 2004: 255).

Fiercely independent and brutally confrontational, Grace's spirit is that of a survivor, one who realises the necessity of matching herself, chameleon-like, to the voyeuristic sensibility of her time and place. Consequently, she commissions Parks to cover the entire area of her body that would be concealed by clothes with a single, repeated motif: a green-iris eye. Her motivation is entrepreneurial for she wishes to be able to exhibit herself alongside the other tattooed women in Coney Island's arcades. However, as much as she is offering up her body as spectacle, the strategy has a secondary effect of curtailing the controlling gaze. Parks, who somewhat reluctantly agrees to carry out the work, encounters this mesmerising prohibition when he contemplates her design:

> The eye outmanoeuvred his gaze, it failed to be inanimate and resisted being used or judged as an object. [...] Truly, he did not know who was primarily looking at whom, Cyril Parks or the eye, because his gaze was mirrored, deflected, equalled. It was as if the image was playing a game with him. (Hall, 2004: 258)

The appropriative, disempowering power of the gaze is captured and returned by Grace's tattooed body, which exploits its consumers even as it is exploited by them. As an exhibit she reflects not the dead-eyed gawp of the jaded customer but a challenge to the objectification of all the human variety and mutations that act as currency in a society of the spectacle. In explaining her motives for the body art, she locates her desire to turn the gaze upon itself within the context of her gender, for, as she states:

> It will always be about body! Always for us! I don't see a time when it won't. I can't say you can't have my body, that's already decided, it's already obtained. [...] All I can do is to interfere with what they think is theirs, how it is supposed to look, the rules. (Hall, 2004: 274)

This identification of the appropriative gaze as male feels out of step with the rest of the novel, a rather heavy-handed feminist inflection in a text which has consistently implied that the appeal of voyeurism is universal. However, in interview with the *Guardian*, Hall readily contends that body dysmorphia and social pressure on women's appearances figured in the construction of her female characters (Edemariam, 2004). It is certainly true that her characters (Reeda, Claudia, Nina) are independent and decisive, but the determination to shape from them a political message rent from second-wave feminist theory seems unnecessarily instrumental in a novel about how the tenebrous depths of human desire are shaped into art.

What is certainly true is that Grace is far from the passive model of male fantasy. Like Fevvers in Angela Carter's *Nights at the Circus* (1984), with whom she bears a resemblance, her transformed body is a challenge to conformity and a repudiation of the notion of standardised beauty. It is this determination to be judged on her own terms that ultimately leads her assailant, Malcolm Sedak, to throw acid over her in a bid to burn from her skin the markings he regards to be unfeminine. Insane with a religious fanaticism, Sedak immediately douses her with alkali to prevent her death, but her body is horrifically disfigured, turned, as so much else in this novel, to a state 'not quite solid, not quite liquid, but something in between' (Hall, 2004: 297). In this condition, Grace embodies the dichotomy of surface and depth which has become such a recurrent theme in *The Electric Michelangelo*. She is both, simultaneously – the tortured, visceral interior and the worldly worn skin – but she is also the apotheosis of the spectacle, drawing eyes inexorably to the abject juices and mess on another's inner pain. Ironically, as a *bona fide* physical mutant, she holds no appeal for an audience, as the horrified reaction of the lascivious pest who propositions her from behind shows when she turns to face him and exposes her ruined abdomen. There is a biblical justice in the revenge that she and Parks enact on Sedak, the removal of his two eyes for the loss of her many, but the narrative climax is her assault. From there, Hall has to return Parks to Morecambe and to Riley's boarded-up premises.

The Electric Michelangelo is not Hall's most successful nor narratively most satisfying work, but I could not concur with Eileen Battersby that it 'underlines most of what is wrong with English fiction' (Battersby, 2004). It is a novel of originality and ambition, and shows Hall handling with growing confidence the generic, formal, and stylistic elements of her craft. Her writing is strikingly poetic and reveals her willingness to experiment with voice and mood. Most significantly, the novel sees the further development of her interest in the grubby, gritty, and gruesome underpinnings of civilised life to which she has returned in each subsequent work, and which has become her literary calling card.

The Carhullan Army (2007)

Against the baroque verbosity of *The Electric Michelangelo*, Hall's third novel is as spare and bleak as the degraded Cumbrian landscape in which it is set. Gone is the florid artistry of a narrative spanning nations, and gone too is the colourful vibrancy of Hall's carnivalesque vision of history. Instead, *The Carhullan Army* sets its story in a near-future Britain in which financial corruption, creeping environmental despoliation, global geopolitical instability, and resource shortage have brought about an Orwellian nightmare of material austerity and restrictive governance. Under the auspices of the Authority, the country has been 'reorganised' under strict regimes of enforced manual labour, compulsory birth control, and rationing. Paternalism reigns, and women are randomly required to display the presence of their contraceptive coil to any Authority officer on demand. In Rith (a fictionalised town similar to Penrith), the narrator, known only as Sister, and her husband eke out a miserable subsistence, growing emotionally and politically apart whilst they attend their allocated work duties and try to avoid contracting tuberculosis, which, with the perpetual rain, has become rife. Sister dreams of escaping to join the fabled community of Carhullan, where a collective of women exists self-sufficiently, espousing an ideology of hard-line feminist emancipation and political resistance to the Authority.

The novel has clear generic links to the dystopian tradition, and particularly those novels such as Doris Lessing's *Memoirs of a Survivor* (1974), Marge Piercy's *Woman on the Edge of Time* (1976), Margaret Atwood's *The Handmaid's Tale* (1985), and P.D. James' *The Children of Men* (1992), which explore contemporary feminist politics through the dystopian form. The novel also owes a great deal to Cormac McCarthy's *The Road* (2006), and there are strong echoes of Orwell's *Animal Farm* (1945) and *Nineteen Eighty-Four* (1949) and to Joseph Conrad's *Heart of Darkness* (1899).[1] In an article published shortly after *The Carhullan Army* won the John Llewellyn Rhys Prize, Hall acknowledges her debt to Robert O'Brien's *Z for Zachariah* (1974), a children's book describing the struggle to survive of a fifteen-year-old girl after the cataclysm of a nuclear war.

In interview, Hall has suggested two further paths of inspiration for the novel. On the one hand she recalls the floods of 2005 as a shockingly direct reminder of vulnerability. As she says: 'This was one of the worst episodes in my county's history, a history that includes many violent sackings, and the implications of an altered climate became no longer merely imaginable, but visible' (Hall, 2007b). On the other hand, *The Carhullan Army* is driven by an interest in a particular kind of womanhood: 'I was brought up in Cumbria where I saw all these fierce agricultural women [...] they terrified me when

I was young. But they're also quite comforting to be around. I've always admired that strength in women' (in Brown, 2007: 14). Tying this interest to the question of how far such a woman would go in extreme circumstances brings Hall to the conclusion that: 'There is an idea of us, as women, being innately pacifist and kind of reactionary. [...] I'm interested in the idea that women are as aggressive as men but, over centuries, we have been taught not to be. We are – and I think it's increasingly apparent that's the case' (in Guest, 2007). Hall's work is thus infused and enthused by a localism which is at the same time expansive and metaphorical; the Cumbrian landscape in her writing becomes the female body political – desecrated but defiant. By bringing together the themes of environmental degradation and gender politics into this dystopian speculation, Hall manages to achieve something which is both prospective and retrospective.

The Carhullan Army is a novel about fanaticism and the ways in which seemingly rational convictions can spill over into extremist actions. The novel's focal point is Jackie Nixon, a hard-bitten, ex-military intimidation-made-flesh whose second-wave feminist politics are as dyed-in-the-wool as the yellow tunics new initiates to Carhullan are required to wear. She set up the communal farm in the forbidding Cumbrian fells with her American partner, Veronique, over twenty years before the start of Sister's narrative, and has run it as a self-sustaining concern of like-minded women, asking little from the authorities other than to be left alone. Approximately one-third of the novel details Sister's arduous journey to Carhullan, during which she builds Jackie's mystique into near inviolable heroism, making the gradual collapse into mania and paranoia that she seems to undergo in the final third all the more dramatic. Jackie maintains and trains an army of elite warriors whose role is initially unclear but who become increasingly dominant within the community as Jackie develops the belief that Carhullan is to be dissolved by the Authority, and pre-emptive military action is thus required. Filtered through the uncritical eyes of Sister, the division of the community into factions in favour of and against violence becomes a necessary Darwinian struggle through which the elemental aggressive life-force of Jackie and her army are revealed. Pushed to extremity by an enemy that is not only invisible but also whose malign motives may be a product of Jackie's imagination, the Carhullan army become both a case study in women's violent potential and an anatomisation of the appeal of fanatical leadership.

Whilst the novel's gender politics may seem a little dated, much about *The Carhullan Army* speaks to very contemporary concerns. The despoiling of the natural environment, the collapse of trust in international finance operations, the grinding to a halt of capitalism's globalised consumer motor, the dependence of Britain on American paternalism, and the deep suspicion of those in power are all starkly current concerns, and Hall has captured well the sense of anxiety that pervades contemporary British culture. Though published before the calamitous financial crisis that began to take shape in 2007, the novel is uncannily prescient in identifying the weaknesses of the money markets as threatening the stability of the social order. Admittedly the austerity depicted outstrips that which has been widely implemented in advanced economies, but, by conjoining popular fears about a credit system too unwieldy to sustain itself with the increasingly ominous prognostications about climate change, Hall manages to convey a deep and widespread sense of unease. This is only exacerbated by the novel's treatment of authoritarianism; power is leveraged here by institutionalised force but is enacted more insidiously through the logic of benign protectionism – civil liberties must be given up in order to ensure that the people can be properly protected from unnamed but diabolical threats. This seemingly reasonable mechanism is operated as much by Jackie as by the Authority, as we shall see, and it reflects a political strategy of intimidating populations into consensus that has been a defining feature of Anglo-American governance in the years since 9/11.

If these years have been defined by anything it is the increasing sense of threat and a fear of the potential for violence against us which could be perpetrated at any moment by enemies we never knew we had. The benefits of firm and visible government have been extolled alongside an exhortation to acknowledge that safety comes with an inevitable cost to freedom. The conduct of the novel's Authority is presented (by its apologists) as a rational and necessary circumscription of civilian privileges in the wake of rapidly declining resources and technological capabilities. Its conclusions are 'logical' steps intended to maintain social cohesiveness and manage welfare crisis. As such the fitting of women of childbearing age with mandatory contraception is the unavoidable consequence of diminished resources. The Authority's dictats are enacted by people like Sister's husband, Andrew, who, for all his initial partisan bluster against being controlled, grows to accept the restrictions on their conduct and even takes a perverse sexual pleasure in Sister's reproductive disabling. Such measures inevitably evoke the piecemeal undercutting of individual freedoms following a rhetoric that perniciously erodes each citizen's expectations of safety in her/his environment at the same time that it hands power to an authority that appears less and less accountable. Sister desires to break away from the cycle of diminishing expectations and to free herself into a form of authentic self-determination that is expansive in vision, open-hearted in sentiment, and rooted in a primal landscape. The utopianism of Carhullan's intentional community seems to offer a conduit to this selfhood, but Sister's experience there reveals much about the power of fear.

Sister's journey to Carhullan is motivated as much by nostalgia as it is by a desire to escape the soul destruction of her life with Andrew. She fantasises about the frigid altitude, the purity of the remoteness, the possibility of snow to replace the ever-present rain: 'There were no regulations out here. There was no human mess, no chaos, poorly managed, and barely liveable. There was just me, in my own skin, with my blood speeding up. I was taking a chance on something that felt not like a gamble now but like my only option' (Hall, 2007a: 17). Her adventure is retrogressive in the sense that it represents a retreat to a style of subsistence living more precarious than that she is prepared to give up. Carhullan, she knows, 'was of another age, when utilities and services were unimaginable, before the light bulb had been dreamt of' (Hall, 2007a: 54); it demands a practical collectivism and intellectual solidarity that goes against the kind of individualism on which she has been weaned, an individualism that has become increasingly compromised by the Reorganisation. Politically, Sister is an idealist who understands and rejects the implementation of strict social controls as part of the dehumanisation of women by a society governed by men. She retains a core antagonism towards the objectification of the female body – the doctor is described as fitting her coil as 'efficiently as a farmer clipping the ear of one of his herd' (Hall, 2007a: 28) – and, when Andrew characterises the nation as a female, she reacts angrily: 'She's a female, is she, this country that's been fucked over?' (Hall, 2007a: 31). She believes strongly that the potentiality for resistance lies within her, unschooled and waiting to be called into words, and her rejection of life in Rith is driven by this desire for a political self-actualisation. Her initial idealisation of Carhullan derives from a belief that it is a place beyond such coercive politics, somewhere which can draw out the latent power and self-belief that she contains. With Andrew, she has been unable to find 'a voice with which to make my arguments' (Hall, 2007a: 32), deferring to his opinion and allowing his words to speak for her, and, with the egalitarianism and companionability of Carhullan, she hopes to 'be able to find the right words' (Hall, 2007a: 33).

So far, so utopian, but, as she approaches her destination, Hall's tone becomes darker, her mode more gothic. Sister is given a lift by a man whose sexual designs on her are clear; hikes through abandoned villages filled with the uncanny remnants of their last owners; and is eventually pounced upon and disarmed by two members of the community's security force. Far from being welcomed as she had hoped, she is, on Jackie's orders, confined to a 'dog box' – a tiny, filthy pen – and imprisoned there for a number of days. The purpose of this hazing – to flush out any devious intent – indicates how some in Carhullan function on a reflexive suspicion of the intentions of those in the outside world, a conviction that their independence and ideological resistance cannot have been unnoticed by the Authority and must subsequently be destroyed, the 'Unofficials' made official within the redrafted boundaries of society. The dog box episode is a visceral first step that Sister is forced to take towards being 'unmade' (Hall, 2007a: 94), but it is also an indication that that process is likely to be not just depersonalising but also dehumanising. The torture temporarily strips away her reason and renders her animalistic, scrabbling in the dirt for food only to put excrement in her mouth. If Sister is to be remade by Carhullan, it will be from scratch.

Once her *bona fides* have been accepted by Jackie, she is treated with kindness and welcomed by other members of the community, falling in with their rituals and absorbing herself with physical labour, which makes her feel 'active and real and connected' (Hall, 2007a: 131). In these middle sections, she is intimately connected to the landscape, revealing herself as she pulls back the surface of the earth to cut the peat turves. She identifies with the camaraderie of her companions in the fields, begins a sexual relationship with one of the other women in her work party, and glories in a sense of 'basic usefulness and dependence' (Hall, 2007a: 131). Yet, for all the gratification she experiences, these sections are undercut by a palpable dissonance within the community and a growing sense of menace. Sister finds not a collection of women who, like herself, have wrestled themselves from the inert dominance of men but rather a diffuse coincidence of leftist feminist idealists, the socially dysfunctional and disillusioned, and those needing a place in which they can disappear. She is surprised that 'There were fewer victims at Carhullan than I had imagined. Often it was the women themselves who had committed a crime or were misfits: they had been violent, outspoken, socially inept, promiscuous, drug-addicted, and aware they needed some kind of system to bring them in to line' (Hall, 2007a: 130).

This blend of backgrounds, with the range of political ambitions that it engenders, generates an underlying tension within the community as those wishing to maintain their splendid isolation from society come into conflict with those who increasingly believe that the only way to retain an independence is to actively eliminate opposition. The creeping suspicion that this second group are shaping the community's agenda is exacerbated by the lack of reliable information about what is planned by the Authority. Jackie's word is law, and she is the one who informs the others of the death of the king and interprets how the consequent redrawing of civil laws will impinge more significantly on Carhullan. There is no external viewpoint to substantiate her evidence, and the reader is left wondering at the extent to which she employs an exaggerated or bogus scenario as a pretext for her own territorial ambitions. The threat that Jackie envisions and inspires in others is nebulous, but, in locating it outside Carhullan, she is able both to demonise it and draw the community into itself sufficiently to stifle and disarm serious resistance. In this, her strategy is similar to that of the Authority, citing the unquantifiable menace of an ill-defined enemy as justification for increasingly draconian restrictions on those around her.

From Jackie's first physical appearance in the narrative, her depths are portrayed as murkier and her motives less susceptible to explanation than those of the other women Sister encounters. 'The territory had somehow gone into the making of her' (Hall, 2007a: 78) for she is 'indigenous' and has 'a durability' and a 'worn and coarsened exterior' (Hall, 2007a: 82), but also, tellingly, she has the presence of 'someone to whom others would bow' (Hall, 2007a: 82). Where Sister is an idealist, Jackie is a pragmatist, and she quickly identifies the tactical advantages offered by her newest recruit's naivety. Exploiting Sister's dewy-eyed idolisation of her, she influences Sister's political and moral education through subtle prompts designed to draw her gradually into the view that peace can only be maintained by violence. To read, she gives her *The Green Book*, an induction and training manual for the Irish Republican Army, and initially refuses her request to join the corps of raiders, thereby intensifying Sister's desire.[2] For all her conviction that politics is 'all about body and sexuality for us' (Hall, 2007a: 51), she reacts to the disruption that Sister's arrival might cause with a distinctly practical frustration: 'I don't need these bitches squabbling over new cunt' (Hall, 2007a: 85).

Jackie manages the community as a cross between a military boot camp and a farm, never allowing principle to fully get the better of *realpolitik*. The initiation process which Sister undergoes under Jackie's tutelage is intended to produce a retroactive reshaping into something prior to the contamination by the world. It is the kind of stripping away that is seen as a natural function of landscape: 'Rock was beginning to show through the grassland; the bones of an older district, stripped by the wind, washed clean by fast-flowing becks and rain' (Hall, 2007a: 50–51). It is also a stripping back to the animal, as we see in the dog box confinement, where a dehumanisation far in excess of that experienced in Rith is inflicted on Sister. This figurative reduction to a shit-eating animal, driven by thirst to the point of physical and psychological breakdown, might be seen as the necessary detoxification for one entering Carhullan, but it is primarily a rendering down of the human into an animalistic rawness in order that it might be reconfigured along the lines of the community's (or Jackie's) precepts. Once Sister's reconfiguration is complete, she asks to be put back into the box to test the authenticity of her deconstructed animality.

By the time of Jackie's face-to-face confrontation with the community, Sister's self-slaughter is complete. As determined as she was to escape being the mouthpiece for Andrew's opinions, she smoothly falls into a ventriloquial role to support Jackie's forecast that the peace of Carhullan is in jeopardy: 'Her words had always clarified my thoughts. And her voice was the one I had always been listening too from inside my own head' (Hall, 2007a: 162). She finds that, though she is aware of her own manipulation, she has little to resist it, and, once she succumbs, it is a short step to exalting Jackie in messianic terms: 'It was the morning of her annunciation, her arrival' (Hall, 2007a: 164). Before a woman to whom others bow down, Sister bows. By the point of the novel's violent dénouement, Sister's body and mind have been reshaped by Jackie's ruthless training, and, though she describes herself and her companions as not 'monsters', she does admit that they are the 'inviolable creatures the God of Equality had intended us to be' (Hall, 2007a: 187). The brutality of the regime is intended to strip away the indoctrinated 'disabled versions of our sex' (Hall, 2007a: 187), which, because they run so deep, require extraordinary methods of extirpation. What this process readies the women for is the 'fresh red field' of war 'that history had never let us gather' (Hall, 2007a: 187). Like Jackie they now have the bodies of fanatics, voided of their 'femininity', finally at one with the male as an animalistic equal. Hall's point through Sister is of course that women's violence is just as instinctual as man's violence and that, once stripped of the culture of feminine idealism, they function without reference to the notions of nurture, domesticity, and maternal instinct. All those ideals are functions of history, for beneath lies an archaic aggression that is not specific to either sex: 'If we had stood together on the shoreline two thousand years before, facing the invading ships with fire in our hands and screaming for them to come, they would have called us Furies, and they would have been afraid' (Hall, 2007a: 204).

Yet we are left with questions about the extent to which the women's actions are manipulated by the logic of Jackie's mania and paranoia. Sister's narrative unapologetically allies with belligerence, and, if Jackie is a female Kurtz, then Sister is a Marlow who has no issue staring into the face of 'the horror'. The stripping away of the ground cover of socialised identity, to tap into the igneous sub-strata of selfhood, creates a group that are drilled into obedience and cannot, as a consequence, acknowledge the value of the other women's desire to retain elements of the peaceable and holistic principles of Carhullan. The hunting down and execution of Martyn and Chloe is a sobering example of an extremism that cannot brook any dissent, but the killing is not frenzied or disorderly; it is carried out with detachment and ruthless objectification: 'I stared down at Chloe's white foot [...] until it looked like something other. Until it was abhorrent, and did not seem human' (Hall, 2007a: 202).

For all its futuristic setting and retrospective gender politics, *The Carhullan Army* is perhaps Hall's most contemporary novel. It explores, like so many of the other texts covered in this book, the search for an authentic solidity that legitimises our being in the world and makes us more than victims of ideological, political, or environmental instability. Just as the downtrodden citizens of Rith want to believe and want to be exalted, so Sister invests herself in the possibility of transcendence in Carhullan's nostalgia. But that wanting, that need for the reliable, makes them vulnerable to those with swift answers and ready promises. Fanaticism has returned as a historical driver in the twenty-first century, and, as Hall suggests, it is finding fertile ground in the current age of anxiety.

How to Paint a Dead Man (2009)

Hall's fourth novel marks a return to the theme of art, and, whilst *How to Paint a Dead Man* is less lusciously artistic than *The Electric Michelangelo*, it is more formally wrought, having four distinct but interweaved narratives exploring the relationships between, to use Hall's own words: 'Oh, life, sex, death, art...' (in Guest, 2009). Such a broad canvas would seem to warrant comparably broad strokes, but this novel achieves its effects through intimate portraits of characters facing traumatic physical and psychological situations from which they appear to have no escape and for which they are unprepared. Structurally this is Hall's most ambitious work to date, and, for all the flippancy of her run-down of themes, is a finely balanced and serious work which explores the necessity for art in mediating our reception of life's inevitable catastrophes. It is sufficiently intricate in both its style and structure to require the kind of leisurely, careful, and reflective attention that one might pay to a work of visual art. The reader must establish a contemplative distance from the novel's artifice to appreciate the common architectural features as well as the formal idiosyncrasies of each separate narrative. For all the intersections across time and space, each of the panels of this tetratych offers a distinct reading of the interpenetration of life and art, sympathetic to but not dependent on the work as a whole.

The artistic metaphor can be extended to Hall's structural method for the novel, which is based on a technique of layering tone and detail on each narrative in turn, as layers of paint might be added to produce depth and verisimilitude. The novel's postscript, taken from Cennino d'Andrea Cennini's *Il libro dell'arte* (*The Craftsman's Handbook*), describes this process of layering as the most effective way to paint a dead man, and Hall adopts a similar accretive realism to the dead of her narrative. Each of the four strands is underpinned by the inexorability of mortality, but 'The Mirror Crisis' – set in the first decade of the twenty-first century – focuses most viscerally on the consequences of a sudden death. It is the narrative of Susan Caldicutt, voiced unwaveringly in the second person, whose pleasant life as a promising photographic artist and curator is shattered by the death in a traffic accident of her twin brother, Danny. Utterly inconsolable with grief, Susan spirals into increasingly dark and self-destructive behaviour in a bid to obliterate the remaining thinking, feeling parts of herself. In 'The Fool on the Hill' – set in the early to mid-1990s – Susan and Danny's father, and celebrated landscape artist, Peter Caldicutt, contemplates the death of his first wife whilst trapped by a boulder in the fells around his Cumbrian home. The self-destructive Raymelia's collapse into drug addiction and either suicidal or accidental death in the 1960s haunts Peter as much as the sense that he has lost touch with the inspired young artist he had been when he contacted Giorgio, the protagonist of 'Translated from the Bottle Journals'. These journal entries are penned in the last months of the life of an Italian still-life artist during the mid-1960s, who from a hilltop retreat outside Bologna bickers with his housekeeper, mourns his dog, and adjusts himself to the inexorable growth of the cancer that will kill him. Regarding his fast approaching demise, he takes solace in his memory of teaching art to a young girl whose fading eyesight and eventual blindness becomes the subject of the remaining narrative 'The Divine Vision of Annette Tambroni'. Annette's loss of vision means the death of possibility as her devoutly religious mother circumscribes her life within ever narrower parameters of acceptable conduct. One of Annette's few duties is to tend the graves of her father and Giorgio, whose instruction she venerates but in whose tomb she is raped and (possibly) murdered. In one final, and not fully articulated, plot resonance, Annette's brother Tomasso may be the translator of the bottle journals and the Tom with whom Susan indulges in a reckless affair.

This focus on death is appropriate to a novel that takes the still-life (or *nature morte*) as its central artistic reference point. The semantic nuances of the term are explored throughout, with Hall exposing the paradoxes between still/dead and life/nature in both literal and figurative contexts. Particularly in Giorgio's narrative, she plays with the oxymoronic qualities of the term; nature for the painter is anything but dead, as we see in his description of the view from his hilltop retreat: 'The land often seems like an ocean below – the hill moves through leaves, wheat, lavender tides. It never reaches the mountains of the horizon, but still we can hope' (Hall, 2010: 13). Here there is a commutation of 'dead' substance into sentient, striving life, one that Peter similarly perceives in the bleak hillscape around him: 'The rocks seem to have their own gelid circulation; they seem reptilian that way' (Hall,

2010: 152). Both men subscribe to an unalloyed Romanticist's belief that the world about them thrums with recuperative energy; as Giorgio comments, 'when we limp away afflicted through the spirit [...] we go to the sea for its salt. We find shade under the sycamores on the great avenues. Or we go to the rivers where water tells us modestly of its own sickness' (Hall, 2010: 13). Giorgio's narrative, and his artistic practice, is driven by his insistence on looking intently at the world, of regarding it both in its singularity and its plurality. For him, the complacent acceptance of our surroundings robs them of their truthful and creative qualities, of the difference in sameness that becomes insensible through daily routines. Modern life, he suspects, over-complicates the authentic relationship with nature, and he abjures the narcissism of theoretical understanding in favour of the simplicity of seeing and noticing the ways in which the natural world enfolds our lives. The still-life for him becomes the simplified contemplation of the ordinary, the stripping away of custom to look anew at the object in its haecceity.

Like those of Giorgio Morandi – on whom Hall seems to be drawing – the character Giorgio's paintings capture everyday objects in relations of intimacy and extimacy, at once self-referential and turned outwards towards the world. He can become lost in the unpretentiousness of the collection of bottles that he paints, for he discovers in them the reduction of the world to a purely material quintessence of plane and form that is nonetheless spiritual on contemplation. Tiny repositionings create new reflective patterns, new tones, fresh densities, forcing the observer to regard the same materials in different inflections. The undemonstrative simplicity of Giorgio's bottle still-lifes makes them central to his mystique as an artist and as a character. To others – journalists, art critics, the Italian cultural elite – the paintings are a mystery because they do not offer direct and explicit comment either on the purpose of the artist or on the nature of art. Moreover, they are believed to lack a dynamism consonant with the political and ideological reshapings of Europe in the mid-twentieth century; the stillness, their deadness, is somehow a rebuke to an expressionistic urgency. Yet, as Giorgio explains in advising Peter to study Velázquez's still lives, he 'must feel the temperature of the bream, the death-shroud of seas over it, and the cracking of the garlic skin as it is peeled. [...] I would present him with the timeless gifts of the *nature morte*. [...] Only then will he begin to understand living art' (Hall, 2010: 150).

The lives that Hall presents in *How to Paint a Dead Man* are all momentarily bestilled. Each is in some way pinioned by circumstances beyond their control, caught within the intersections of their lives with others, with religion, with art, with mortality, with politics, and with history. The still(ed)-life provides a context for the framing of their quarrels with the world, a metaphor with which to engage with the forces and beliefs that have shaped them. One literal interpretation of a still-life is Susan's best friend, Nicki, who after suffering an asthma attack is left vegetatively brain-damaged. She is kept alive and tended with assiduous care but, without hope of recovery, she is transformed into symbolic occlusion, an abject space impenetrable to knowing and yet always open to interpretation. Susan wonders at the extent to which she is conscious of the comings and goings around her bed, but exploits Nicki's muteness to vent her own inner anguish over Danny's death. Nicki's stillness thus provokes self-reflection in the same way that the ordinariness of a still-life might.

A more developed version of a still-life occurs in Peter's narrative when he is literally trapped within, and by, the same landscape he has used to carve out a celebrated career as an artist. Peter's lifelong fascination with painting rocks underlines the irony of his becoming caught beneath a boulder, but the night that he spends in the ravine strips away the confidence, even imperial nonchalance, with which he has represented the natural world in his work. There is a certain amount of just desserts in his predicament, for the Peter who emerges in his early sections is boastful, hubristic, flamboyantly arty, and irresponsible. Much as he is devoted to his family, he requires compromises that accommodate his needs and rolls this selfishness up within the larger-than-life persona of the eccentric, if affable, artist. On accepting that he will be passing the night in the open air, his arrogance rapidly begins to fade as he is beset by morbid anxieties about the unexplained scuttlings and gurglings he hears around him, convinced that they herald the presence of rats and other unknown predators intent on eating him. The excruciating pain from his injury forces him to acknowledge his own fleshy impotence in an environment of timeless processes and instinctual needs, and he is soon fantasising about the unadventurous comforts of home – the fish pie, the drink, and the ribald bonhomie of his family. He is disempowered by a landscape over which he has executed an aesthetic command, and his lack of ability to influence his situation throws him into a form of existentialist introspection that is profoundly unwelcome for him.

Circling around the penumbra of his conscious mind is the thought of his first wife, Raymelia, an American art student with whom he shared an often tempestuous, occasionally non-monogamous, and always drug-fuelled few years. Her bitter dysmorphic view of the world embraced a self-destructiveness that ultimately drove Peter away, and her towards an early death. In contrast to his customary cavalier egotism, Peter's memories of her, which become more vivid as the night progresses, reveal tenderness and sensitivity. His regret and despair about her loss speak of a love that does not match the bluff cynicism of his public persona. The knowledge that he has failed her by protecting himself sits with him uncomfortably, but it insistently inveigles its way into his mind as the night passes. Hall gradually reveals the caring man with whom we are familiar from Giorgio's narrative.

From their separate narratives, Peter appears to be the antithesis to Giorgio in his conviction that an image should 'tip you off your comfortable perch' (Hall, 2010: 24). He holds that art should be dynamic and interventive, and semi-seriously produces a series of rules of artistic practice that he amuses himself by rehearsing in his head so that he can pass them on to his children. Where Giorgio's methodology is reverential, Peter's is whimsical, his 'rules' showy and narcissistic, designed to be contrarian and to make a name for himself. The Peter of the 1960s who emerges from Giorgio's narrative is the polar opposite to the later incarnation: an enthusiastic student, vivaciously schooling himself in the traditions of his craft and unpretentiously absorbing the intricacies of others' practice. He writes admiringly to Giorgio about his work, impressing the older man by asking not about meaning but about matters of technique. In Giorgio's narrative, Peter's mind is flexible and his spirit enquiring whereas in his own he is curmudgeonly and self-possessed.

Why Peter moves from idealism to cynicism is revealed in a passage of acute sentimentality where he recalls the fragile beauty of Susan and Danny as babies: 'They were both so pale as children that he could see through to the red scribble of capillaries in their cheeks and their ankles. He could see absolutely how they were made, the remarkable pattern of cells' (Hall, 2010: 52). Within a few lines he has countered this with the melancholy summation: 'All innocent mechanisms are muddied up with experience. Children become less and less translucent. Layers of guile and suspicion grow. It's the law of paternal disenchantments' (Hall, 2010: 53). Peter's description of the loss of clarity through the layering of experience is directly comparable to Cennini's advice about the careful laying down of coats of paint to generate the effect of reality. Life, like art, Hall suggests, amounts to a palimpsest of experiences whose accumulating colours blend to produce the depths of an individual but in the process obscure the clarity and simplicity of the underlying state.

Peter's narrative details this darkening in his movement from enthusiastic and committed student, through a gradual hardening at the hands of his tutor Ivan and Raymelia, to his present condition in the 1990s, when he is a celebrated but egotistical artist. Beneath the cynicism of his present demeanour lies the ebullience and wonder of someone struck by art, but that has been lacquered over by a hearty but insincere mien. His enforced night spent as a still-life brings him gradually closer to the painful memories of his losses, the nagging suspicion of his own fraudulence, and the unedifying costs that his craft has demanded. At the same time, it has the effect of re-focusing him on the present and re-engaging his vision on the land-scape, on 'gorse and moor grass, rowan and elder, and the summits of the blue and yellow fells' (Hall, 2010: 275). The dawn brings him to an accom-modation with the past as past –'Life goes on, and the pain hangs around' (Hall, 2010: 275) – and enables a new kind of vision, one that allows him to escape his imprisonment.

Peter's still-life experience forces him into a process of shaping his mem-ories through self-reflection, but for his daughter the death of her twin threatens her entire world with dissolution and reminds us that, for the *nature morte*, death is central. Susan's narrative begins with the enigmatic 'You aren't feeling like yourself' (Hall, 2010: 3), a rather prosaic opening that mutates on the reader learning that she is not describing another's off-colour mood but her own inability to connect emotionally with herself. Danny's death throws her deeper into crisis than the grief of a lost love might entail; it rips apart her sense of herself as a self-cohering monad, projecting her into a perimeterless obscurity where the concept of an 'I' no longer has any resonance.

As children the closeness of Susan and Danny's bond transcended the physical and verbal distance between them; they experienced each other's bodily sensations, shared mental playgrounds, and, in the case of Susan, could not distinguish between 'you' and 'I'. Concerned that this 'ulterior proximity' (Hall, 2010: 4) would retard her development, Susan is sent by her parents to a child psychologist who drilled into her the mantra 'Say I do, Sue, say I do, Sue' (Hall, 2010: 6). Like all the other principal protagonists in the novel, she is forced to accept the shape of the world around her, but her discovery of self is problematised by her fear that the process of becom-ing an individual involves the violent extraction of one part of the self from another, a reduction of a collection of multiplicities and possibilities to sim-plistic binaries of me and not me. Multiplicity is pathologised, the text sug-gests, because the world demands simplicity of form over complexity, unitary definition rather than ambiguity. Being consequently requires the not being other, or even not being the whole of oneself; it demands the creation of a copy in Susan's case, one that is expelled and abjected as the second-person voice. Hall draws a parallel here between the disambiguation of Susan's iden-tity and the hermeneutic orderliness of the art criticism establishment that wishes to dispel the mystery of Giorgio's bottle paintings by labelling them 'relativist, existentialist, totalist' (Hall, 2010: 73) because it cannot accept the unknowable. Susan's rote-learnt 'Me, me, me. I,I,I' (Hall, 2010: 6) is undone by Danny's death, which recuperates the primary trauma of separa-tion in which she was forced to disarticulate herself from him in order to establish her own identity. The shape that she has been forced to construct for herself in the world, the work of artifice that is 'Susan', collapses inwards, leaving a form without substance, an outer without an inner. Her torment of being without the other manifests in the self-destructive intensity of her affair with her colleague, Tom, who is translating Giorgio's bottle journals.

Suspended in a kind of atemporal present, Susan and Tom's illicit relationship is based purely on physical sensation; description focuses on the heightened sensory reception of their encounters – the feel of his hands, the taste of his body, the susurrus of his presence behind her – rather than any emotional coincidence between them. Their fucking is driven by the danger involved in their transgression; moments are grabbed when Tom's wife and Susan's friend, Angela, is engaged elsewhere. Tom's motivation for engaging in the affair are never accounted for in the narrative, but Susan's involve the complete and unrestricted submission of an opened body to another's intentions. Such is the case in the following description where her body is literally pulled apart demanding the entry of the other:

> You'll feel him stroke your legs, and move you onto his lap. He will pull your buttocks apart as if he is separating pieces of a fruit. He will rub you wet with his thumb, open the fastening, and move the tip of himself into place. You will hurt yourself slowly, your legs either side of the chair, and he will continue to open you outwards as you move. (Hall, 2010: 259)

This corporeal rending matches the psychic disintegration that her grief initiates, her mindless bodily secession an erotic manifestation of her drive towards self-obliteration. Sex and death are her only routes to the bliss of non-being, and they converge at the point when Susan wildly surfs the Internet in an attempt to discover material sufficiently disturbing to shock her back from the morbid abyss that she faces. She discovers enough 'Graveyard doggers. [...] autopsy pornography. Auto-strangulation pornography. Transplant donor pornography' (Hall, 2010: 173) to sate the most jaded appetite, but all she sees is 'loss and longing' (Hall, 2010: 173) tied to the banal logistics of money-making: 'The film paused a second later and a window appeared asking you for payment details' (Hall, 2010: 174). Her own emptiness can only come to a conclusion when her body is once again filled by a living presence – the embryo created by her affair. At this point, loss gives way to replenishment and allows her to move, at the novel's conclusion, towards a position of affirmative subjectivity. Like Giorgio's quiet acceptance of his death and Peter's determined desire to live in the world, Susan's narrative resolves with a moment of self-reclamation. Her final exclamation on realising the confirmation of her pregnancy is a resounding affirmation of herself as a singularity and as a meaningful work of art: 'Yes, you say. I'm here' (Hall, 2010: 286).

Violent self-negation leads Susan back to selfhood and to herself as a physically embodied individual, and can thus be regarded as a liberating transgression. For Annette Tambroni, transgression is to be feared and not embraced. Her life is dictated by the frames that are placed around her and within which she must negotiate the shape of her life at the very time when she is losing her eyesight. Unlike the Tambroni men, Annette is not free to explore the world around her, or to escape the overbearing domination of her mother; where they express their passions freely, she is required to subdue, ignore, and, if possible, eradicate hers. Her increasing blindness metaphorises the limited vision she is allowed as a young Italian woman in the 1960s. It moves from a gentle snow falling before her eyes to an ability to discern only shapes and patches of darkness and light, and, as she is increasingly confined to the memories of her surroundings, she falls further beneath the conservative yoke of her mother's Catholicism. The rigorous circumscription of her expectations and conduct lead to her being removed from school and largely restricted to interactions with the outside world which can be carefully policed, including her job selling flowers for the family business and her regular pilgrimages to the cemetery to tend the graves of her father and Signor Giorgio. Her whole life falls under the constraints of her mother's opinion 'that a frame should be placed around her life so that everything is contained and manageable. She is at risk. She is vulnerable' (Hall, 2010: 169).

The vulnerability that her mother emphasises is primarily a sexual one, for she believes that Annette will fall prey to the inveterate desires of men and must be constrained from viewing herself as in any way sexual. The onset of menstruation is deemed a reason for shame and Annette's physicality is acknowledged only by the incestuous flirtations of her brother, Mauri. As she is increasingly forced back on her imagination for a understanding of the world, she develops vivid fantasies of being stalked by the 'Bestia', a slavering, leering demon in a painting of the crucifixion that she saw as a young girl on a visit to church and that continues to haunt her as an adult. Her mother colludes in the mythologisation of the creature by crossing herself vigorously and changing the subject whenever her daughter asks about him, so for Annette the Bestia becomes the compacted manifestation of all the worldly fears against which she has been warned. Her life is framed by the fear of violation and by the fear of the frame that surrounds her life being crossed. In her increasingly lurid visions of the creature, he is freed from the painting and intent on seeking her out, reflecting not just her internalisation of the devouring sexuality of men but also an anxiety about the literal truth of art. If the Bestia can descend from his painting and exist in her world, then the boundary between what is art and what is real disappears; art and reality become intertwined in a more malevolent way than that she has learnt from her classes with Signor Giorgio.

With him she has sourced ochre in the hills outside her village, ground it, and made it into yellow paint, and from him she has learnt 'that as artists you are free to paint whenever you choose' (Hall, 2010: 145). Signor Giorgio's artisanal tutoring, which stresses that the space between reality and its depiction is full of all imaginable things, counteracts the doctrinaire strictness of Annette's mother's prohibitions, so it is appropriate that when Annette finally encounters the Bestia it is in Giorgio's tomb. The scene brings together the dominant worldviews that she has inherited from both her mother and her tutor. As she is raped by an unknown assailant, she submits herself as if the act is an inevitable culmination of her own unexamined desires. There are echoes with Tom and Susan's sex as her attacker covers her face with her dress, and, as he bears his weight down on her, the narrative infers that Annette is killed:

> Small fireworks detonate inside her skull. Her legs kick. Her eyes feel as if they will break like yolks. The fit throwing her body up will snap her ligaments and break her spine, but she cannot stop it. There is one last flash in her head, and then she calms, and her feet still. (Hall, 2010: 267–268)

There is ambiguity about Annette's experience here, and Hall deliberately draws us back to the sex–death duality of 'The Mirror Crisis' in order to muddy the water. Are we witnessing Annette's final breath, her first orgasm, or both? In the paragraphs that follow, Annette dreams that she is restored to sight and witnesses all in the village going about their daily business; she also witnesses her attacker/murderer hastily leaving the scene. The culmination of the narrative is thus an obscure fusion of the themes of the novel – sex, death, art, and life – and, like Annette, we are ultimately left in the dark. But, just as the Bestia descends from its frame into the real world, so we might see Annette's post-mortem paragraphs as an escape from her narrative into the realm between art and life.

At an early point in the novel, Peter wonders about the psychological effects of a disfiguring accident on a poet friend and ponders why he had not engaged in 'some kind of formal quarrel with what had happened' (Hall, 2010: 82). This seems to me a neat way of approaching each of the narratives in *How to Paint a Dead Man* for it highlights perfectly the rancour and difficulty these protagonists find in accommodating their inchoate experiences of the world within formal settings. Each is engaged in quarrelling with the world around them, attempting to wrestle with the intractable and the unpropitious circumstances of their lives in order to construct a way of looking at the world that is artful. For Giorgio, this happens in his bottle paintings, which reduce the world down to a depthless materiality that can be endlessly shaped and reshaped; Susan is lost within her reckless adultery, which threatens her relationship and her profession but enables her to connect with the world through unfeeling self-obliteration; Annette is framed by the precepts of Catholic doctrine and her imagination; and Peter is lost in the kind of bohemian narcissism that protects him from acknowledging his duty to others. Each of these protagonists struggles to craft her/his life into an order that s/he can accept, but Hall's use of the term 'quarrel' is apt in another sense, for it conveys a kind of discordance that is born of intimacy, of knowing the world in a very personal way yet finding it obdurately resistant to interpretation. There is a domestic quality to the term 'quarrel' which implies ongoing struggle for mastery, but for Hall this is not incompatible with the frozen 'deadness' of the still-life. In fact the dominant artistic motif in her novel effectively captures the world in mid-quarrel, pinning it at a moment of hiatus in the ongoing struggle between 'Oh, life, sex, death, art....'.

The Beautiful Indifference (2011)

Without doubt, Hall is a writer of great formal and technical skill who has produced strikingly different fictions at each turn. A pastoral tragedy, an extravagantly described historical drama, a sci-fi-inflected dystopia, an intricately mirrored tetratypch, and, in 2011, a collection of short stories characterised by the ghostly, the brutal, and the threatening. Though there are threads which unite all these works, Hall's experimentation with form marks her out as adventurous in a literary fiction market that has become saturated by sameness. She has commented in interview about the pressure to explain her work to readers, and suggested that her writing is only ever partly a reflection of her as a novelist: 'people always try and label you by your work. But my work is of me, it's not me' (in Allfree, 2011). We see this sense of her channelling something both personal and indistinct most effectively in her short stories. It is a form which is particularly suited to her interest in the sub-strata of the eventual, the layers of disorderly semi-perception which underlie the experiences of the world around her protagonists, and which reflect their sense of provisionality. Very little is determined in Hall's writerly universe – however things are, they could have been other. This is a quality which has certainly developed in her work, and it runs curiously counter to the flinty solidity of her Cumbrian settings. The hardness of her landscapes and their skeletal quiddity blend with the frailties and caprice of the humans that inhabit them to create an uncannily ethereal, yet materially substantial, universe.

It is a determinacy in indeterminacy that is perfectly captured by her use of the short story format.

Two phrases from the stories stand out as illustrative of Hall's overall vision in putting *The Beautiful Indifference* together: 'The shock of the real' (Hall, 2012: 50) and 'managed tension' (Hall, 2012: 17). Both phrases point to consistent thematic threads that run through the stories, as well as to Hall's methodological approach in this collection. The former comes from the title story, a tale about an early-middle-aged woman's largely sexual relationship with a considerably younger man, set against a backdrop of low-level violence and disruption after the York horse races. The latter is taken from the opening story, 'Butcher's Perfume', and describes the emotional state of the Slessor household in Penrith but more broadly relates to the barely suppressed undertow of violence that, for Hall, characterises the borderlands between the north of England and the south of Scotland. Both phrases, and both stories, are exemplary of the collection as a whole for they focus the short story's formal disquiet through the shocking irruption of violence and threat into otherwise ordinary existences. Hall is interested in the kinds of tension that are released as the usual gives way to the extreme and the known suddenly becomes dangerously obscured. Across the stories, forms of threat lurk in the penumbra of the protagonists' awareness but only become palpable in moments of jarring realisation. Hall manages the build-up and release of tension repeatedly through these stories, but nowhere better than in the gothic 'She Murdered Mortal He' and in her own take on Scandinavian noir, 'Vuotjärvi'.

The latter describes a young couple's seemingly idyllic summer holiday by a Finnish lake through the point of view of the woman. Wrapped in the perfect isolation of their retreat and glorying in the unbroken time spent together, the couple are disporting themselves in the water when the woman is suddenly gripped by the kind of nameless terror that occurs when one is out of one's depth:

> The lake depth was unknown and the pressure against her limbs was a trick: it felt no greater than in the shallows. Underneath was vestigial territory. Rotting vegetation. Benthic silence. The scale of her body was terribly wrong. Something was reaching up, pulling down. (Hall, 2012: 172)

The otherworldliness of the water's depths – 'no more than a black imagining' (Hall, 2012: 171) – induce an uncanny horror that spooks the woman and opens in her a sense of the place's potentiality for darkness. It is an unspecified anxiety that grows when her partner, having departed to swim to a distant island in the lake, disappears from view, and becomes unmanageable the longer he remains invisible. Taking their small dinghy, she begins to track his path only to discover that she has omitted to replace the bung designed to drain the bilge water, and her small boat is rapidly taking on water far from shore. The story ends with the woman desperately rowing for land whilst the water rises. It is a work of carefully managed tension; the woman's anxiety grows and recedes as the dangers move from the abstract to the real and back, but the reader is left with a sense of the ominous imbalance of control between the individual and the environment, a control that is based, in part at least, on the asymmetry of the known and the unknown. Nothing categorically catastrophic happens in the story, but the story leaves the ineradicable sense that it could have done and might still do.

'She Murdered Mortal He' conveys a similarly progressive sense of tension but concludes with a more conventionally gothic twist. Again, the focus is on a young couple in the transitional phase of their relationship where novelty is succumbing to the uncertainties of permanence, and, like in 'Vuotjärvi', the setting is alien – a newly constructed resort in a war-torn southern African nation. The man's revelation that he is unsure about the future of the relationship drives the woman from their beachside hut and into an environment suffused with multiple threats. Suddenly open to vivid fantasies of being preyed upon – by leopards, local men, the voracious sea-waters – she plunges forwards caught between a self-righteous recklessness and a nagging suspicion that her bullishness is self-defeating and ultimately risky. When she notices a distant white shape moving swiftly towards her, she is torn over whether it represents her regret-filled and solicitous partner or some animal spirit with violent designs on her. It turns out to be a dog, but the immediate release of tension does not last long. The men in the bar she visits offer her no harm, but there is a palpable sense of her vulnerability in a context over which she has little control. There is a compelling gothic quality to the story (appropriate considering that it was originally included in a special issue of *Granta* magazine on horror) which extends to the female protagonist's job as a ghost-tour guide. Yet the true tension of the story lies between the man and the woman and the different visions of the relationship that they have developed over the preceding year. The woman wonders at one point about the parallelism of their worlds, about how that which has brought them together has been kept company by that which pulls them apart:

> But the true argument had seemingly come out of nowhere. As if with her arch invitation to speak his mind, she had conjured from a void the means to destroy everything. As if he had suddenly decided it could end. Like deciding he wanted her phone number. Like deciding to get a spare door key cut for her. How easily inverted the world could be. How dual it was. (Hall, 2012: 135)

Hall emphasises the proximity of comfort and threat here, drawing attention to the balance in which they are maintained. Far from domesticity succeeding novelty, or the known replacing the unknown, such phenomena co-exist in both time and space, displacing simplistic binarism with indivisibility. Though the story oscillates between tension and relief, Hall's writing suggests their natural complicity rather than antagonism. This comes more fully into focus at the conclusion when the woman returns to the beach hut to discover her partner has been badly mauled by an unknown animal, perhaps the dog the woman has befriended and which had returned to her with blood on its muzzle. The ironic sting in the tail is thus the woman's complicity in a form of displaced violence against her lover at the very moment at which she seemed to be most in danger. The story's title also points us towards this reading as it quotes a lyric from the Bob Dylan song 'Love Henry' which tells of a woman who murders her lover on finding out that he has another woman.

The threat of violence is ever present in the stories of *The Beautiful Indifference*, and the thinness of the veil of civility is constantly at risk of being exposed. Throughout, violence – though, in the present context, wildness may be a better term – is associated with the animal and with the animalistic behaviours of the human. Whether it is wolves ('Vuotjärvi'); dogs or leopards ('She Murdered Mortal He'); bees or foxes ('Bees'); horses ('Butcher's Perfume'; 'The Beautiful Indifference'); mink ('The Nightlong River'); or non-specific preying creatures ('The Agency'), animals feature heavily in this collection. Most are undomesticated, some embody an intensity of instinctual drive that sets them clearly apart from humans, and others are exploited by the human world. But in each story there is a clear familial relationship that suggests that the borderline between the human and the animal is indistinct and that underlying the interactions of the social world are predatory and atavistic impulses. In 'The Agency', a story about a middle-aged woman's adventure into buying sado-masochistic sex from a discreet and well-heeled agency, Hannah is introduced to the idea by her friend Anthea, who is described at one point as sitting 'in almost predatory stillness, for almost an hour or more [...] mobile face set, and only her eyes moved as she surveyed the scene, marking, biding' (Hall, 2012: 95). 'The Beautiful Indifference' contrasts the gentility of York's medieval streets with the casual, anti-social destructiveness of the drunken race-goers, and describes the meetings between the couple in analogous terms: 'They were perfectly capable of having conversations, about politics, their occupations, anything. But they were not capable of corralling the animal necessity of ruining each other first' (Hall, 2012: 43). There is such elision of culture and nature throughout the collection, focusing often on sex and violence as points of intersection, where the illusion of human exceptionalism is exposed to the presence of the animal as a harbinger of the uncanny. In 'Bees', sexual violence within a marriage rends the mask of acceptability from the face of domination, but it is in 'Butcher's Perfume', perhaps the most original story in the collection, that Hall articulates her theme most fully.

The story is set in Hall's familiar Penrith and is self-consciously northern in its frequent use of Cumbrian and Border dialect ('lajful', 'chor', 'gannan', kessen') and also in the construction of a particular attitudinal bite in her protagonists. The north, Hall has argued 'is separate. Particularly Cumbria, because it's so cut off. You get into the interior and you are surrounded by mountains. There's a lawless aspect in terms of people's opinions' (in Allfree, 2011: 41). Her characters have what Sister calls in *The Carhullan Army* 'Northern Brio' (Hall, 2007a: 84), and there are certainly familial similarities between Jackie Nixon and Vivian Slessor both in the ways in which they manage tension and in their impatience with the weaknesses of others. Above all, though, 'Butcher's Perfume' is a story of Cumbrian landscape as a space of brutal contestation; it is 'burnt-farm, red-river, raping territory. A landscape of torn skirts and hacked throats, where roofs were oiled and fired, and haylofts were used to kipper children' (Hall, 2012: 23). Hall's Borders embody a history of tension and violence, and, as major cities give way to 'the last run before Scotland' (Hall, 2012: 22), the land retains a sense of temporary ownership. It is still a forbidding, dangerous land, one where ancient slaughter has given way to car accidents as drivers 'leaned hard on the accelerator [...] through these stretches, not checking the rear-view mirror' (Hall, 2012: 24). Hall repeatedly emphasises how the county's violent past underpins the character of the people who live in it, and, just as the dialect words punch their way through the standardised English of Kathleen's narration, so her story is punctuated by moments of regurgitated brutality. As the story opens, Manda Slessor, a study in teenage alienation, is threatening a fellow schoolgirl but is not required to inflict retribution because the threat of violence is sufficient to make the girl droop 'like rabbit-skin, like carrion' (Hall, 2012: 6) The knowledge of Manda's hardness, like Vivian Slessor's children's awareness that the opinions of their mother are not to be challenged, militates against explosive confrontation – the possibility of violence is enough.

Sexual tension is managed in a similarly ungainly but customised fashion. The story is sensuous in the way it maintains a balance between sexual threat and erotic desire, and there is fecundity in the kind of unconstrained, unapologetic, unselfconscious sexual urgency that the Slessors display. It is a fecundity which is inextricably linked with decay and death, and reintroduces Hall's interest in kinds of sex which are stripped of their sanitised and commoditised safety nets. Sex is filthy in her writing, as when Aaron Slessor boasts of having being fellated by a girl kneeling in horse-shit, and the intensity of it grows from its proximity to that which is truly unmanageable – death. In the moments before Kathleen shows him a stricken horse, dying from its owner's neglect, Aaron grabs at her, believing that she has led him into the barn for sex. Though the sight of the horse kills all sexual desire, it releases its violent relative; that which has been restrained beneath the surface of the story is liberated with an outburst of violence against the owner which leaves him, like his horse, unlikely ever to walk again. The narrator emphasises that the retribution that the Slessors inflict is not sentimental; it stems not from a sense of offence about the rights of animals but rather from the necessity of maintaining the proper balance between the worlds of manifest and latent desires. As horse-trainers, the Slessors have constructed a means of managing the conflicts of instinct and sociability through animals, and the violation of one of those animals threatens to undermine the hierarchy of control by which they live. So, where the borderline between safety and danger in 'Vuotjärvi' and 'She Murdered Mortal He' was brought shockingly to mind but (possibly) not crossed, the shock of the real in 'Butcher's Perfume' is exactly the moment when the distinction gives way. As Kathleen stands before the unbearable suffering of the animal, the knowledge of the darkness beneath and around is not just glimpsed but squarely regarded.

In modified forms, the same knowledge is apparent in all the other stories. Even in 'The Agency', where the numbing influence of commercial transaction displaces the danger of transgressive sex into a carefully moderated exchange as banal as rinsing yoghurt pots for recycling, the nexus of sex, violence, and death is present. Detailing her desires as if selecting from a well-judged wine list, Hannah ponders more extreme offerings: '*Film, Restraints, Doll, Defecation*' (Hall, 2012: 109, italics in original), all part of the *smörgåsbord* of personal choice in a consumerist society. That society may cordon such desires behind fantasies of consequence-less invulnerability, but, as Hall makes clear, the anxieties that attend danger and wildness are irrepressible. However, it would be false to apply a negative reading of wildness in these stories. Instead it is the proximity of sex, violence, and death that breeds spiritual vitality. The closeness to catastrophe is frequently what defines the temper of safety in Hall's view, and acknowledging or embracing the darkness of the unknown healthily maintains a link to the animal that is trammelled by socialised behaviours.

In 'The Nightlong River' we are presented with the loosening of those restraints, as the protagonist, Dolly, hunts mink with her brothers in order to make her dying friend a warming stole. Killing in order to commemorate life unleashes an atavism that makes Dolly feel not only in tune with the animal world but also the master of death: 'The truth of death is a peculiar thing. For there was a fascination to these evenings that went past utility or sport. We were in the hinterlands, a wilding place, where the reign was entirely ours. We were the wolves. We were the lions' (Hall, 2012: 159). 'The truth of death', she later modifies, is the simple fact of no longer being alive when the moors and mountains persist. Impermanence is an irreducible and ineluctable given of life and it is one which is variously accepted and denied in *The Beautiful Indifference*. Life cannot, Hall suggests, be rescued from the mud, blood, and shit of the past, of the landscape, and of the animal, by a clean, safe, efficient, and predictable modernity which replaces magical thinking with a watertight rationality. Nor can life be separated from death, or sex from violence. Whichever imaginative tools are used to fashion their distinction, we are inexorably drawn back to their points of intersection and to the reminder that, regardless of the advancement of civil society, it is never entirely possible to outdistance the mayhem on which it was built.

'Mrs Fox'

Hall won the 2013 BBC National Short Story Award with 'Mrs Fox', a narrative which uses David Garnett's short novel *Lady into Fox* (1922) as a model. The story focuses on a woman's metamorphosis into a vixen and the phases of her husband's horrified, grief-stricken, accepting, and ultimately respectful reaction. It is a tale with a strongly political through-line: gradual urban encroachment and settlement into the edgelands of cities transforms the landscapes and desecrates with modern 'arable' (Hall, 2014: 4) coloured houses the 'protean' (Hall, 2014: 27), fecund (Hall, 2014: 28), and 'mythical' (Hall, 2014: 30) environment. The ancient woodlands on the edges of the housing estate in which the couple live are being haggled over by 'councillors who dine in expensive restaurants with developers' (Hall, 2014: 29–30), the only thing protecting them from destruction being a 'tenuous council ruling' (Hall, 2014: 29). But the story has allegorical import too which ties back to Hall's work in *The Beautiful Indifference*.

Sophia's wildness as a fox strikes her husband as a deliberate turning away from the 'disease of being human' (Hall, 2014: 15), a stripping away of the comfortable social self to find an uncorrupted authentic animality. On researching mythical transmogrifications, he is pained to learn that they are reputed to come about as 'an act of will' (Hall, 2014: 21), which strikes him initially more as a rejection of him than of a world-weariness at the couple's middle-class insularity. His despair at his wife's metamorphosis manifests as an unwillingness to accept the necessities of her new condition. He keeps her locked in the house, attempts to feed her processed food rather than acknowledge her killing instinct, and even wonders about the possibilities of sexual congress. Thus, for all his grief, his instinct is territorial and it is only grudgingly that he accepts he must allow her her freedom. Once this act of generosity has been granted, she returns it by leading him to her den and revealing to him the cubs that he immediately asserts are his to nurture and, 'if it comes to it, lie down in front of the diggers before they level this shrine' (Hall, 2014: 32). Both are thus ultimately introduced to a new way of being, whilst the remorselessly acquisitive society of which they are a part trundles on its journey of destruction. Finally, it is not the loss of the human that the man abhors but the loss of the animal: 'he thinks of the fox, in her blaze, in her magnificence. It is she who quarters his mind, she whose absence strikes fear into his heart. Her loss would be unendurable' (Hall, 2014: 36).

The Wolf Border (2015)

In embryonic form, 'Mrs Fox' contains many of the elements of Hall's fifth novel. The threat to wilderness of economic expediency, the misguided impulse to dominate the natural world, and the symbiotic co-existence of the civilised and feral are all considered in greater depth in *The Wolf Border*, but the trope that transfers most insistently is the porosity between the condition of human and non-human animality. Where 'Mrs Fox' employed an extended transmogrification metaphor to articulate the easy slippage between states, the novel relies on naturalist characterisation to suggest the consanguineous continuum between human and wolf. Rachel Caine – the novel's chief protagonist – spoors, marks, and displays much as the wolves that she conserves do, and, though she retains her human shape, Hall makes clear that she should be read as a hybrid. As such, she represents the contestation of instinctual and rational drives that have underpinned the representation of human behaviour in all Hall's fiction. Organised yet frenzied; creative yet destructive; familiar yet alien; managed yet wild – these are the characteristics of both her human actors and the environments that they inhabit, inseparably co-determined. Rachel, like Janet Lightburn, Jackie Nixon, Sarah Cauldicutt, and Vivian Slessor before her, straddles the border between the human and non-human, drawing and channelling a fierce energy derived from the uncertainty of the both/and dichotomy.

The Wolf Border feels like the natural coalescence of Hall's constellation of writerly concerns into a narrative that is deliberately shaped by the political timeliness of the mid-2010s. Hall has commented that the novel contains 'everything I've learned about writing over the years' (in Crown, 2015) and there are familiar hallmarks: the speculative scenario of *The Carhullan Army* is there in the counter-historical victory of the independence movement in the 2014 Scottish referendum; the Cumbrian landscape with all its 'sweet, spermy fragrance' (Hall, 2015: 85) is as ever present as is an agonised female protagonist trapped between duty and desire. But the novel elicits fresh ideas as well, in particular a dramatisation of the emotional conflict arising from childbearing and a more trenchant political engagement than previously.[3] The plot centres on an experiment in rewilding – the reintroduction of wolves to Cumbria – dreamt up by Thomas Pennington, the Earl of Annerdale, who brings Rachel back from her work on an Idaho reservation to act as the project's manager. In many ways, however, the context for the experiment is more significant than the content, for it functions in parallel with the Scottish independence referendum of September 2014 to address questions of freedom and self-determination in the face of rigidly upheld hierarchies, whether on the scale of the pack or the nation. As required by a plot device that involves the erection of inescapable animal pens, the wolves escape, cross the border in the days immediately after the electorate has voted to secede from the United Kingdom, and are enthusiastically embraced by the Scottish nation as a symbol of its return to an authentic wildness.

In all this there is a discourse of political critique, one reminiscent of *The Carhullan Army*. The United Kingdom is governed by a social set committed primarily to maintaining its privileged position and perpetuating an order of conservative patriarchalism based on exclusivity and calculated blindness to change. The satire of the Conservative and Liberal Democrat coalition administration (2010–2015) is impossible to mistake, as is the caricature of David Cameron in the fey, aristocratic prime minister, Sebastian Mellor. Hall paints a political class – from which the new Scottish first minister, Caleb Douglas, is not exempted – as haughtily self-absorbed and ideologically opportunistic, but they are also rapaciously single-minded when it comes to the defence of their privilege. As their representative, Pennington is characterised by Rachel as a supreme predator, positioned in relation to other social classes as the wolf is to its prey; he is 'a behemoth among ordinary men; he resides at the apex, above all trophic levels' (Hall, 2015: 232). This reference to the aristocratic class as the pinnacle of the food chain explicitly parallels the predatory dynamic that governs the natural world, and it associates the upper classes with the ills of a rigid and formalised social hierarchy against which the Scots, and Rachel, grate.

Rachel's is a politics of upheaval that regards the complacency of inherited privilege with disgust; such elitism is not just morally abhorrent, as far as she is concerned, but fundamentally unhealthy to the social ecosystem. The lack of a mobile, adaptable political ethos has resulted in the stultification

of the nation as a whole for 'the English, bred to feel superior for generations but lacking any real desire for improvement or vision, seem intolerable' (Hall, 2015: 227). The vitrified advantage of the aristocratic classes she
believes – mistakenly in Pennington's case – has produced a morbid resistance to change and has thereby become increasingly entropic. Everything
about Pennington she despises on principle: his casual accomplishment,
relaxed good humour, and cultured dishevelment are the by-products of the
leisure that wealth endows as far as she is concerned, and should be rejected
as little more than window-dressing. The ample salary and indentured
estate cottage that she accepts as part of her contract represent a necessary
noblesse oblige that she finds tolerable only so long as she considers them a
sop to the earl's social conscience. She immediately takes against the pol-
ished finishing-school sophistication of Pennington's daughter, Sylvia, and
dismisses her desire to work on the project as trustafarian dabbling. She ste-
reotypes Pennington's son, Leo, as a self-styled black sheep, and concocts an
unsubstantiated narrative of his complicity in the death of his mother. She
resents the stand-offishness of Pennington's staff, convinced that they are
working against her, and condemns individually and severally those of his
associates with whom she is required to mix. In short, she is about as sceptical of the value of wealth as she is certain that the earl's rewilding ambitions
are shallow and vain.

For Rachel, involving herself in the Annerdale project is primarily therefore a means to a zoological end, and, as cynical as this seems, it is consistent
with a character raised to regard the world around her with an aggressive
distrust of the ambiguity of complex interpersonal and social signification.
From childhood, Rachel has learnt a utilitarian semiotic vocabulary from
a mother, Binny, for whom children were a hindrance to the well-honed
seductive persona that she cultivated. Binny's testiness with the needs of
Rachel and her half-brother, Lawrence, is prompted by an impatience with
the inefficiencies of intimacy, which require the navigation of complex emotional and affective waters. Binny prefers the simple sign systems of desire
without attachment, pleasure without responsibility; her erotic relationships have been a question of 'arriving in the village, taking the spoils, then
razing everything to the ground' (Hall, 2015: 72) and, through the walls of
their home, Rachel has frequently heard 'the sound of male weeping, a sound
exotic and horrendous. And her mother's vexed responses. *Buck up, man,
there was never anything to it. Go back home to her*' (Hall, 2015: 72). Such
serial drama has driven Lawrence away from home at the earliest opportunity and has sent Rachel into career itinerancy, moving between conserva-
tion projects and investing her libidinal energies in understanding the social
structures of the wolf pack. When sexual desire overcomes her, she satiates

it with practical, uncomplicated couplings that mimic the performance of availability that she witnesses in her charges: 'She braces against the cab wall and he holds her hips. There is just movement and noise, flesh slapping. [...] Then it is automatic, impossible to stop. A man's identity is revealed in the habit of climax; it is the real introduction' (Hall, 2015: 41). Given that Rachel has learnt from Binny that passion does not endure, she discards the human pantomime of romance in favour of a more instinctual release.

This self-severance from the emotional dimension of relationships involves a turning inwards that is familiar from many of Hall's other female protagonists, but here it is given more aetiology. Rachel's fascination with wolves is closely associated with her mother's bitter selfishness, for her first encounter with the animals occurs when Binny dismisses her on a visit to a zoo to leave the field clear for her flirting. Coming across the wolf pen, Rachel experiences an early presentiment of her vulnerability within the world, a vulnerability that is tied to a 'pre-erotic fear' (Hall, 2015: 6) and a sense of herself as viscera: her fast-beating heart 'smells bloody' (Hall, 2015: 7) under the gaze of the wolf. The consciousness of herself as prey sustains throughout her life and informs her relationships, particularly with men. She is dismayed and disarmed by power, submitting to it at the same time that she resists because she associates it with a timeless immanence deriving from a predetermined order. There is a distinction to be made here between Rachel's submission to men and her submissiveness in a negative sense. She is in no way presented as a weak character but rather one that is determined by her conviction in the healthfulness of orderly systems and the placedness of individuals within those systems; to submit is not necessarily to be submissive but to recognise one's place of belonging. The controlled, almost casual supremacy of the wolf matches that of Pennington, for whom the security of class belonging is given forth in an easeful command of the world around him; neither needs to display their power for it is embodied and understood. Coming into contact with it is profoundly disconcerting and disabling for Rachel, however, for she struggles to maintain a sense of her own capability in the face of it, exacerbated by her tendency to accept her place within the food chain.

This quarrel with herself illustrates the novel's engagement with a duality between free will and predetermination. For Rachel things are as they have always been and are dominated by the codes, inhibitions, and narratives that have grown to accommodate instinctive and animal behaviours. She thinks rigidly, dismissing her relationship with her mother as an example of predetermination: 'Nothing would have changed the dynamic, no more than the elliptical orbit of planets can be altered by human hand. She had the only version of her mother she could have had; Binny had the only daughter. In some ways they were motherless, daughterless' (Hall, 2015: 70). In many ways she is a poor reader who extrapolates from animal behaviours to understand the world through a system of reductive and unsubtle signs. As immersed as she is professionally in the signification of instinctive behaviour, she cannot see beyond that to any more sophisticated psychological nuance, and, because she cannot understand her mother's indifference towards her, she regards it as being the only possible course that events could have taken. Towards her brother she exhibits a similar lack of faith in the human will, falling back on biology to explain her distance from him: 'She even used to think, once she'd learnt enough biology, that her programming meant she wasn't supposed to care for him – they had different genes' (Hall, 2015: 126). This conviction in predetermined patterns and outcomes renders her thinking inflexible, her prejudices unnegotiable, and her decision-making programmatic. Once she discovers that she is pregnant from a one-night stand with a co-worker, there is little jeopardy in the pages where she tries to make a decision about whether to undergo an abortion – she has little room for manoeuvre either psychologically or narratively.[4] Such a mindset also determines her acceptance of the offer to lead the Annerdale project only after Binny's death, for, like the wolf pups who bear no children of their own until one of their parents dies, her life is dictated by the domination of the previous generation. Once relieved of her duty to her mother to remain powerless, she can return home to give birth to her son.

Back in Cumbria, the narrative bifurcates between the gradual introduction of the wolves onto the estate, and the birth of Charlie and the closening of the relationship between Rachel and Lawrence he produces. For many of the novel's reviewers this splitting of focus diminished the narrative's tension, and certainly the increasing attention on Lawrence's struggles with drug addiction and marital break-up – sub-plots on anyone's terms – reduce the diegetic drive to walking pace.[5] The two strands are, however, woven together by modulations on the themes of wildness and belonging, with Rachel's increasingly unfamiliar pregnant body metonymising the uncanniness of the alien within. Where the wolves alter the ecology of the Cumbrian landscape, Charlie effects a similar transformation on Rachel, overtaking her body and causing mutations that she experiences as profoundly disconcerting. He represents a different kind of submission on her part that she indulges equally grudgingly but from which she cannot extricate herself. Hall details the territorialisation of the mother's body by her child as an abjectifying retreat from control as the internal stranger grows to influence every aspect of Rachel's physical and mental life. After birth, the demands are no longer solely physical but attain a hermeneutic dimension as she is forced to attune herself to the barrage of non-verbal signs that are

Charlie's way of conveying his needs. Having stripped back her interpretational apparatus to bare semiotic functionality, the intensity and immediacy of his demands leaves her struggling to read his otherness with any degree of acuity. Charlie provides the narrative with a human analogue for the wolves' strangeness, and, though it moves towards a sentimental dénouement, the novel never comfortably reconciles this notion of the wolf in human skin.

Hall draws very clear parallels between the wildness of the human and the non-human animal, making explicit the consonances between their distinct social systems and highlighting the instinctual drives that energise both. That human beings are dressed up animals – like the mysterious protestor against the Annerdale project who wears a business suit and papier mâché wolf head – is a point frequently iterated, and Hall's characteristic theme of the civilised veneer veiling only thinly the undertow of aggression and predation persists. But the text adds something new to this, which is the exploration of the sublimated fear of savagery. The Annerdale project is haunted by anxious protests and archaic prejudices about the wolves' rapacity. They stimulate subterranean and pre-social fears about human isolation and weakness precisely because they inhabit an imaginative, cultural space that has been safely cordoned behind the myth of extinction. That they had been eradicated from the British landscape had enabled the human animal to overcome the fear of predation and to assume the position of trophic supremacy. Their reintroduction acts as a reminder of the precariousness of the domination over nature that has been assuaged by centuries of control.

The wolves' reintroduction also discloses the latent desires for confrontation that Hall sees as underpinning human behaviour. Fear of the wolves' untameable nature is really a displaced anxiety about tensions in human packs, and, in the broader context, between the social and national structures that those packs erect. The Pennington family is fissured by resentments that gravitate around the accidental death of Thomas' wife, just as the Caine family is as rent by internal strife as that of its biblical namesake. On the national scale, the novel articulates the separatist aspirations of Scotland as part of the same sibling rivalry – Caleb Douglas and Sebastian Mellor are cut from the same fraternal cloth for all their political differences. The relationship between Scotland and England is one of managed tension, but the wolves have a catalytic effect on the release of the underlying aggression. They allow fears of otherness to be openly expressed, acting as a prompt not just for the public expression of antagonism but also for a triumphal glorification in incipient violence. The farmer who shoots dead one of the escaped wolf pups does so with a barely suppressed pride in his masculinity, but he is only the last in a line of those seeking to provoke the tension to such a degree that it erupts into violence. The fence is vandalised and the locks eventually sabotaged in the hope that destruction will be released, that the border will be crossed, and that there will be no retreat from the ensuing mayhem. The wolves are thus the expression both of unconscious fears and latent desires, contused symbolic representatives of humanity's death drive. They instil such anxiety in the protestors not for their innate predatoriness but for their status as cultural scapegoats, vicarious distillations of the urge for destructiveness that fills human beings.

However, the violent emotions that the wolves release may be seen as purgatives for they are associated throughout with the creation of a healthy ecology and with processes of cleansing and growth. One of the first things that Rachel notices on arriving at Annerdale manor is a statue of Romulus and Remus being suckled by a wolf, and this nurturing instinct that so goes against preconception is a consistent feature in their presentation throughout, where the raising of the pups is paralleled with the raising of Charlie. At the peak of the food chain, the wolves are intended to naturally regulate the deer populations, which otherwise need to be expensively managed, and the impact of this organic biodeterminism is total, filtering down the ecosystem to create a healthy balance between the land and its inhabitants. Everything Rachel sees as positive in this pyramidal structure she regards as negative in the social hierarchy, where power seems to coagulate at the top, starving the entire system of healthy winnowing. Yet she is as mistaken in her prejudices against the Pennington clan as the protestors are in their demonisation of the wolves. She grudgingly has to accept that Sylvia is a committed and willing worker; is proved wrong in her suspicions about estate manager Michael Stott and Leo as the saboteurs; and comes to realise that Thomas is a force for revolution rather than reaction. It is he who engineers the wolves' escape as a symbolic rewilding of the new Scottish nation, and he who enthusiastically assists the bureaucratic realities of independence. The symbolic violence that is involved in the secession of Scotland is ultimately purgative, for it cleanses – at least in the short term – the political ecosystem of a deadening conservatism. Rachel's anger is directed less at Pennington's calculated manipulation of her and the Annerdale project and more at the frustration of her own prejudices about the inertia of social privilege, but she ends the novel appreciative of the hope that is born from chaos:

> The plane flew over, looped round, following their trajectory. She and Lawrence watched as the four wolves loped onto the outskirts of Rannoch, its turf still bloody from autumn, as if battle-worn; the red bracken beginning to disappear under the first low-lying drifts. (Hall, 2015: 431–432)

The Wolf Border's counter-historical speculation deliberately foregrounds its contemporaneity in a way that nonetheless points to the broader issue of the management of a healthy society under capitalism. The wolves may find freedom in the Scottish midlands, but the politicking and manipulation that accomplish that freedom are anything but romantic. As she did in *The Carhullan Army*, where the autocratic leadership of Jackie metaphorised the dangerous appeal of ideological certainty in the post-9/11 world, Hall has produced a novel timely in its concern at the barely contained aggressivity that characterises the drift towards right-wing politics in the 2010s. The discrediting of collective action by a dominant neoliberal worldview, allied with the hollowing out of the political commitment to democracy in the West and the consequences of the global financial insecurity on nations as much as individuals, has seen the resurgence of well-worn fears of entropy and the collapse of social order. The potential dissolution of the United Kingdom, though historically averted in 2014, is for Hall an indicator of the increasing precariousness of the argument for commonality in unpropitious, politically reactionary times, for what is enabled by the prospect is rarely enlightened progressivism and more often the kinds of shallowly interred antagonistic recidivism that she has made a career out of charting.

Coda

Whilst Hall's writing intersects with others in this volume in its concerns with the disruptive effects of technology, the difficulties of shaping authentic selfhood, and the compensatory qualities of art, her commitment to a fiction of specific locale and regional mindset makes her distinct. Andrew O'Hagan and Jon McGregor gravitate around familiar topographies and incorporate transtextual resonances that build worlds with convincing texture and depth, but their engagement with place contains a restless desire to look outwards, to embrace the bigger picture of which their settings are a small part. Hall's gaze is always inwards, not in a parochial sense but as a function of the intensity that she sees in the affective relationship between her protagonists and the places from which they derive. As Rachel in *The Wolf Border*, Cyril in *The Electric Michelangelo*, and Susan in *How to Paint a Dead Man* demonstrate, her characters are drawn back to Cumbria through loyalties that they don't fully understand but that are connected to a noumenal anxiety. When they are away from the wildness of the fells, like the narrator of the story 'The Bees', they experience themselves as lost and feel compelled to recreate in miniature the bitter taste of a landscape that is indifferent to their nostalgia. For home represents a very conflicted kind of solace, and family a dubious consolation, in Hall's writing. The pull to return is matched by an equally powerful push away that stems from a landscape intent on rejecting any colonisation and which infuses the worldviews of those who inhabit the hills with a similar acrimony and an unyielding temperament. This contradictoriness is the real draw of Hall's writing and is where she stands apart from the lyrical revisioning of the pastoral evident in the current popularity of Simon Armitage, Richard Mabey, Robert Macfarlane, and Alice Oswald. Their desire to reconnect language to landscape in the face of irreversible change is not Hall's objective. Rather she portrays the necessary tearing away of self from the forbidding authority of place, a parturition that is as violent as it is ineffective. If the way to authenticity is through returning to nature, as much contemporary pastoral writing suggests, Hall's estimation is that the journey would be quarrelsome.

Notes

1 Hall acknowledges the influence of McCarthy on her writing in 'Stories of My Life' (Hall, 2008); she illustrates her familiarity with Conrad's text in Brown, 2007.
2 Later in the novel, Hall introduces another reference to the IRA when she has Sister quote Terence MacSwiney, Commandant of the 1st Cork Brigade and hunger striker: 'It is not those who can inflict the most, but those who can suffer the most that will conquer' (Hall, 2007a: 158).
3 Rachel Cusk has written equally eloquently about the moral ambivalences of motherhood in *A Life's Work: On Becoming a Mother* (Cusk, 2001).
4 In her review, Lionel Shriver wryly comments that 'fictional characters never have abortions any more' (Shriver, 2015).
5 See for instance Clark, 2010; Shriver, 2015; Tait, 2015; Taylor, 2015.

5

Jon McGregor

When Jon McGregor won the prestigious International IMPAC Dublin Literary Award in 2012 for *Even the Dogs*, his disturbing, polyphonic rendering of the lives of a group of drug and alcohol addicts in a midland city, Erica Wagner headlined her profile of him: 'Jon McGregor: The Best Novelist You've Never Heard Of' (Wagner, 2012). Though somewhat exaggerated, there is an element of truth in Wagner's description; for a novelist who has twice been longlisted for the Man Booker Prize, and who won a Somerset Maugham Award and the Betty Trask Prize for his first novel, *If Nobody Speaks of Remarkable Things*, McGregor has, to some extent, remained under the critical radar. He did not feature in either the 2003 or 2013 editions of Granta's *Best of Young British Novelists* collection, a decision which is astonishing given the maturity and technical accomplishment that his writing shows. Whilst Granta's selections can be hit and miss, and one should be wary of any such heavily publicised canonisation, however speculative, it is the case that McGregor's omission is an oversight.

To date, McGregor's output amounts to three novels – *If Nobody Speaks of Remarkable Things* (2002), *So Many Ways to Begin* (2006), *Even the Dogs* (2010) – and a collection of short stories, *This Isn't the Sort of Thing That Happens to Someone Like You* (2012). His writing falls somewhere between a northern social realist tradition and a modernist-inspired stylistic experimentation that employs extended narrative interventions – minimal punctuation, framing devices, prosopopoeia, typographical disruption – in order to portray contemporary experiences of (often urban) anomie and isolation. For some critics, these interventions are too intrusive and over-extended, becoming mere authorial quirks which inhibit the quality of expression, but often the fragmentation and defamiliarisation that these devices produce accord with McGregor's vision of a contemporary Britain in which isolation and provisionality have become markers of neoliberal individualism's

effects. In a narrow sense his writing is parochial – it focuses on the functioning and often dysfunctionality of small communities in specific locales – but to
regard it as limited in scope would be wrong. McGregor's pathos is human-
istic and his empathy universal; the limited frames which he sets himself –
whether they be the inhabitants of a street on a single day or a series of stories
about the fen landscapes of eastern England – mediate the reader's attention between the local and the global, the extrinsic and the immanent. His
narrative frames are merely the shapes he establishes in order to reveal how
shapeless and disconnected the experience of the contemporary world can
be. Though his characters seek the resonance of connection to others, and
the security of understanding their places in the social realm, these safety
nets are often denied them or at best are obliquely recognised as they retreat
into the distance.

For McGregor, the contemporary experience is identifiable with problems
of visibility, and, more often, invisibility. His fictions resound with the need to
be known, the need to be acknowledged for all the impenetrability, unknowability, and contradictoriness that attends subjectivity. The McGregor self is
never stable in the world in which s/he lives and is always dominated by an
overpowering sense of provisionality and by the fear of falling out of sight
completely. This is most sharply evident in the invisibility of the addict community in *Even the Dogs*, pushed to the city's edgelands in a novel where more
conventional citizens are all but absent. As dispiriting as these recurrent concerns sound, they reflect profound anxieties about the relationship between
the individual and the social body in a historical moment characterised by
the ideologically solipsistic and dividual. However, for all its pessimism,
McGregor's writing is never cynical. There remains, always, the fleeting possibility of absolute connection between the self and other, or the self with itself,
a moment of epiphanic convergence that he identifies in his first novel as the
'remarkable thing'. Becoming aware of how the ordinary world is infused
with extraordinariness is a romantic conceit that acquires real currency in
McGregor's writing. The simple act of touching another, hearing the fall of
the rain, assisting another to achieve her/his desire, or cherishing the shape
of familiarity are momentary transcendences which, though they never take
McGregor's protagonists far from their worlds, allow their limits to be seen
for a split second with untrammelled clarity.

If Nobody Speaks of Remarkable Things (2002)

McGregor's first novel depicts the comings and goings of the inhabitants
of a single street in a northern English town on 31 August 1997, the day on

which Princess Diana was killed in a car crash in Paris and the day on which a freak car accident injures one of the street's younger occupants. McGregor's street is a cosmopolitan mix of immigrant families, students, long-term indigenous residents, and those able to afford only the price of once stately, but now shabby, accommodation. One house is derelict, others have rubbish piled in their gardens, and low expectations, allied to the late summer heat, lend the setting an air of lethargy. Children play in the street whilst adults go about their routines with varying degrees of commitment and precision. Neighbourly relationships are characterised by casual acquaintance and the kind of low-level restless tension that has come to be accepted as the by-product of the cheek-by-jowl nature of modern urban living.

Despite the proximity of others, the lives of the inhabitants are underscored by isolation, provisionality, and private sorrows that they feel unable to share even with those closest to them. Life is lived, and small traumas are experienced, largely within the personal realm, contained by architectures of psychological reticence as solid as the bricks that physically separate the residents. The narratorial eye cuts between the houses, invading and inveigling into private space with an inquisitive prurience but rarely focalising through the perspectives of the characters. Rather we see them from the outside, pressed into shape by the weight of their lives and unwilling to contemplate the scale of what troubles them. Ironically, what goes unaddressed are often the things that they share most with their neighbours but guard as private sorrows: the loneliness of being unrecognised; the fear of death; the burdensome responsibility of others; anxiety about what the future holds; terror of not being in control. All these emotional states are heightened to pathological proportions by the particular pressures of individualism on contemporary consciousness, but it is the combination of the general existential fear and the particular diurnal manifestation that McGregor balances so well. In so doing, he accomplishes the task of expressing distance in closeness and alienation in identification: defining contradictions, he suggests, of the modern urban experience.

If Nobody Speaks of Remarkable Things is a novel about urban space and about the way in which that space conditions its inhabitants to see, and not see, the extraordinariness of the world around them. As a debut, it could never be charged with lacking ambition: not only does McGregor channel Virginia Woolf's *Mrs Dalloway* (1925) in its intensive temporal focus on the events of one day but he also evokes Joycean tropes in his depiction of the city as a place of grim and desensitising materiality. As with Joyce's Dublin, the deadening repetitiveness of life on the small scale is leavened by momentary glimpses of aesthetic possibility – the epiphanic potential of the 'remarkable thing' that can transform the everyday and personal into the rarefied and universal. The debt to modernist sensibility and technique is evident also in a multi-perspectivalism through which McGregor narrates the events of the day as a collage of partial and casually intersecting viewpoints, ultimately drawing the gaze of all to a single dramatic point at which the young Shahid Mohammed Nawaz is knocked over by a car. Visual perspective, and, in particular, the difficulties of seeing with fresh eyes, is at the heart of the novel's thematic and stylistic construction. It quietly articulates the paradox of the modern subject's intertwined fear of invisibility in the indifferent gaze of the other and the practised self-limiting of vision to the confines of subjects' immediate material environs. McGregor's characters crave recognition but blinker themselves into tunnels of perception that include only the proximate and immediately relevant.

McGregor's background in media technology – the subject of his undergraduate study at the University of Bradford – informs his writing with a visual sensibility that is accentuated by the imagistic precision of many of his descriptions, and stylistically *If Nobody Speaks* exploits the vocabulary of film-making to shift swiftly between individual perspectives and a prying omniscience. The novel cleverly modulates close-up intimacy with distance work that offers at once the textural detail of lived life and the expansive vision of the social stage. In balancing the opening sweep across the city or the giddying view from the top of a crane with the intense specificity of a man trying to wash life back into his damaged hands or the butterfly sunlight as it struggles through closed curtains, McGregor combines the particular and the general. Detail and context are thereby kept in frame, reminding the reader that, for all the sharp focus on the street's residents, the novel's vision is social and historical in a broader sense. This dual perspective is instantiated from the opening sweep across the sleeping city, which owes as much to a film's establishing panning shot as it does to the rhythmic narration of W.H. Auden's 'Night Mail' in the 1936 documentary of the same name and to the soft nocturnal monologue that introduces Llareggub in Dylan Thomas' *Under Milk Wood* (1954) – two texts which equally celebrate the beauty of the ordinary.

The narrative eye here is mobile and expansive, manoeuvring across the city as if perusing a living organism whose 'long breaths layered upon each other' recall 'a lullaby hum for tired streets' (McGregor, 2003: 1). For all its distance, the narratorial voice is enticed into the sensual evanescence of the city in the moment of an unregarded out-breath. McGregor interweaves panoramic views with the lilting susurrus of the narrator's call to hear the specific cadences of the city's night song. The resting pulse of the streets creates an intense beauty and sensory harmony that blends into tunefulness the city's man-made elements and natural phenomena:

> And all these things sing constant, the machines and the sirens, the cars blurting hey and rumbling all headlong and the shouts and the hums and the crackles, all come together and rouse like a choir, sinking and rising with the turn of the wind, the counter and the solo, the harmony humming expecting more voices. (McGregor, 2003: 2)

This choral fusion of the organic and the inorganic celebrates the 'crackled voice crying street names for taxis' alongside the 'treeful of birds tricked into morning' (McGregor, 2003: 3), incorporating the banal residues of the day before with the nascent possibility of the one to come. The entwined couple have 'not been a couple long, a few days perhaps, or a week, and they are still both excited and nervous with desire and possibility' (McGregor, 2003: 5). There is an attention here to the lyrical potentiality of the world, its immanence evident in a moment of unadorned *déshabillé*, and such fulsomeness infuses the panoramic method with an inclusive communality that contrasts dramatically with the insistence of the singular perspective that narrates the following chapter.

Here, we shift to the point of view of the 'girl with short hair and glasses', whose alternating chapters will counterpoint the disinterested observation of the third-person narrator. The clipped, end-stopped sentences that proleptically introduce the drama of the novel could not be further from the enjambment and inclusiveness of the prologue. They are dominated by personal pronouns, particularly 'I', and instantly arrest the movement of the camera eye, focusing it instead on the central moment of the day in question: the car accident, whose gravitational force draws the narrative strands unstoppably together. This sudden shift from expansiveness to singularity introduces another of McGregor's visual conceits: the tableau. Here, as elsewhere, he momentarily freezes the frame, reducing potentiality to a point of actuality and holding within his gaze the multiple threads of his story. 'I can see all these moments as though they were cast in stone, small moments captured and enlarged by the context, like figures in a Pompeii exhibition' (McGregor, 2003: 8), comments the narrator, broadening the historical frame but emphasising the importance of the participants' immobile responses both physically and mentally. She 'watched him moving across the street, the boy from number eighteen, and I tried to understand' (McGregor, 2003: 7), a snapshot that presents a decontextualised moment of seeing but without a frame of logic or causality, only uninterpretable data.

McGregor's use of tableaux facilitates a narratorial omniscience because it enables him to establish a scene and then move within it, assuming a number of perspectival positions and moving his actors around. This is notable in this early chapter, where the girl with short hair and glasses attempts to discern the import of the accident by plotting the positions of those involved, but it is used most effectively, and more critically, in the ultimate description of the accident scene. Here the pace of the action slows to a crawl, and the omniscient voice presents the tableau from a number of close and wide angles, introducing an imaginary CNN news team reporting on the incident in real time. The effect is to reintroduce movement, in contrast to the depiction of the scene by the girl, presenting the incident in its totality and from standpoints which go beyond the purely subjective. By positing the televisual newsworthiness of the event, McGregor draws attention to the shift from the ordinary to the remarkable and from the local to the global. For instance, as he stands watching in horror, the man with burnt hands experiences an urgent desire for interconnection:

> He imagines what would happen if the whole street called his [Nawaz's] name, joining with the mother's small voice, the whole street lifting the words and the words spreading through this city, taking flight like a flock of birds at dusk, clouding the sky, the voices all-present, across fields and forests and oceans, sent out, transmitted, broadcast, on BBC and CNN, satellite and terrestrial and international optic fibres, on billboards and buses and videoscreens, on flyers and posters and news-journals and magazines, the information, the name, pouring down from the sky like electronic rain, out from this one street and sucked down into the lightning-rod antennas that bristle from mansions and shantyhouses across all our misconnected world, a chorus of name-saying, a brief redemptive span of attention. (McGregor, 2003: 271–272)

There is desperation here; fear that, in an age of informational excess, the small details of individuals' lives are eclipsed by the restless cut to some more arresting novelty. But what is most striking about this passage is the re-emergence of movement: the perspective soars above the particuliarity of this street to embrace the ceaseless noise of human life. A moment of sublime recognition is being conjured, a fantasy of complete attention that allays the experience of deracinating anonymity. Yet the shift here is neither emancipatory nor redemptive; it lacks the hope of the prologue's flight, acknowledging the loss of the self as part of the contemporary condition and the unlikelihood of connection.

As a cry against the anonymising effect of contemporary society, the desperate plea for a collective enunciation of Shahid Mohammed Nawaz's name reminds us emphatically of the namelessness of the street's other residents. By referring to each of the protagonists only by the number of the house in which they live or by physical traits (the man with the moustache, the women with henna-red hair), McGregor deindividualises them, producing a flattening effect which is at odds with the depths of feeling through which so many of them struggle. Again the tableau is an appropriate analogue, for the withholding of names distances the reader from the characters to the point where our observation of their lives feels intrusive, as if we were examining them as pinned butterflies in a case – helpless, categorised, but darkly familiar. By positioning the numbered residents relative to each other, McGregor forces the reader's gaze through the speculative camera eye as it cuts from one house to another, glimpsing the flux of daily life but settling only briefly, and regarding the various psychodramas only obliquely.

The narrative's refusal of recognition here corresponds with the quality of forgetfulness that characterises the city's memory. Urban space is recycled space, and many of the residents on McGregor's street are painfully conscious that they are placeholders for those who will come after. The students in particular are sensitive to their transient condition, aware that 'a time of easy certainty had come to an end, and most of us had lost our nerve' (McGregor, 2003: 37). At the end of their studies, and at the end of a summer which marks the final period of adolescent insouciance, they await their calling into the world with a trepidation that it might never come. Each somehow seeks to make peace with the world that they are leaving, to negotiate a legacy that will substantiate the passed time. The female narrator peers behind posters attached to the walls of her bedroom, searching for unfaded wallpaper which would mutely attest to her impact; she thinks of all 'the other people who've slept in this room before me, about what traces they've left behind' (McGregor, 2003: 66) and wants 'to leave a note for the next tenant, leave a trace of myself behind, I wanted to be able to go back years later and find a plaque with my name on it screwed to the wall' (McGregor, 2003: 65). Similarly the unnamed young man from number eighteen leaves a 'jar between the floor joists, nesting it among the dust and the cables and pipes like an egg, a bundle of memories waiting to hatch into the future' (McGregor, 2003: 56–57). These acts of self-memorialisation emphasise the importance of the trace as a sign of continuity, an indelible mark of presence in a place that will be reused indefinitely.

One house on the street articulates the poignancy of this ambition to be remembered. Standing derelict, it is filled with the abandoned, unwanted debris of its last residents' lives – a school textbook, a radio, photographs – all gently deteriorating under a carapace of mould and fungus. The reader's voyeuristic observation of seemingly half-completed activities gains an uncanny quality with the recognition that the record on the player will never be heard and the textbook never closed. There is also an intense pathos at the unfulfilled hope that these objects' continued existence generates, as if the traces left behind might resonate a permanent connection to inhabited places. Yet the house's first floor recounts a different history to the prying gaze of the young girl through whom this section is focalised:

Mice, making nests from scraps of magazines and bedding, their tiny pink eyes staring back at her. Bats, hanging in wardrobes like tiny folded umbrellas. Pigeons clustered in the corner of another room, murmuring and scratching and loosening their droppings onto the threadbare carpet. Spiders' webs woven thicker than net curtains, skirting boards honeycombed by woodworm, blue-green algae blooming in the bathroom sink. And in the attic, if she had managed to find her way up the steep and crumbling steps, she would have found the one room left open to the light, she would have stood breathless, picking cobwebs from her fingers and her face, staring at a whole meadow of wildflowers and grasses, poppies and oxeyes and flowering coriander, all flourishing in bird droppings and all lunging pointedly towards the one square of available sky. (McGregor, 2003: 135)

Here is not just decay but reoccupation and transformation; a palimpsest of the old and the new, the faecal and the fecund in a riot of biological determinism. Such description does not negate the value of the immutable human trace, but it does suddenly shift the reader into a longer perspective, which suggests the sublimation of those traces into an archaeological process of change.

It is this archaeological instinct that is picked up in the obsessive collecting of the boy from number eighteen. Afflicted with a pathological fear of the world's multiplicity – 'too much of everything, too much stuff, too many places, too much information, too many people, too much of things for there to be too much of, there is too much to know' (McGregor, 2003: 216) – he seeks methods to rationalise it with a form of forensic archiving. His painstaking collecting of urban jetsam – discarded receipts, used syringes, bits of broken glass – and obsessive photographic detailing of the street's inhabitants represents a ritualistic shaping of reality that allows him to control the world and reduce it from one incomprehensible mess to a structure which can be documented and understood. By capturing the too-muchness of the urban environment, he can suspend change and absorb the complexity of the urban ecological system through its concrete traces. But the boy's obsessive compulsive behaviour is not a simple collocation of random objects; there is an art to his efforts, and a determination to valorise the ordinary. He describes his finds as 'urban diamonds' (McGregor, 2003: 153) and constructs display cases to house them, fixing them within a museological frame that trans-values them from worthless rejectamenta to exemplary artefacts. These objects are recycled, up-scaled from the ordinary to the artful in a way that emphasises the potential for beauty in the most unpromising material once one observes with fresh eyes. The boy's fetishisation highlights the thin line between the ordinary and the extraordinary and the subconscious ways in which the desire to leave a trace verges on ritualism. Like the 'girl with short hair and glasses', desperate to leave something of herself, he buries his jar of receipts and bus tickets as a totem, a future-oriented guarantee of his presence that is designed to function in the same protective way as the oriental clay figure which he has obtained on his anthropological travels and which is inherited by his brother Michael, and ultimately by the female narrator. In this way the legacy of the trace is honoured, the individual becomes social, and the moment in time is transformed into the historical.

The importance of the clay figure is picked up again when Michael and the female narrator attend an exhibition of 'thousands and thousands of six-inch red clay figures [...] a pair of finger-sized sockets for eyes, heads tilted up from formless bodies' (McGregor, 2003: 231), which unmistakably refers to Antony Gormley's *Field for the British Isles* sculpture (1996). This project involved 'thousands of unglazed, fired, small clay figures, standing closely together, all staring towards the viewer and filling a large enclosed space. There are more figures than can be counted, more still disappearing out of sight into a further space. Their number seems to be endless' (Searle, 1996). Each is a familiar spirit which stands for the individual, but also for the collective, blindly calling to the viewer to reflect on the relationship of the one to the many and asking whether what one sees is a society or a group of individuals. McGregor's reference is clear: modern urban environments operate on the same monocular principle; the gaze is fixed ahead on the horizon of personal circumstances with little regard to the hinterlands that incorporate others, the unanticipated, the multiple, and the uncanny potential of unpromising stuff.

The question of whether society is any longer anything more than a collection of individuals is one that many of those on the street answer by wondering how they fit into the wider narratives of the world around them. For the students, this question is particularly acute as they launch themselves into the future, but, for the old man in the upstairs flat of number twenty, the anxiety is retrospective. Regarding his life and marriage in the light of a cancer that is likely to kill him, he pulls at the threads of memory to discover which are connected. The defining moment in his life – the calling into 'place in the way of things' (McGregor, 2003: 107) – should have been the Second World War, a moment when the individual could be subsumed within the collective need. However, his experience is a disappointing one: 'he had travelled half-way across Europe, and when it was over he had travelled back, but somehow the war had passed him by, as if he'd been asleep when the others had started and he'd spent the whole time trying to catch up' (McGregor, 2003: 178). Being assigned to an auxiliary role burying the combat dead brings him into contact with all the misery of war but none of the heroism that he anticipated; he wades ashore on the Normandy coast long after the cataclysm of D-Day to clear up its consequences, but utterly excluded from the life-enhancing brotherhood of its survivors. Instead the legacy of the war for him is one of traumatic morbidity:

> And they are the memories he's been shuffling around with all these years, unspoken because there is nothing to say, burying them deep down and finding them risen up again, the faces of the men, the smell of the soil and flesh, the stumbling words of the chaplain drowned by the distant noises of war. (McGregor, 2003: 180)

At least for the old man the national cause was clear and urgent, but, as they fret over the last days of a dying summer, the students wonder what narratives of belonging remain for them to inhabit. 'For fucksake', bemoans one of them, 'didn't our parents used to make stuff for a living?' (McGregor, 2003: 174), identifying the diminishment of the post-Thatcherite manufacturing sector as carrying a concomitant social loss. Another casts his sense of displacement in gender terms, describing his struggle to deal a fatal blow to a fish he has caught as evidence that the role of the 'masculine hunter' is beyond him. So, if traditional social and gender narratives fail the students, what avenues of being remain? One offers a more contemporary, but similarly limited, mantra of self-actualisation:

> You've got to travel light she says, start in a new place with empty hands. It's good for your karmic energy she says, and the other girl looks at her and laughs. Where did that come from she says and the girl in the pyjamas shrugs, she says I don't know I read it in a magazine or something and she drinks her tea. (McGregor, 2003: 190)

Even the baby boomer clichés of self-fulfilment echo hollowly when mashed up with the horizonless banality of celebrity culture, posing the question of what sustains the modern subject if the narratives of both society and self are becoming increasingly meaningless. What hope is there for coalescence when even the moments of intersection between public and private are as empty of symbolic permanence as the narrator's experience of the 1997 general election, which brought Tony Blair's New Labour administration to power?

The story she tells is of exciting exceptionality – watching the results come in with her friends and feeling how the evanescent 'excitement of history' (McGregor, 2003: 40) brings people together in uncommon ways. Yet, her final comment is telling: her friends were 'already looking like ghosts' (McGregor, 2003: 40), a phrase that indicates the fleeting insubstantiality of these moments of coherence. As with the infectious and conspicuous mourning for Princess Diana that would follow the other car accident within the novel's timeframe, a togetherness which breaches the impermeability of late-capitalist individualism is installed and almost immediately undermined. The moment of transition where the country moves into a different phase of self-recognition is paralleled with the students' unspecific sense of the ending of one comfortable phase and the beginning of a less certain period. National and personal are thus tied together at moments when some sort of direction of travel is visible, but that quickly becomes negated, compromised, or obscured.

If narrative certainty about the world has collapsed, ushering in only impermanence and invisibility, then, McGregor suggests, we need to turn to the poetic to be reminded that such negative qualities can offer succour and transcendence. The emptiness of an urban modernity can be turned around to reveal a plenitude that is masked only by the unwillingness to regard it. The physical and the metaphysical are neighbours in McGregor's writing, with the latter articulated through the ordinary in a familiarly Joycean manner. However, the unspectacular materiality of stuff is never merely a means to the revelation of a higher order of meaning or truth. Instead, it contains its own quiet beauty and transcendent potential, which, in the correct visual frame, becomes apparent. It is not too grandiloquent to describe McGregor as a poet of the unregarded: his fiction consistently addresses marginal experience, and, whilst I would not wholly agree with Caroline Edwards (2010) that he prioritises descriptive precision over political message, it is true that he frequently de-emphasises the bigger picture in favour of the liminal and the obscured. Whether it's the fenland setting of some of the stories in *This Isn't the Sort of Thing That Happens to Someone Like You*, the drug and alcohol para-world of *Even the Dogs*, or the obsessional gathering together of life's debris that figures in the first two novels, McGregor's attention is devotedly 'excentric'. Here, that gaze is directed towards the poetic possibilities of the mundane. The banal and the extraordinary facets of the world are tightly rolled together, and, whilst perceiving the remarkable requires no skill, it does demand a willingness to misrecognise the ordinary. The prologue's swooping envisioning of the sleeping city prepares the reader for the necessity of seeing the world in an open and receptive way to appreciate its intrinsic beauty, but what largely follows is sight enclosed by the limits of the everyday.

This novel could equally have been entitled *If Nobody Sees Remarkable Things*, such is the focus on the visual perception of the ordinarily beautiful, but the failure to look beyond the limits of one's vision, to acknowledge the possibility of the transcending horizon, is a consequence of instrumentalised living which promotes the idea of self-determined individualism over and above the recognition of other, more communal values. Seeing the remarkable requires a different kind of focus, one which is open to enlightenment, but it does not demand the rejection of modernity's materialism; rather it needs a romantic receptiveness to the transformational power of perception, as we see in the following two examples:

> he ['the architecture student from number eleven'] thinks about a place he worked in the spring, an office where they had a stack of empty watercooler bottles against the window, and how he would sit and watch the sun mazing its way through the layers of refraction, the beauty of it, he called it spontaneous maths and he wanted to build architecture like it, he looks at the row of houses opposite and he pictures them built entirely of plastic and glass, he imagines how people's lives might change if their dwellings shook with endless reflections of light, he does not know if it's possible but he thinks it's a nice idea. (McGregor, 2003: 212)

> He ['the man with the scarred hands'] says do you want to see another special thing, and he points to the rooftops opposite, he says can you clap your hands for your daddy, and when she does so the whole ridgepole of pigeons springs up in the air, ballooning off down the street as a group, circling, landing on another rooftop in a matching single line. (McGregor, 2003: 239)

These moments of insight do not request or require explanation; they are simple, pure exposures to a clarity that need be neither meaningful nor meaningless. Their evanescence as much as their contingency determines their epiphanic quality, granting an instant of insight into an alternative sensibility that suggests the possibility of otherworldly experiences. In the two examples quoted above, that insight is aesthetic in terms, offering a visual encounter with the beautiful in a raw, unmoulded state, but the remarkable is also perceptible in moments of empathic connection.

The habitual and unconsidered shapes of relationships with others still have the potential to be revelatory if they are acknowledged: small acts of loving kindness, moments of tenderness in the run of things, dutiful attention to others, momentary escape from regret, even the shared wonder at a torrential rain storm allow McGregor's protagonists breaks in vision which temporarily surprise them into a fresh relationship with the ordinary. And that shift of perception, however brief, carries an ethical importance, for through it the protagonists evaluate their lives as ventures that extend beyond themselves. In a moment of respite from the needs of their twins, the couple at number nineteen retreat to their bedroom and a lovemaking that because of, rather than despite, its familiarity reveals a time-wrought intensity:

> And in a moment the door will be locked, and the stillness and quiet will be left on this side of the door. They will both drop their politeness and reserve to the floor with their clothes, he will close the curtains and she will unveil her body, she will stand against the wall with her arms raised high, waiting for him to drink in his fill of the sight of her, she will lick her fingers, each in turn, as though sharpening them, and then they will be together. (McGregor, 2003: 192–193)

The consummation gains in eroticism from its ordinariness; as the woman adopts her seductive pose, the performance transforms the oft-repeated act into an echo of originality. McGregor would reprise and extend this scene in *So Many Ways to Begin*, in which David and Eleanor's lovemaking is heightened by the familiarity of each other's aged and imperfect bodies. Such moments are transformative not because they reshape reality or perception but because they highlight what is always already present. McGregor's point is that the magical is ever present but is rarely perceived and even more rarely venerated. The touch of another can be exotic in its sheer simplicity precisely because it counteracts the egoistic imperative that dominates contemporary Western notions of subjectivity. The other may represent foreign and impenetrable territory, but, McGregor suggests, the spaces that divide individuals are not as unbridgeable as one may imagine.

Often, the remarkable stands outside the vocal, but McGregor's title points towards the importance of sharing, of bringing into speech that which is ignored. In the dialogue from which the novel takes its name, the man with scarred hands exhorts his daughter to see and hear the extraordinary but concludes that, unless we speak of remarkable things, 'how can they be remarkable?' (McGregor, 2003: 239). The remarkable has no freight unless it is remarked, a point which draws us back to the novel's presentation of modern communal living as alienating not only in a social sense but also linguistically and perceptually. It is thus important that the novel's central remarkable event – Shahid's accident – unfolds as an act of collective and unifying enunciation. Its first rendering, in the staccato narration of the girl with short hair and glasses' initial chapter, is characterised by stasis and denial. Characters are presented as turning away, covering their eyes, mouths open, fists clenched – immobile and silent. Disconnection prevails, and the possibility of overcoming it is rendered impossibly awkward – 'If we'd been closer, or younger, we might have held hands, tightly, but we didn't' (McGregor, 2003: 11). Returning to the scene, the final chapter unfreezes events from the one-dimensionality of the narrator's perception, depicting it instead from the third-person point of view and adding the flow that is missing from her account. Here we have the streets' residents moving together towards a central point, momentarily united in concern for the child. Geometrically, the hermeticism of the rectilinear boxes in which they live is dissolved by a single, collective point to which their attention, action, and empathy are directed. Thereby randomness unifies in a vocal affirmation of the recognition of the other: Shahid Mohammed Nawaz. The exclamation of the singularity of a name is an articulation of the remarkable as a shared and spoken event, and it is this, rather than the death of the boy from number eighteen or the survival of Shahid, that is the true climax of the novel.

So Many Ways to Begin (2006)

Where *If Nobody Speaks* is characterised by a poetic vision and a visual sensibility, McGregor's second novel, *So Many Ways to Begin*, is rooted tonally and thematically in the prosaic. Its primary mode is diegetic rather than mimetic and, where its predecessor is punctuated by moments of striking lyrical intensity, this tale unfolds with the delicacy and poignancy of a story related at length. It is consequently more halting and dilatory in its development, though, as with *If Nobody Speaks*, the dénouement is prefigured early in the novel and then worked towards with a shortening stride and a sense of ambivalence. The sensory shift from the visual to the tactile displays a growing interest in the textural materiality of the world that accompanies McGregor's impressive capturing of the immaterial, emotionally loaded relations between people. The novel contains fewer imaginative flights than his debut, drawing in its reader instead with a melancholic contemplativeness which, by comparison, seems positively repressed. Reviews tended to pick up on this restraint, praising the quality of McGregor's writing but describing it as 'low-key', 'excruciatingly undramatic', 'subdued', 'poignant', 'tender', and 'undecorated' (see Cross, 2007; Hickling, 2006; Koning, 2007; Mahawatte, 2006; Merritt, 2006). His exaltation of the everyday was, ironically, generally regarded as lending itself less well to the prosaic than to the lyrical, but few critics saw *So Many Ways to Begin* as anything other than a solidification of McGregor's promise.[1]

The most striking structural aspect of the novel was generally considered a success by critics. This involves the narrative's division into sixty-two chapters each framed by an item or group of items associated with the life stories of the protagonist David Carter or his wife Eleanor. These objects – 'Model fishing boat, handmade c.1905', 'Examination results, Scottish Highers, July 1967' etc. – are intimate and personal keepsakes gathered over the course of a curatorial life that speak not only of one individual but also of a century of social transformation. Varying between the intrinsically valueless and the historically loaded, these mementoes represent an eclectic jetsam of the intersection of the private and the public, reminding us that the presence of the past in the here and now is neither predictable nor affectively discriminating. McGregor's use of this random collection as a structuring device provides a natural frame for the unfolding of the narrative, but, as with the compartmentalisation of point of view in *If Nobody Speaks* and the third-person-plural narration in *Even the Dogs*, it has a limiting effect on the reader's vision that is both productive and counter-productive. On the one hand, the rigidity of the structuring principle perfectly captures David's aleatoric meticulousness in chronicling his life, but, on the other, it situates narrative development fully within the protagonist's problematic understanding of the world. Insisting on such formulaic structures could swiftly lead McGregor towards accusation of tiresome whimsy or imaginative inflexibility, but the fact that he transcends these repetitive stylistic quirks to produce fiction of depth and subtlety is a testament to his careful attention to the detail of feeling.

So Many Ways to Begin balances two core narrative strands which function in opposing chronological directions but which continually interleave. At the heart of both strands is David, a museum curator from Coventry who, made redundant in his forties, determines to seek out the mother who gave him up for adoption as a baby and of whose existence he became aware only as a grown man when the dementia of his Aunt Julia caused her to let slip the truth of his parentage. Unable to reconcile himself with the charitable intentions of his adoptive mother and gnawed by irresolvable feelings of rootlessness, he grows increasingly obsessed with tracking to Ireland the 'Mary Friel' he believes to be his birth mother. This search for a reliable link to selfhood in the past is counterbalanced by the forwards-moving narrative of his marriage to Eleanor, whom he meets as a schoolgirl in Aberdeen and with whom he constructs a life that must accommodate not only his lack of belonging, but also the legacy of her brutalisation by a domineering and jealous mother. The life they shape together is notable only for its ordinariness: their trials, triumphs, temptations, and tantrums are the ordinary stuff of lower-middle-class life in post-Second World War Britain, and, for all the piquancy of their private traumas, they endure them with muted stoicism and realistic horizons.

A love between them similarly endures; from passionate intensity through sentimental resignation to a mature openness, it incorporates the kinds of frustrations, emotional suppressions, recriminations, and regrets that characterise any long-term commitment. As in *If Nobody Speaks*, the unsaid becomes part of the furniture of a life, and these lacunae offer the kind of quiet insights that fascinate McGregor, as he has stated in interview: '[I'm] interested in two people sitting at a table not quite able to explain to each other how they feel. [...] There's something very interesting about listening to people, realising they're not saying what they mean, that they expect you to read between the lines' (Mansfield, 2007). The growing darkness of Eleanor's depression and David's desperate need to know the circumstances of his birth colour their story, but McGregor has created them as spectacularly unspectacular, seeking the paths to themselves amidst the distractions of domestic and employed life.

McGregor's first two novels are of a piece in the sense that they share similar formal experiments, comparable tonal palettes, common themes, and

referential crossovers. Incidental correspondences such as both novels containing funerals in Aberdeen, or the motif of boxing videos, reiterate this kinship,
as do the themes of social alienation and the affective load of space. David and
Eleanor would not have seemed out of place in one of the numbered houses
of *If Nobody Speaks*, and the second novel gives the reader the sense of spend-
ing an extended stretch of time in the company of those characters captured
so fleetingly. McGregor has commented that *So Many Ways to Begin* was an
attempt to thematise some of the more inchoate ideas of the first novel and
to render the visual qualities into fully realised literary forms (in Edwards,
2010: 220–201). It is certainly no great stretch to imagine David Carter's gen-
esis in the nervy, anonymous collector obsessively recording urban detritus for
some future archive. Both characters display a form of pathological anxiety
about being lost or forgotten in a socially fluid and migratory cityscape where
the ability to imprint themselves on the world around them is diminished by
quondam social relations and a sense of compromised authenticity.

Circumscribed by the painful consciousness of their rootlessness,
both invest huge amounts of emotional capital in things, entrusting their
psycho-social fixity to the resonance of the material. But, where the archival
instincts of the young man in number eighteen are confined to the margins
of worldly traffic, David's ambitions are more capacious. For him, museums
represent the possibility of orderliness and interconnection that enables
sense-making on a cultural as much as a personal level. In childhood he fantasises about owning his own museum, whose organising principle would be
complete transparency; all exhibits would be on display with nothing that
could augment understanding hidden from view. On discovering during a
visit to a museum that a Viking longboat on display is a replica, the young
David condemns the lie: 'It didn't mean anything. [...] It wasn't real, it was
made up. You can't learn anything about history by looking at made-up
things, he said talking quickly and urgently. It's stupid, it's not fair. It's a lie, he
said' (McGregor, 2007: 42). His anger is driven by what he perceives to be the
symbolic emptiness of the simulacrum; because it is not 'the thing itself' it is
devoid of weight and meaning, disrupting the clarity of the observer's gaze
into the truth of the past. Such is his conviction in the accessibility of origins
through things that:

> It seemed perfectly natural to him to be amazed by the physical presence of history,
> to be able to stand in front of an ancient object and be awed by its reach across time.
> A thumbprint in a piece of prehistoric pottery. The chipped edge of a Viking battle-
> axe, and the shattered remains of a human skull. The scribbled designs for the world's
> first steam engine, spotted with candlewax and stained with jam. It seemed like some
> kind of miracle to him that these traces of distant lives had survived, and that he was
> able to stand in front of them and stare for as long as he liked. (McGregor, 2007: 37)

So Many Ways to Begin is a novel that explores the ways in which the material is endowed with whole architectures of emotion. Even the most mundane of objects functions ritualistically, condensing unspoken, and perhaps unspeakable, relations with the world and others. They are thingly representatives of whole worlds of interconnection, and singular distillations of the multiple. David's relationship with his 'finds' is fetishistic in the sense that in them he discerns both intrinsic and extrinsic structures of feeling that transcend their banal utility. Some cigarettes preserved from the First World War transport him imaginatively to the trenches with such a powerful jolt of excitement that 'he couldn't move and he couldn't bring himself to look away' (McGregor, 2007: 34). What fascinates him most is the contingency that governs the survival of these artefacts, the thought that they could have been lost and yet have found their way into his hands. They are 'at once indestructible and hopelessly fragile' (McGregor, 2007: 34), and, to David, speak of the paradoxical availability and yet impenetrability of the past. Furthermore these exhibits, many of which are catalogued in the novel's chapter headings, coalesce histories of beginnings, endings, and trajectories of ownership that are more eloquent than the object itself can articulate. Thus the thing becomes a decontextualised material memory, silently encapsulating voluble stories. Gathered over time, these things accrue an increasing emotional poignancy and value even as the original contexts of their being become more distant. Discovering a photograph of his adoptive father in uniform, David enjoyed 'feeling the rough and crinkled texture of the greying card, turning it over to read the soft pencilled dates and numbers on the back, running his fingers across the scratches scored into the photograph's dull surface' (McGregor, 2007: 21), a description which evokes the fullness of the past in the same moment that he is distanced from ever attaining it.

Shaping the bricolage of David and Eleanor's material traces allows McGregor to beg the question of whether by gathering these objects together in a catalogue of a life the whole transcends the parts to speak coherently of that life in a manner that offers purpose and value. Is the reader being presented here with a story determined by a teleological linearity, or with a vitrified collection of discrete moments that are reified as exemplary instances of an individual life? In other words, what kinds of narrative possibilities are realised by the dramatic technique of assembling a life's archaeology? These questions cut to the heart of the novel's relationship between history and story and force us to consider the complexity of the novel's diegesis.

As has been established, the novel is dominated by sixty-two chapters, each identified with a specific object related to the lives of the protagonists with the content of each chapter generally (but by no means always) focusing on the relation of that object to the story of David and/or Eleanor. These chapters tend to be retrospective accounts of the protagonists' post-war upbringings, the development of their marriage, the birth of their daughter (Kate), and the challenges that David's sense of betrayal and Eleanor's depression impose. The chapters do not unfold chronologically and the narrative incorporates both a backwards look to the development of David's adoptive parents' relationship and a forwards look to the narrative present in 2000, when David and Eleanor travel to Northern Ireland to meet Mary Friel. Alongside these, the novel contain three other unnamed chapters, two of which are set immediately prior to the trip across the Irish Sea in the aftermath of David having delivered Kate to university for the first time. The third of these unnamed chapters concludes the novel after the meeting with Mary. There is, in addition, a prologue, set in the early decades of the twentieth century, which follows a young girl from the north of Ireland, travelling for domestic work to England, becoming pregnant by her employer, and abandoning the baby before returning home. The whole creates a complicated temporal sandwich in which the beginnings of the twentieth and twenty-first centuries bookend a narrative that has both forwards and backwards momentum whilst being simultaneously statically located on decontextualised objects. The unfolding of the narrative thus presents us with, at least, two versions of historical understanding: that presented by the trans-generational story and that by the catalogue of objects. The former depends upon a linear model of the outcomes of causal factors; the latter on a vision of history as random, discontinuous, provisional, and modelled through its telling. The former seeks a point of origin as the authentic truth; the latter recognises the necessity of reshaping life from disorder.

Eleanor and David offer two contrasting routes to exploring these versions of the past. Eleanor's narrative is dominated by a sense of causal inevitability and trans-generational inheritance. Her life is plotted out as a story of consequences – her tempestuous relationship with her mother giving rise to psychological distress, introversion, limited affective connection to her own child, and a deep bitterness about her inability to be more than she is. This circumscription she passes on to Kate. Like the narrative through-line which charts the story of Eleanor and David's marriage in a roughly chronological manner, Eleanor's story offers one version of a history which is basically ordered through cause and effect. Contrastingly, David's history is less a story of influence because he cannot reliably trace the generational lineage or identify any of the people from whom he may have inherited his sense of selfhood. He, like the objects he curates, is decontextualised, able to muster a sense of place only through the collocation of equivalences and differences within a broader social context. Without the kind of genetic link that

Eleanor can boast, he cannot tell a story of himself that is developmental or organic. Instead, the only story he can relate is one of contingency and self-shaping, ordering *ex nihilo* a collection of discontinuities. David's life is dominated by what he doesn't know, whereas Eleanor's is dominated by what she does know. But, McGregor asks, what actually constitutes a life? Is it dictated by where it begins, where it ends, its formative influences, or the construction of a factitious continuity?

Without a pre-determining shape, David's life narrative depends for its robustness on the ways in which he recounts it. It equally depends on the willingness of a listener to indulge him, a necessity that induces in him an existential anxiety of recognition manifested in multiple variations of the phrase 'If he was asked', or the more poignant 'if there was anyone who wanted to know' (McGregor, 2007: 26). The possibility that nobody wants to know is a deeply worrying one for David, and for McGregor, for it suggests the ubiquity of the kind of self-regarding atomisation that afflicted the characters of *If Nobody Speaks*. The ability to shape the self – and the external world – through the stories that are told hinges on the willingness of a listener to indulge and encourage the telling, but David's fear is that such altruism is rare and easily rescinded. Just as he fantasises about constructing a personal museum, so he also imagines himself into the role of guide, drawing the attention of onlookers towards the depth and resonance of his constructed past, pointing them to the connections to their own stories, thickening the intersubjective commonality between them as a reminder that all stories cross and co-determine. By this means he gives substance and layers to his precarious sense of identity, pulling from the links with others and the material stuff of the past a density of being that his 'official' genealogical story lacks.

Telling and hearing these stories is particularly important because to engage with the material relics of the past is always to experience silence and to acknowledge the loss of the voices and lives tied to passed time. For all the resonant volubility of the object, its stories are only enlivened in the retelling, and David recognises that the performance of history is vital to both its mystique and its availability to the present. He imagines addressing a group of dinner guests, dramatically expostulating on the tattered photograph of his father before passing the picture around for examination. All is stage-managed to heighten the sense of historical realisation but also to ensure his guests appreciate the interdependence of artefact and story. The self-catalogue that David constructs is not made in a vacuum, nor is it conceived without an audience anticipated. The stories both he and Eleanor tell of their lives are seeking validation through the commitment of others, and performance is important for it is only through the listener that history (personal or public) gains an ethical load. What the listener chooses to do with those stories is equally important, if less manageable, because the self-construction is fragile; without reciprocation there is an underlying fear of being lost, history-less, and alone – to oneself as much as to others.

In a novel filled with stories – some which have beginnings and endings, some which don't; some which need to be told, some which exist outside the telling – the undramatic continuity of David and Eleanor's marriage offers the most compelling narrative arc, which ultimately brings us back to the opening pages. Does this circularity repudiate David's illusion of historical traceability, or Eleanor's desperate struggle with the cause and effect of her own emotional brutalisation? I would argue that it does neither, but proffers instead another historiographical methodology, one based on contingency. David's life is directly shaped by two moments of contingency: the first meeting with Eleanor in the museum café (McGregor, 2007: 66) and the momentary indiscretion of Julia in revealing the lie of his parentage (McGregor, 2007: 92). Both dominate the narrative, but one of the novel's constant refrains is 'Isn't it funny to think we almost never met?' (McGregor, 2007: 69), a recognition of the potentiality for otherness of what seems inevitable. McGregor identifies the fragility in the web of a life story, the multiple possibilities of things having been otherwise, of having developed in a completely different way and with alternative outcomes. Many moments in the narrative are fraught with this imagining of what could have been different if a particular moment had pivoted on a separate, but equally possible, emotion or motivation. McGregor repeatedly utilises versions of the following construction to highlight the alternative potential of history's breaking points:

> Stewart [Eleanor's father] stood, with one hand on the door frame, one foot on the front step, watching the pair of them until they'd rounded the corner at the bottom of the hill, waiting to see if one of them might turn round, just once. Or he went back inside as soon as they'd said their goodbyes, closing the door sharply behind him, breathless with rage and regret. Or he waited a moment, went inside to put the kettle on, and came back out to see whether they might not, after all, still be there. (McGregor, 2007: 148)

Life is made in these moments of unmaking or otherwiseness, and McGregor offers his reader an idea of history susceptible to continuous reimagining and retelling. And each of those possible retellings offers an alternative way to begin; in each fracture there is a new story told which moulds the past in different ways. This is why the above construction is so important: it represents not just the possibility of difference but also the concrete presence of different shapings of being in the same moment. This co-presence of historical multiplicity sits alongside aetiological determinism and the inaccessibility of the truth of the past as a third way of deriving narratives of memory and continuity. It is an idea which, in essence, McGregor was imagining in the co-terminous lives of the street's residents in *If Nobody Speaks*, where a plethora of pasts and futures collided in a single dramatic moment, but it finds a much more expressive metaphor here through David's relics.

The struggle to matter to the wider world is a common feature of McGregor's fiction and a condition of the societies he represents. The post-war Britain of *So Many Ways to Begin* is a place of social transition, and Coventry is emblematic of that landscape of change. McGregor alighted on the city as his setting because of its protean status: nearly flattened by German bombing, it emerged as a symbol of industrial regrowth and social progressiveness in the war's aftermath (Edwards, 2010: 218). Its ancient and modern cathedrals reflect a double-facing temporal orientation towards past and future, but the influx of migrant populations, the expansion of the car manufacturing industry, and the endowment of the University of Warwick (located in Coventry) all point to McGregor's interest in the city as a microcosm of contemporary social change. David's family are beneficiaries of the kind of class mobility initiated by such progressiveness: his parents move to the city from London, able to take advantage of cheap, new housing; Eleanor attempts to enrol in a geology degree at Warwick; and David's role in the newly opened museum brings into focus the process of rapid demographic change that characterised the decades following the war. His most successful exhibition involves bringing together the stories of migrants to Coventry such as himself, combining both the utopian hopes of the new and the nostalgic thrall of origins:

> He'd learnt working at the museum, how many people wanted someone to tell their family's story to, how often the children of people who died would bring their parents' possessions to the museum to be archived or put on display, assuming that because these objects had belonged to someone who was no longer alive they would naturally take on a historical importance, assuming that the words museum and mausoleum were somehow the same. (McGregor, 2007: 209–210)

Historical change intensifies the need for stories to have shape and for those stories to be heard and valorised, but the need for public commemoration of that which has been lost reveals a deep-seated anxiety about the obliteration of meaningful attachments to the past and, more obliquely, the disappearance of a set of common narratives which, however imaginary, foster collective belonging. As in *If Nobody Speaks*, the shells of shared myths are still discernible and socially functional, but their contents have been largely hollowed out, leaving the imaginary residue of collective belonging without supporting material evidence. McGregor's characters are conscious of the lack of grand narratives that shape their social subjectivity, just as they are aware of the lack of any determining forces (other than chance) that order their lives on the smallest level, but this consciousness does not completely diminish the nostalgic yearning for completeness and meaningfulness. For David's sister Susan, the connection to the past is also a connection to something substantial; the stories she liked to tell of the past 'made her feel a part of something bigger than herself, tied to a time when there were bigger things to feel a part of' (McGregor, 2007: 19).

McGregor's engagement with the political frame is subtle and indirect, but it is also trenchant. McGregor's writing co-locates the public and the private in the same physical and imaginative spaces, intricately weaving the two together from the same fabric skeins. The cherished object retained across a lifetime is imbued with a significance beyond the personal, just as the discarded ephemera of daily life represents something more than itself; both are endowed with the trace of social memory. But equally the political is always personal for McGregor, as the conditions of late twentieth-century social life are reflected in a looking inwards for connection with points of reference outside the self. David's profession fulfils his desire for both inner and outer order, but it also encompasses the public's need for the significant and the insignificant to be jointly valued. That the political quality of the personal cannot be underestimated is evident in the novel's engagement with the domestic.

It is characteristic of McGregor that a moment of cataclysmic personal significance is framed by the banal. This is the moment when David tells Eleanor what he knows about the lie of his life:

> They did the washing up together, scraping the uneaten food into the bin, standing in close silence while he stacked the pans and filled the bowl with hot water and she waited with a clean tea towel. She touched his arm. You okay? She said. He nodded, not looking at her. She slid her arms around his waist, pressing her face against his chest for a moment. I don't know what to say, she told him. I don't know how to make it better for you. [...] You could start by drying these, he told her. (McGregor, 2007: 162)

Rather than being an indication of the distance between them, this undramatic reaction is a testament to their intimacy, for the repressed emotional excess of the revelation is contained by the mutually understood task in which they are engaged. The juxtaposition of the ordinary and the extraordinary lends the scene a comic pathos, but that adds to the intimacy, for it speaks of the tender circumscription of their love, moulded through trial and error across the years to reflect the unique temper of their relationship.

That is not to say that the pain of David's discovery or of Eleanor's depression is swallowed by their togetherness, only that they are framed within an enduring closeness that can give shape to disorder through the ordinariness of domestic living. To borrow one of the reviewers' clichés, McGregor is very accomplished at underplaying the familiarity of the everyday whilst not diminishing or trivialising its weight. Actually, by doing so, he elevates the unspectacular to the aesthetic, displaying the quiet beauty of a marriage that can accommodate the momentous and the insignificant without a jarring emotional gear change.

The answer to so many of the questions that Eleanor and David have of the world is contained within this intimate domesticity and is not really an answer that offers any kind of closure that narrative would recognise. As David's journey moves to a (false) conclusion, his desire for self-completion moderates to accept the restorative powers of storytelling – the fiction of their kinship proves sufficient for both him and Mary Friel – and the truth of his marriage. That truth involves the gradual accumulation of experience, unnoticed across time, and the accruing of material and immaterial freight along the way. It also involves an attritional wearing-away of hopes and expectations. It is thus a dynamic exchange of positive and negative, gaining and losing, knowing and not knowing, growth and recession, and failure and success. As in the older married couple in *If Nobody Speaks*, most of the work of the relationship is done not only in silence but also at the edges of intentionality, happening with and without conscious organisation.

Without quite being aware of it, David builds a meaningful life based on loyalty, care, and fidelity to Eleanor and Kate, and it is on this tenderness that he falls back when the futility of his mission to Ireland becomes apparent. The palpable truths of fixed identity disappear into the shared togetherness and mutual understanding of a life lived in partnership. The culminating scene of lovemaking gains in eroticism from the knowledge of the other's needs, but also from an awareness of the other's failures and limitations. It is a profoundly human moment that, for the reader, feels intrusive and voyeuristic because one is being allowed access to an intensely private consummation of love over time. It emphasises the importance for McGregor of touch, of physical connection as a way of rooting the self in the reality of the other, a theme that would be more strongly articulated in *Even the Dogs*. McGregor doesn't suggest in any naïve way that love is any kind of answer, but he suggests that it is a baseline human affect disclosed over time that retains a value and, like the other objects of the novel, is always tied to the particular context. Love is not transcendent here, but it is the best compensation for the lack of knowledge and the absence of authenticity.

Even the Dogs (2010)

'Who wants to open up the discussion' (McGregor, 2011a: 71). Who indeed, McGregor seems to ask in his bleak third novel about addiction, alienation, and suffering on the fringes of society in a nameless East Midlands city. The setting for *Even the Dogs* is contemporary, as are its concerns, and in particular its questioning of a British welfare state system that voids itself of empathy as it grows in bureaucracy. The statement – for, as the absence of a question mark indicates, this is no interrogative – is spoken by one of the counsellors during a therapy session designed to confront the collected drug- and alcohol-addicted audience with their potential for change and the necessity of taking personal responsibility for the problems that afflict them. Only by acknowledging, owning, sharing, and staying free of judgement within an inclusive environment can these addicts lay claim to their narratives of personal catastrophe and move towards self-reconciliation ... and towards the closure of an hour which will reward them with a sanctioned script for drug-substituting medication. For, whilst one narrative of social reclamation is being enabled, another, less holistic narrative of need is undermining the discursive openness of the session. The bargain is uncomplicated: attend the group, tick the box on the form, and receive medication intended to wean the taker off harder drug choices. That both sides know the terms of the deal, colluding in it for different ends, renders the question mark redundant. But only in one sense. For McGregor the question is far from rhetorical; who, he asks, wants to know, to acknowledge, to talk about the condition of the urban underclasses, of those jettisoned by the 'System'? Isn't it easier simply to collude in the bargain?

Given the contemplativeness of his first two novels, McGregor was conscious that his readership would be divided by *Even the Dogs*. He described the novel as

> very dark, fairly unpleasant to read, full of swearing and unpleasant images [...] fragmented and non-linear but within a strict structure. There's going to be a whole bunch of people who don't like it; and quite a lot of them are going to be those people who did like my first book. And they're going to dislike this for the reasons that they did like the first one. (in Urquhart, 2010)

Critically at least, *Even the Dogs* was a huge success, winning the prestigious IMPAC Dublin Award and being received by reviewers as a significant and darkly powerful anatomy of social exclusion. Diegetically the narrative follows the journey that the corpse of alcoholic Robert Radcliffe takes from a puddle of bodily decay on his living-room floor, through police investigation, autopsy, and cremation, to the coroner's court and an official recording of the circumstances of his life and death. But the simplicity of this journey belies the complexity of the novel's intertwining of voices as they recount not only their responses to Robert's death but also their own discomforting stories. Danny, Steve, Mike, Ant, Ben, Heather, and Robert's daughter, Laura, produce a chorus of pain out of which their individual stories of drug addiction emerge as specific, yet familial, strains. As Robert's death moves from one stage of official resolution to the next, the unresolved chaos of the lives of these addicts weaves back and forth, simultaneously revealing and obscuring the reasons behind their descent into addiction and the desperation of their struggles to co-exist with their self-obliterating desires. The narrative *coup-de-grâce* is that the voices – with the exceptions of Laura and Mike – emanate from beyond the grave as one by one they succumb to their addictions.

Even the Dogs is by far McGregor's most political novel, but, that said, it is primarily politically conscious rather than stridently ideological or didactic. In their attention to the conditions of twentieth-century social change, his first two novels were quietly engaged in political observation, but *Even the Dogs* represents a significant step-change in his rhetorical position regarding the contemporary condition of England. Where historical forces of social transformation were expressed through the smallness of an individual's struggle with life in the earlier novels, *Even the Dogs* presents a more visceral exhibition of cause and effect on the levels of individual and society. McGregor's politics are never hectoring, nor are they partisan; he simply lays bare a vision of inequality, moral indifference, and despair. That the degradation is as much a reflection of the country as it is of the individual is left very much for the reader to infer. McGregor's writing is not generally regarded as politically tendentious, and reviewers have tended to cast him as the miniaturist for whom wider concerns are secondary. McGregor himself demurs from attributing a strongly politicised purport to his writing, suggesting that 'I'm always very conscious of not setting out to write something with a theme or an agenda in mind, because then you kill off the story and the characters' (McGregor, 2010b). Elsewhere he expresses a wariness of 'standing on platforms' (in Urquhart, 2010), believing instead that 'the act of describing this world properly and authentically is in itself quite political' (McGregor, 2010b: 22). He wants, in James Urquhart's view, to 'raise his readers' baseline engagement with the world' (Urquhart, 2010), a statement that suggests an increasing normalisation of empathy depletion but also implies that the political is primarily personal. This is a feature that we have encountered elsewhere in the writers in this volume, and it is suggestive of a reticence to envision the writer as an intervener in the public sphere. This reticence is curious but is reflective of an unwillingness within contemporary

British literary fiction to engage in matters of public import, a fear that to be saying something, anything, that effects a knowledge of collective, social feeling is to indulge in a hubristic, politically incorrect humanism. By focusing on the microscopic, the personal experience, the uncontestable, novelists are protected from claims that they do not understand the bigger picture – the picture that, as James Wood has argued, is precisely the domain of the novelist (Wood, 2001b).

At the centre of *Even the Dogs* is the grotesque, bloated, deliquescent, and lumpen body of Robert Radcliffe, festering in a condemned flat in which no one is officially recorded as living. Discovered on a frost-rimed morning shortly after Christmas after a neighbour complains to the police about an unpleasant smell, Robert's body is the literal and metaphorical object of analysis and interpretation, dissected as much for its symbolic import as for the cause of its squalid death. From the moment of its discovery, the body represents a problem that draws into view interlocking systems of welfare management, community dependence, social subjectivity, and symbolic valence. It channels previously discrete discursive eco-systems into dialogic relationships, opening up for discussion their interdependence and frailties. Robert's abject body thus becomes a crossing-point of interpretative systems – bureaucratic, welfare, symbolic, diagnostic, capitalist, libidinal – which McGregor interrogates to determine how, in an advanced, wealthy society, it is possible for someone to die alone and anonymous. This question haunts the novel as potently as the spectral chorus of lost souls that, by employing the third-person-plural point of view, pull the reader into their world through their questioning, accusatory gaze. This ordinary tragedy is the natural extension of the kind of urban disregard that we saw in *If Nobody Speaks*, but here it is given a wider resonance and more stringent moral frame. Where *If Nobody Speaks* mournfully accepts the invisibility of modern communal living, *Even the Dogs* offers a more determined examination of how that invisibility is perpetuated.

Robert is an empty space. His life has effectively ceased since his wife and daughter left him; he continues to exist, but only in a broken and hopeless manner, drinking, smoking, and opening a flat which is no longer officially his to anyone who will exchange food and alcohol for a secure place to feed their habits. Beyond this, he is nothing but a bloated bundle of regrets, false hopes, and damage. Yet, his body is a problem. For all his anonymity, he needs to be accounted for in the official record – his death produces a crisis of knowledge within a bureaucratic system that requires resolution. We might interpret this as representing a tear in the fabric of symbolic understanding which introduces the real threat of the unknown and must therefore be patched and repaired. The mechanisms employed to effect that repair are objective and forensic in method, designed to establish the factual trace of Robert within the record and close the hole created by his death.

McGregor structures his novel around the initial police investigation at the scene; the autopsy, which determines the physiological cause of death; and the coroner's court of inquiry, which seeks to structure the evidence into an acceptable narrative of cause and effect. These fixed official processes invest time and attention on the morbid body of Robert in a way that they never did during his lifetime – an irony not lost on the observers. They are all performed by functionaries of an arch-system of legal processes who seek to position Robert within a series of categorical certainties; to pull him back from the margins and into accountability. Each site of investigation evidences a bureaucratic system that is dispassionate in gaze and disinterested in judgement, yet, McGregor asks, what kind of knowledge can they hope to establish, and what value is that knowledge in the production of meaningful interactions with the other systems that contain and control the lives of the protagonists? These are important questions, for the practices detailed in these investigations produce only the kind of evidence that their underlying assumptions permit; they generate knowledge that is orderly, logical, and linear, the kind of knowledge, in other words, that reflects the mode of inquiry. Chronologically, the novel unravels with the same rationality, tracing Robert's trip from floor to furnace with systematic linearity. But, though bureaucracy offers a formal and procedural shape for containing the world, it is a sterile, anti-empathetic vehicle for understanding the complexity of a life.

The same is true of the welfare mechanisms designed to deal with the human costs of addiction. The intersections of the protagonists with the institutional framework are not wholly alienating in the sense that there are limited services available to them (day centres, wet centres, night hostels) but the price of accessing these services is often humiliating infantilisation. The counselling session is a prime example of the inflexibility of a co-ordinated system in conflict with the chaotic expediency of the protagonists' desires. The narrative that underpins the provision of care – and, more urgently, the access to legitimate drugs and substitutes – is rooted in a therapeutic self-exposure intended to be confessional and recuperative. The bureaucratic diagnosis for the addicts' behaviour is that they have made a series of bad choices which have been driven by a lack of self-knowledge and an unwillingness to engage with personal failings. The 'meaning' of the addicts, their place within the social substructure, is therefore managed via both a drip-feed of narcotics and a story of failure into which the addicts themselves have to buy in order to guarantee their own supply. From both sides, this arrangement enables a blind eye to be turned: for the wider social body, the provision of baseline services offers a sop to liberal concerns for the underclasses, whilst the addicts recognise that the unrealistic mantras of personal growth and responsibility need to be endured for short-term ends to be fulfilled. McGregor is not critical of the intentions of the talking-cure welfare, but he does present the effort to produce self-realisation as hopelessly theoretical and impractical. It reflects a rigid, institutionalised thinking where the actions of the addicts are driven by contingency, desperation, and often creative need.

This tension between the rigid and the chaotic is figured in the structure of the novel. Spatially, the text oscillates between points of fixity (Robert's flat; the morgue; the coroner's court; the choric viewpoint of the observers) and a restless itinerancy. Following Danny around the city in the second chapter as he searches for Laura and for his next fix, the narrative presents a vision of a run-down and impoverished hinterland, unregarded and unclaimed. He circuits this cityscape with a charged urgency and restlessness totally in contrast to the bloated immobility of Robert's body and the official frame into which it has fallen. He inhabits an edgeland that exists outside the gaze of bureaucratic governance and officialdom – wastelands, underpasses, canalsides, alleyways – as much a part of the rejected flotsam of life as the rubbish through which he navigates. The same is true, albeit in a different register, of the third chapter, where the interminable inertia of the counselling session is undercut by the spiralling and intersecting narratives of Steve, Mike, Heather, and Ant, who through a contrapuntal torrent of memories and experiences open up the discussion in a way that totally defies the straight lines of the counsellor's cause and consequence model. They clearly have plenty to say, but cannot shape their experiences into the codes and clichés that are presented to them.

Whilst official welfare spaces are disablingly paternalistic, it would be wrong to suggest that the spaces outside the formal, institutional network are more egalitarian. Life in the edgelands is underscored with the constant possibility of violence, exploitation, and despair, and the cruel arbitrariness of dealers, panhandlers, and other entrepreneurs of misery is equally as alienating as the official superstructure of compliance. Only Robert's flat, with its sense of carnivalesque communality, acts as a temporary relief from intimidation. It is a space to which all have access – through the window above the garage – and in which its visitors find protection, companionship, and acceptance. By supplying him with food and alcohol, the addicts buy themselves a space outside the judgemental network of the official welfare system and beyond the random dangers of the streets. Robert's death destroys the freedom of that space, in the process disarticulating the ecosystem which has been constructed to sustain all the addicts. The breakdown of the unofficial care ecosystem represents a much greater anxiety to the protagonists than the deficiencies of the official counterpart, for it highlights the fragility of the bonds of commonality which binds them. Without Robert, the lack of social kinship between the addicts becomes apparent.

Though Robert's death may be a problem then for the authorities, who don't know him, it is a much greater problem for the people who do. Robert is the focus of the others' sympathy, the means by which they channel their capacity to care out and beyond themselves. It is not that he demands attention but rather that he licences the acknowledgement of others in a way which is democratically indifferent. In many ways, therefore, it is not Robert himself who inspires this concern; rather, the space that he represents in the narrative and in the lives of the protagonists condones altruistic intent. An otherwise bleak novel is enlightened by McGregor's abiding faith in the recuperative potential of small acts, such as when Danny and Mike help a desperate Laura find a vein in her neck to inject herself:

> Laura with her chin right up looking way past Mike to the sky, her eyes spilling with tears and holding her breath while he eased in the pin. Clinging on to his arms to keep still, like he was her only hope or something. Like he was the one who could make her body new. A new body and what though but. A new heaven and all that. All Laura wanted was one more vein. One more chance to begin again. (McGregor, 2011a: 152)

The sacred and the profane combine here; a desperately squalid act of self-destruction is transformed into a momentary transcendence based on the help of others. Danny and Mike display a genuine care, a willingness to help the other that is unconditional and non-judgemental. It is an attempt to help Laura to 'begin again', to capture a moment of hope through self-obliteration. The novel contains other such moments of uncomplicated sympathy – Danny's desire to tell Laura of Robert's death before the police do; the horror with which the others regard Ben when he tears a pigeon apart; the pure joy of being touched tenderly and without prejudice. As individual moments of kindness and recognition are possible within the official welfare framework, so they are in the parallel unofficial structures that determine the lives of the protagonists. The two worlds exist side by side with their own logics, their own ethics, and their own hierarchies. But, whilst the death of Robert threatens one of those worlds with an administrative burden, it threatens the other with collapse.

If Robert's flat is the only space in which the addicts can fully allow themselves to escape from the systems of order that alienate them, the loss of that space, and with it the loss of the freedom that Robert represents, dismantles the imagined community and all its structures of support. Without Robert the world is split between the instrumentalised rationality of institutional welfare and the brutalising irrationality of dog-eat-dog street reality. More importantly, his loss contracts the forum for mutuality, and, as it does, the possibilities for mutuality similarly contract. Robert's informal offer of shelter for food and drink creates a space for beneficial exchange, but, without it, the protagonists are thrown back on a world of supply and demand. His loss thus creates more than a literal emptiness; it generates a far more damaging crisis of hope and a rupture in the ethical and symbolic structures of their community. The anxiety that this releases is apparent not only in the reflections of the characters on their experiences of Robert but also in the underlying question of accountability that permeates the disembodied vigil they maintain over his body.

Who is to blame for Robert's death becomes an important strain of the intertwining narratives, and blame here is understood not as an institutional failing – which social services failed to prevent it – but as an abnegation of individual responsibility. Who was the last person to see him alive? Who forgot to take him the food he needed? Who let him down the most? These are questions of accountability which the urgency and self-centredness of a drug addict's need do not negate. In the absence of a formal structure to help these desperate individuals 'begin again', they erect their own structures of support, but, when those fail, the moral consequences are all the greater for being small-scale and informal. In his chapter, Danny intercuts his search for Laura with an imagined interrogation about what he knows of Robert's last days; Mike stutteringly admits, 'by the way, like it don't mean nothing, that he's not sure but he maybe might have been the last one there before Robert died. Don't matter no more anyhow la but it's just worth mentioning' (McGregor, 2011a: 131); and Laura tells the coroner that she was too afraid of losing her place in rehab to take the time to deliver her father's food, a task she delegated to Ben, who, focused on his next fix, forgot. This catalogue of errors, miscalculations, and self-recriminations reveals the protagonists' consciousness of the fragility of their care ecosystem and the key role that Robert played in it.

Danny reiterates that role in his eulogistic imagining of a more appropriate fate for Robert's desecrated body:

> Should be different, should be like it would have been in the old days, like we should be carrying his body ourselves, like bearing him high on a what on a bier of broken branches, hurrying him out to the burying ground. Burning bunches of herbs and that to hide the smell, and people coming out of their houses and lowering their heads. [...] They should be closing the streets. There should be a piper or a fucking what a Sally army band or something, TV cameras, helicopters. (McGregor, 2011a: 36)

This send off, with all its ceremony and marks of grief on a collective scale, is totally out of keeping with the shabby, utilitarian death that Robert suffers. It harks back to a nostalgic ideal of the person as part of a community first and as an individual second. There is sadness in Danny's encomium at the lack of collective recognition of loss and the passing of the rituals of death, but there is also glorification, for the kind of burial that Danny fantasises is that of a hero rather than that of an alcoholic outsider. Elsewhere he considers that a Viking sea burial would be a fitting mark. Such tributes identify Robert as the symbolic constant of the community, elevating him to a monarchical level that is entirely consistent with McGregor's contention that the homeless and socially abjected are the heroes of the age of modern individualism.

The novel's epigraph is drawn from Canto 4 of Dante's *Inferno* – 'Cut off from hope, we live on in desire' – and, in a short article written for the *Guardian*, McGregor gives an insight into why he chose this particular line: Dante's 'doomed souls represent, for me, the authentically heroic voice of all those who, in impossible circumstances, fight on' (McGregor, 2011b). This comment draws Robert's death into a mythical frame of reference that includes the cussed Scots drunk Sammy, whose eye problems recall Tiresias, and the nameless wheelchair-bound character whose efforts suggest a Sisyphean archetype. These readings are not fanciful; they correspond with the choric prosopopoeia which frames the narrative, and point us towards the otherworldliness of McGregor's edgeland. Save for a few key workers in the social services, the novel is strikingly absent of representatives of other social classes, creating a strong sense of separation between this and other worlds. We might indeed be navigating around a Dantean circle of Hell, and if so, McGregor's *Guardian* article seems to suggest, these characters display a heroic spirit for facing the challenges of living in a world without any kind of financial, social, or psychological security. By elevating the characters to the level of myth, it becomes clearer to see why Robert's death represents such a threat to the balance of the micro-social order that congregates around his flat. His death is a literal loss, but it is also the loss of a disorderly orderliness which all the addicts understand and appreciate. He was a cynosure for his small community, a significatory point of meaning, and, just as the authorities have to dissect him and his past to account for his death, so the addicts seek to account for his loss through a sepulchral honouring and search for meaning.

The circles of Dante's inferno have another important function in the novel. Their shape mimics the unending circularity of the protagonists' search for the means and the connections to sustain their habits. McGregor emphasises the routine involved in the continuous flight from the world: 'Three or four times a day, measuring out the hours, filling their pockets with shrapnel until they could change it for gear. Having a dig and a nod and then getting up and starting all over again' (McGregor, 2011a: 38). This ceaseless cycle of accumulation and consumption obviously has parallels with contemporary consumer society, the same logic of supply and demand – or as Danny describes it the 'law of supply and desire' (McGregor, 2011a: 38) – being played out beyond the official marketplace. Danny's phrasal twist is interesting for it subtly shifts the attention away from the purely mechanistic laws of capitalism and towards the more amorphous, open-ended nature of desire. If demand is associated with need (for things to fulfil functions, real or perceived gaps in life), then desire is more closely attached to unconscious and primitive psychic drives. Desire is unquenchable; a constantly replenished drive which cannot be negotiated with and which precedes demand is, in fact, the agency behind demand. What Danny draws attention to here is the unfathomable depths of the libidinal excess in the kind of modern consumer society that McGregor's characters inhabit.

The neediness of desire stimulating us all may get turned towards drugs or alcohol, but it is simply a function of the cyclicality of the capitalist system. To a market driven not by prejudice but by blind currency, the novel's protagonists are not invisible or unpalatable; they are first and foremost consumers who maintain an economic system which thrives on the stimulation of individualistic desire and which devalues communal, empathetic values. The systems of exchange have become formalised into patterns which all understand but which are hopelessly alienating. Take the example of the day centre therapy sessions: in order to obtain what they need to sustain their desire, the addicts have to sit through a degrading simplification of their problems shaped through a theoretical model of social subjectivity to which they do not feel they have access. Empathy, or its lack, is irrelevant because the system of exchange does not require it. Instead, if one submits oneself to a particular discourse of social and self-belonging, one receives the beneficence of the system. Welfare becomes, in other words, part of the apparatus of the exchange system and tied to the discursive practices of power which will forever keep the addicts in their place as needy, subaltern consumers.

This unbreakable cyclicality is most strikingly demonstrated in a standout section (McGregor, 2011a: 114–120) where the narrative focus shifts to the global cycle of production that enables the drugs trade. Beginning with the image of Ant, a wounded British solider, bleeding into the earth of Afghanistan in a hubristic war to maintain the West's supremacy, the focus shifts to the poppy fields in which he lies and to the farmers who harvest seed heads and begin the process of producing heroin. Following each step and each procedure, the reader's gaze shifts between the repatriation of Ant's wounded body and the grotesque subterfuges necessary to bring the drug to British streets:

> The strange journey the seeping poppy gum takes across continents, from an Afghan field to an English city street, carried by mules and men and pickup trucks, through shacks and labs and mountain passes, across borders, through hotel rooms and tea-shops and dark-windowed cars, stuffed into bags and suitcases and petrol tanks, coffee jars, coal sacks, butcher's vans, freight containers, arseholes and vaginas and crudely stitched wounds, forced in and out of desperate bodies, glued in under wigs and false beards and fake-pregnant bellies, squeezing into Europe through the narrow gateway of Istanbul and on through the transit routes of Kosovo and Macedonia and Bosnia [...] shipments bought and sold by men with dark glasses at café tables looking over the sea, suitcases of money changing hands in backrooms and bathrooms, arguments settled by fists and knives and boys with borrowed pistols buzzing past on scooters, the cargo gathering weight and value and bloody narrative as it hurtles through Italy and Germany [...] until a bald-headed man in a baggy tracksuit gets out of a BMW on the Milton Estate, jogs up the concrete steps of a towerblock to the ninth floor, knocks twice on the steel door, and walks in past a young man in a baseball cap who nods and closes the door behind him. (McGregor, 2011a: 118–119)

At each point in the chain, someone benefits, and those gains are fed back into the production system, guaranteeing that the cycle will continue. It is the relentless logic of capital that, whilst a desire that can be exploited exists, whether that be for growth or detriment, a system will emerge to supply it, feed it, reproduce it, mutate it, perpetuate it, and institutionalise it. The logic of supply and desire guides the formal as well as the informal structures of our capital-driven society, organising thinking as well as behaviour along the lines of procedural, consequential outcomes. McGregor's point is that there are degrees only of cultural tone between exchange systems that supply legal drug substitutes and those that supply illegal products; the question of legitimacy might be moot, but the process is the same.

By the novel's close, the facts of Robert Radcliffe's death have been established to the satisfaction of institutional inquiry, but the gaping hole of 'why' is left untouched – beyond the remit of the court. It is left to his collection of dead witnesses and the reader's gaze, which is directed through them, to draw back the veil and peer at the jumble of consequential and inconsequential factors that may have brought Robert to this pass. Lives, McGregor has established, cannot so easily be disaggregated into straight lines of intentionality; success and failure can only ever be spoken of in the same breath. If the ultimate question of this novel is 'who is to blame?' – for Robert's death; for the fate of the dispossessed and excluded in society; for a culture of indifferent welfare; for the instrumentalisation of officialdom; for the ubiquity of capital's acculturation – then the answer has to be a collective admission of responsibility. The failure of human beings is merely the failure of systems writ small, but it is human beings that create and sustain the systems that disempower them. We are left, at the end of a very bleak novel, with a plaintive rhetorical refrain – 'what else can we do' (McGregor, 2011a: 195).

This Isn't the Sort of Thing That Happens to Someone Like You (2012)

With his fondness for conversational titles, McGregor exceeded even himself with his 2012 collection of short stories. Rambling and undramatic, the title is in stark contrast to many of the thirty stories' sharpness and dark tonal immediacy. As a whole, the collection has a brooding, understated violence which often threatens the peripheries of the action, perceived but rarely comprehended fully by the stories' actors. Its after-taste is bitter in the sense that, in many of the stories, the reader is left with a fear of what follows, beyond the narratorial gaze – how will the accumulated tension resolve itself? What will be the fates of the protagonists? Thus described, *This Isn't the Sort of Thing That Happens to Someone Like You* might be expected to deliver narrative drama, but generally this could not be further from the case. McGregor's subject is the ordinary and the potential for violence that becomes subsumed within the architecture of the prosaic and the everyday – a potential that is rarely actualised but is instead deferred, pushed down, or reabsorbed into the sub-strata of ordinary lives. The stories here involve the kinds of individuals who have become familiar in the longer fiction, living the kinds of worried, uncertain, regretful lives which many of us endure. They are married couples, students, office workers, labourers, and parents caught up with their quotidian concerns and unaware of the proximity of the precipices they skirt.

Two of the collection's most striking stories illustrate the co-presence of the banal with the violent in particular. In 'We Wave and Call' a young man swimming in the Adriatic watches his friends on the beach before realising in his attempts to reach them that he is being dragged by the current further out to sea. In 'Wires' a freak road accident puts a young female student in the hands of two, ostensibly helpful, men, whose motives she realises in a final, black sentence might not be as altruistic as she had assumed. As McGregor's title suggests, in the normal run of things, 'this' isn't the sort of thing that happens to someone like us – our lives proceed within parameters of predictability that obscure the threats that govern us. But, McGregor's collection asks, what if they did? What happens in the collision of the ordinary and the extraordinary, and what conflicts might be exposed or resolved by such concomitance? Describing Philip Larkin's poem 'Wires' as the inspiration for his story of the same name, he draws attention to the moments when the predictable gives way to the unknown:

> I'm fairly confident that nothing awful does happen to Emily Wilkinson while she's waiting by the side of the motorway for the police and breakdown services to arrive. But that's not really the point. The point is that it could have done, and her realisation, later, that something could have happened is, for her, the moment from the Larkin poem when she 'blunders up against the wires, whose muscle-shredding violence gives no quarter'. (McGregor, 2011c)

A series of stories concerned with exploring the edges which determine experience are appropriately enough set in a landscape where determination is a complicated issue. Each of the stories in *This Isn't the Sort* is subtitled with a location in the fenlands which extend across Lincolnshire and Cambridgeshire in the east of England. These notoriously flat, largely featureless areas consist of land reclaimed (originally in the seventeenth century) from the North Sea, and are predominantly given over to arable farming. They require, however, continuous vigilance and frequent draining to maintain the balance between land and water, and it is this inbetweenness that McGregor utilises to explore the lives of his protagonists, who teeter perilously between the solid and the insubstantial. These are characters for whom the past is never completely buried; its secrets always have the potential to rise to the surface in a landscape which is forever transforming and blurring the relationship between what is and what has been. In 'In Winter the Sky', George is a man who has lived much of his adult life with the knowledge of how he accidentally killed a pedestrian whilst driving and then buried his body in the fens. Haunted by the randomness of misfortune, he 'keeps watch on the land and the sky' (McGregor, 2012: 22), fearful that the body will be discovered, which it duly is when flood waters disturb the soil and bring the remains to the surface. What is literalised in this unearthing is metaphorised in the long-nurtured tensions and resentments between George and his wife, which push to the surface with a grim inexorability. The momentary violence of the killing and the extended violence of the marriage are equally brought to light by the pitiless indifference of the landscape.

The litany of towns and villages that are invoked at the beginning of the stories – a litany which is transformed into an incantation in the final story, 'Memorial Stone' – refer less to the locations or subject matter of the stories than to a particular fenland mindset, one seeking to maintain a personal order and meaning against the dwarfing openness of the universe. Two literary reference points are worth bearing in mind when exploring this relationship between place and meaning: W.G. Sebald's *The Rings of Saturn*

(1995) and Graham Swift's *Waterland* (1983). Sebald's narrative is set on the coastal fringes of Norfolk and Suffolk, and it details in a hallucinatory blend of travelogue, memoir, history, and fictionalisation the author's walks around England's easternmost counties and the spirals of introspection and historical reflection that they induce. Sebald's influence on McGregor might be most immediately perceived in the specificity of location and the psychogeographical intermingling of place with palimpsests of individual and community history, but Swift's sensibility for the indeterminate space of the fens comes closer to the tonal palette with which McGregor works.[2] Swift's portrayal of the fens emphasises the bleak monotony of horizonless vistas, enormous fields broken only by occasional drainage ditches, and the impalpability of a land that continuously wishes to flow backwards to a watery origin. But it is the effect that this landscape has on the individuals who inhabit it that is so important, for, as Swift writes: 'To live in the Fens is to receive strong doses of reality' (Swift, 1983: 24). For Swift, the fens dictate a concentration on the immediate nature of the world; they forestall understanding and inhibit vision because they are pitiless in their reality, and, as T.S. Eliot concedes, 'human kind / Cannot bear very much reality' (Eliot, 1963: 190). Far from enabling perspective, the seemingly limitless views blind the observer to the external world and force the gaze back inwards and onto the mixture of truths and lies contained there. There is no escape from ourselves there for Swift, and for McGregor the fens seem to produce a similar painful self-examination.

In some cases, this introspection is only obliquely related to the fen-landscapes; 'Close' and 'We Wave and Call', for instance, are forwarded by 'Gainsborough' and 'Wainfleet' but are respectively set in Japan and a war-torn country that appears to be Croatia. By contrast, stories such as 'In Winter the Sky', 'New York', and 'We Were Just Driving Around' draw heavily on the topography of the fens to iterate a sense of remorseless sameness which, for all its austere beauty, is deadening to the urge for movement, difference, and escape. In the last of these, a group of young friends discuss their plans for the future as they drive along the seemingly endless, straight roads that circumscribe fields of produce. One character describes his plan to establish a business selling gourmet snacks and, as the others tease him about his ambitions, a form of hysteria builds:

> It just kept sort of growing, getting louder and louder, like something sort of swelling up until it filled the car and we couldn't hardly breathe and the noise of it was making me dizzy and then Amanda said Josh will you slow down a bit and he turned round to ask her what she'd said so that must have been how come he never saw the corner? (McGregor, 2012: 54)

The black culmination to the story shatters the joviality, but the narrative has already established that the group's emotions teeter between *joie de vivre* and uncontrolled anxiety. The straightness of the road giving way to a sudden corner is a well-honed metaphor for the radical changes in life's trajectory that awaits these characters, and their lack of preparedness for life and for the approaching corner draws us back to the idea of the fens as a place where ambition meets the smack of reality.

Many other stories contain characters who are similarly limited or trapped by the pre-existing shapes of their world, unable or unwilling to see beyond the horizons that define them. The old lady in 'French Tea' who has been to France once but had been unable to procure a proper cup of tea; a man pathologically afraid of cracking eggs lest he discover a foetal chick ('The Chicken and the Egg'); couples caught in the nets of their own familiarity, unable to articulate the nagging sense of dis-ease that afflicts them ('That Colour'; 'The Cleaning'; and the paired stories 'Which Reminded Her, Later' and 'Years of This, Now'). Many of the characters imagined here are familiar from the longer fiction, as indeed they probably would be in a volume that collects together stories of the previous decade. But, in some ways, what distinguishes this as a distinct collection is McGregor's emphasis on scale as a formal and stylistic tool.

In her review of *This Isn't the Sort*, Maggie O'Farrell argues that 'minor events in human lives assume, in McGregor's fictional world, colossal scale' (O'Farrell, 2012), a comment that could be applied equally to any of the novels. However, in the short story genre, this interest in scale becomes crucial to the fabric of the form as well as a means of shaping characters' experiences of their world. A number of the stories here take this to extremes: in 'Fleeing Complexity', 'Song', and 'Thoughtful' show, McGregor plays with the kind of micro-fictional technique that Lydia Davis has employed. 'Dig a Hole', 'The Singing', 'The Remains', and 'That Colour' are barely longer, and they display a willingness to strip back his narrative technique to focus on the imagistically striking or the linguistically playful, and the disparity in scale that is engendered as a consequence of positioning these micro-fictions in the vastness of the fens is striking, if not always entirely successful. The strength of McGregor's writing lies in the resonance that his observation of the ordinary creates; it is less the piercing acuity of an image that is moving than the accumulating and interdepending cadences that he manages over a sustained breadth of writing. Satisfaction comes from the textural layering that McGregor is able to build into his narratives and from the gradual downward pressure on the reader's imagination of the weight of his characters' lives. This is less manageable in the course of a few lines, or pages, so it is noticeable that the most successful stories – and the ones generally praised by reviewers – are the longer ones.

Of those, 'If It Keeps on Raining' illustrates O'Farrell's point about scale very effectively. The dramatic content of the story concerns nothing more notable than a man urinating by the side of a canal and wondering how he will pass the day ahead of him. From this unpromising start, McGregor weaves an intriguing narrative about aloneness in the face of group mentality, the reverberations of a traumatic incident in the past, and the possibility of a biblically violent environmental catastrophe. The main protagonist observes the world passing on the canal, critiquing the indifference of all to anything but present concerns, whilst he ponders on the tree-house and raft he is constructing in preparation for a flood of epic proportions. His fragile grasp on the present and ominous presentiments of the future are contrasted with the moment in his past which seems to have precipitated his current retreat from the world. Involved in a disaster at a football ground – one with similarities to the 1989 Hillsborough tragedy – his errant memory now spirals close to and away from that moment of crisis with a self-destructive fascination. The struggle to assimilate the import of the events is metaphorised into a watery surge which threatens to overflow his coping mechanisms:

> That's what it's like. The river. When it's been raining too much. The momentum of it is huge and dangerous: it makes him think of a crowd of people being swept along and none of them can stop it and they get to a fence and someone says stop pushing. [...] And there's a fence and someone standing behind the fence says: Stop pushing will you all please stop pushing. (McGregor, 2012: 65)

The flow of people dissolves into the flow of memories desperately marshalled behind the protective fence of the everyday, with the cracks beginning to show and the leaks springing. The flood promises indistinction, the retreat from the containable to that which is shapeless, uncontrolled, and meaningless. The scale is personal but the import more inclusive, for we are thrown back onto the constant tussle between land and water that is played out on the fens. How, the story seems to ask, do we grasp solidity from the fluid? What barriers must we erect to prevent the eternal regression to the indistinct? How can we ever know, with any certainty, where the solid edges of our reality lie?

As much formally as dramatically, edges, limits, and the liminal spaces between them are important metaphors for this collection. Stylistically many of the stories begin *in media res* and end without clear resolution; in many the events to which the narrative alludes take place outside the frame of the story, such as in 'What Happened to Mr Davison', in which a neighbourly dispute has led to an act of violent confrontation, the details of which can only be inferred from the guilt-inflected retrospective account of one of the participants. The reader joins most of the stories either before or after the motivating action, but rarely watches it unfold. We are at the moment before a wife chooses whether to leave her bed-ridden husband ('Years of This, Now'); after a village has been abandoned to the encroaching sea ('I Remember There Was a Hill'); before the fate of the young swimmer has been determined ('We Wave and Call'); and after the divorce and restraining order that prevents a father from watching his daughter perform in her nativity play ('Keeping Watch Over the Sheep'). As readers, we are, like the two indolent labourers of 'I'll Buy You a Shovel', on the edge of events that are momentous but of which we have only the vaguest grasp because, in a very real way, we do not belong in this world. This is demonstrated emphatically in the two most formally fantastical narratives, 'Supplementary Notes to the Testimony' and 'The Last Ditch'. Both stories continue the theme of apocalyptic aftermath, being reports into actions that have occurred at some distance from the narrative present, and both, in their quasi-official terminology and use of endnotes, relegate the reader to a position firmly outside the text's epistemology. In fact, the former further queers the text's own structuring of knowledge by situating much of the significant matter in the endnotes, thus displacing the story's centre.

The effect of such techniques is to wrong-foot the reader, throwing her/him into a constant position of interrogation. Who s/he asks is the American woman who descends into the lives of Michael and Catherine in 'Which Reminded Her, Later', and what are her motives? Michael, as a vicar, is practised in the act of empathy, and his generosity in taking the unnamed woman into his home is something that neither he nor his wife is prepared to explore in depth. But the woman herself is a challenge to both the faith of Michael and the distrust of Catherine. The narrative trajectory would suggest that she is an interloper seeking a hand-out, but there is no strong indication that she has any hidden motives, and the reader, like Michael and Catherine, is denied the satisfaction of having her/his prejudices confirmed. Instead the woman is simply the catalyst for the internal tension between the couple to come to the surface; the scepticism/faith divide in the story is between the husband and wife over whether they can maintain their relationship. By misdirecting his reader in this and other stories, McGregor reminds us that we are on unstable ground. We search, as many of his character do, for solidity, but instead we find, in thematic and formal terms, only uncertainty. The safe ground that we believe ourselves to be inhabiting, like the female protagonist in 'Wires', begins to give beneath our feet; the security of a world made around our own realities starts to dissolve – what was land becomes water.

The satisfaction of knowing that this isn't the sort of thing that happens to someone like you is constantly undercut in this collection by the potential for exactly that sort of thing to happen. In this way the ordinary is shot through with its opposite; provisionality can beget violence or benignity, and it can beget both equally. McGregor's interest in the shapes and currents that underlie ordinariness makes him a writer of both surface and depth and one accomplished in the intricacies of short form writing. However, *This Isn't the Sort* lacks an empathetic gentleness that is present in the other fictions; its bleak judgements of its protagonists are rarely leavened by counterbalancing mitigations, and it is this humane quality that distinguishes his longer prose. McGregor has an ability to make the ordinary extraordinary, but, I would argue, that works most effectively when tied to narratives of development and time; the snapshot aesthetic dictated by the short story produces a darker canvas, and one that reveals a tone which, like his setting, is characterised by flatness.

Coda

If the hysterical realist fills her/his page with a multitude of stories, loading the vacuum of understanding with the ballast of minutiae as a prophylactic against silence, then McGregor does the exact opposite. His fiction is stripped back to a skeletal dramatic economy where any action is secondary to the effects it produces. The narrative motivations of his novels tend towards the minor key and the undramatic – an accident in which a boy is not killed; a journey to Ireland to take tea with a stranger; the routine disposal of a decomposing body – and plotting gives way to idiosyncratic stylistic devices. The reader inhabits fictional worlds characterised by detail and emotional intensity, but McGregor's narrative techniques also establish a distance from his protagonists that renders them paradoxically opaque. To spend so long in the company of characters without ever understanding them is a curious effect of McGregor's fiction, and one that reviewer Eileen Battersby found infuriating: of *If Nobody Speaks* she wrote that 'none of the characters emerge as more than aimless pawns set out on a chessboard of sorts' (Battersby, 2002). Battersby hated the novel, but her criticism highlights the persisting expectation that the novel form has a duty to provide fully psychologised, realist characters, rather than the bundle of affective contradictions in a skin that is common currency in the twenty-first century. This present volume has been peopled by ghosts, waifs, revenants, absentees, fleshy machines, and human–animal hybrids, and amongst these McGregor's lost and lonely shells seem at home. But, if indetermination is a quality of his characters, it is matched by profundity, for they are never less than human in their hopes and fears. This contradictoriness offers a way of regarding identity that is totally in accord with McGregor's interpretation of a liquid modernity in which the value attributed to social relations and self-knowing has been exalted at the same time that self and other can only ever be understood as temporary and provisional. That his characters can be both substantial and insubstantial, rooted and history-less, alone and accompanied is not a failure of his fiction; rather it is the consequence of a deracinating, late-capitalist contemporaneity.

Notes

1 Susan Elderkin's review was one exception (Elderkin, 2006).
2 In interview with James Urquhart, McGregor admits to reading Sebald 'voraciously in the past few years' and makes specific reference to his reading of *The Rings of Saturn* (Urquhart, 2010).

Select bibliography

Adair, Tom (2014) 'How To Be Both: Both Sides of the Story', *Scotsman*, 23 August, p. 42.

Adiseshiah, Siân and Rupert Hildyard (eds) (2013) *Twenty-First Century Fiction: What Happens Now?* (London: Palgrave).

Agamben, Giorgio (2009) *What Is an Apparatus and Other Essays* (Stanford, CA: Stanford University Press).

Ahmed, Fatema (2008) '"Nimble Goddess" Sells Us Short', *Observer* (19 October), p. 22.

Akbar, Arifa (2010) 'Marilyn, as seen by her Dog', *Independent* (7 May), p. 26.

Allfree, Claire (2011) 'A Carnal Journey for the Mind', *Metro* (15 November), p. 41.

Apter, Emily (2013) *Against World Literature: On the Politics of Untranslatability* (London: Verso).

Armesto, Fred Fernandez (2011) 'Interview with Tom McCarthy', *The White Review*, http://www.thewhitereview.org/interviews/interview-with-tom-mccarthy-2.

Battersby, Eileen (2002) 'A Pretentious Parade', *Irish Times* (7 September), p. 59.

Battersby, Eileen (2004) 'Tattoo Déjà Vu at the Seaside', *Irish Times* (2 October), p. 13.

Bauman, Zygmunt (2000) *Liquid Modernity* (Cambridge: Polity Press).

Belsey, Catherine (2004) *Culture and the Real: Theorizing Cultural Criticism* (London: Routledge).

Benfey, Christopher (2015) 'Double Take', *New York Times* (4 January), p. 12.

Boddy, Kasia and Ali Smith (2010) 'All There Is: An Interview About the Short Story', *Critical Quarterly*, 52:2, pp. 66–82.

Bourriaud, Nicholas (ed.) (2009) *Altermodern. Tate Triennial* (London: Tate Publishing).

Boxall, Peter (2012) 'Late: Fictional Time in the Twenty-First Century', *Contemporary Literature*, 53:4, pp. 681–712.

Boxall, Peter (2013) *Twenty-First Century Fiction: A Critical Introduction* (Cambridge: Cambridge University Press).

Breitbach, Julia (2012) *Analog Fictions for the Digital Age: Literary Realism and Photographic Discourse in Novels after 2000* (Rochester, NY: Camden House).

Brooks, Christopher K. (ed.) (2013) *Beyond Postmodernism: Onto the Postcontemporary* (Newcastle-upon-Tyne: Cambridge Scholars Press).

Brown, Erica and Mary Grover (eds) (2011) *Middlebrow Literary Cultures: The Battle of the Brows, 1920–1960* (London: Palgrave).

Brown, Helen (2007) 'Floods, Curses, Fanatics', *Daily Telegraph* (1 December), p. 14.

Brownrigg, Sylvia (2011) 'Playing Verbal Games at the Dinner Table', *International Herald Tribune* (20 September), p. 12.

Childs, Peter and James Green (2013) *Aesthetics and Ethics in Twenty-First-Century British Novels* (London: Bloomsbury Academic).

Christianson Aileen and Alison Lumsden (eds) (2000) *Contemporary Scottish Women's Writing* (Edinburgh: Edinburgh University Press).

Churchwell, Sarah (2010) 'Marilyn's Dog Days', *Observer* (2 May), p. 40.

Clark, Alex (2010) 'In Search of Wilderness', *Guardian* (1 April), p. 10.

Clerk, Honor (2014) 'How To Be Both', *Spectator* (30 August), www.spectator. co.uk/books/9296882/how-to-be-both-by-ali-smith-review.

Collins, Jim (2010) *Bring on the Books for Everybody: How Literary Culture became Popular Culture* (Durham, NC: Duke University Press).

Crary, Jonathan (2013) *24/7: Terminal Capitalism and the Ends of Sleep* (London: Verso).

Cross, Stephanie (2007) 'Family Album', *Observer* (13 May), www.theguardian. com/books/2007/may/13/features.review1.

Crown, Sarah (2015) 'Sarah Hall: "I Love Writing about Sex, the Civil Veneer Stripped Off"', *Guardian* (30 March), p. 13.

Cusk, Rachel (2001) *A Life's Work: On Becoming a Mother* (London: Fourth Estate).

Driscoll, Beth (2014) *The New Literary Middlebrow: Tastemakers and Reading in the Twenty-First Century* (London: Palgrave).

Dunant, Sarah (2009) 'Umbrian Shadows', *Guardian* (6 June), p. 14.

Eaglestone, Robert (2013) 'Contemporary Fiction in the Academy: Towards a Manifesto', *Textual Practice*, 27:7, pp. 1089–1101.

Eastham, Ben (2015) 'Sabotaged Parachutes', *Times Literary Supplement* (27 February), p. 19.

Edemariam, Aida (2004) 'More than Skin Deep', *Guardian* (8 October), p. 8.

Edmondson, Belinda (2010) 'Making the Case for Middlebrow Culture', *Journal of Transnational American Studies*, 2:1, http://escholarship.org/uc/item/01j2b4ms.

Edwards, Caroline (2010) 'An Interview with Jon McGregor', *Contemporary Literature*, 51:2, pp. 217–245.

Elderkin, Susan (2006) 'Ordinary Lives Can Be Too Ordinary', *Sunday Telegraph* (20 August), p. 39.

Elias, Amy (2009) 'Post-postmodernism: Are We There Yet?', www.ttbook.org/book/amy-elias-postmodernism.

Eliot, T.S. (1963) *Collected Poems 1909–1962* (London: Faber & Faber).

Fernandez Armesto, Fred (2011) 'Interview with Tom McCarthy', *The White Review*, 1 (February), www.thewhitereview.org/interviews/interview-with-tom-mccarthy-2.

Fig2 (2015) 'Fig-2 12/50 Tom McCarthy', http://fig2.co.uk/#/12/50.

Flood, Alison (2014a) 'Creative Writing Professor Hanif Kureishi Says Such Courses Are "a Waste of Time"', *Guardian* (4 March), www.theguardian.com/books/2014/mar/04/creative-writing-courses-waste-of-time-hanif-kureishi.

Flood, Alison (2014b) 'UK Publishes More Books per Capita than Any Other Country', *Guardian* (22 October), www.theguardian.com/books/2014/oct/22/uk-publishes-more-books-per-capita-million-report.

Foster, Hal (1996) *The Return of the Real: The Avant-Garde at the End of the Century* (Cambridge, MA: MIT Press).

Gans, Eric (2007) 'Qu'est-Ce Que La Littérature, Aujourd'Hui?', *New Literary History*, 38:1, pp. 33–41.

Gee, Sophie (2008) 'Mad for It', *Financial Times* (11 October), p. 19.

Germanà, Monica (2012) 'Contemporary Fiction', in Glenda Norquay (ed.), *The Edinburgh Companion to Scottish Women's Writing* (Edinburgh: Edinburgh University Press), pp. 152–162.

Goring, Rosemary (2003) 'O'Hagan Shows Why Nothing Is Out of Bounds for the Novelist', *Herald* (5 April), p. 12.

Guest, Katy (2007) 'Apocalypses Then and Now', *Independent* (10 August), p. 28.

Guest, Katy (2009) 'Painting by Letters', *Independent on Sunday* (31 May), p. 24.

Haglund, David (2015) 'The Long Shadow of "Two Paths for the Novel"', *New Yorker* (27 February), www.newyorker.com/books/page-turner/long-shadow-two-paths-novel.

Hall, Sarah (2003) *Haweswater* (London: Faber & Faber).

Hall, Sarah (2004) *The Electric Michelangelo* (London: Faber & Faber).

Hall, Sarah (2007a) *The Carhullan Army* (London: Faber & Faber).

Hall, Sarah (2007b) 'Rereading: Survivor's Tale', *Guardian* (1 December), p. 22.

Hall, Sarah (2008) 'Stories of My Life', *Sunday Herald* (30 March), p. 57.

Hall, Sarah (2010) *How to Paint a Dead Man* (London: Faber & Faber).

Hall, Sarah (2012) *The Beautiful Indifference* (London: Faber & Faber).

Hall, Sarah (2013) 'We Need a Story Laureate', *Guardian* (12 October), p. 42.

Hall, Sarah (2014) *Mrs Fox* (London: Faber & Faber).

Hall, Sarah (2015) *The Wolf Border* (London: Faber & Faber).

Hart, Matthew and Aaron Jaffe with Jonathan Eburne (2013) 'An Interview with Tom McCarthy', *Contemporary Literature*, 54:4, pp. 656–682.

Head, Dominic (2008) *The State of the Novel: Britain and Beyond* (Oxford: Wiley-Blackwell).

Hickling, Alfred (2006) 'Local Hero: A Museum Curator Finds Joy in the Everyday', *Guardian* (12 August), p. 14.

Hoberek, Andrew (2007) 'Introduction: After Postmodernism', *Twentieth Century Literature*, 53:3, pp. 233–247.

Hoggart, Richard (1993) *A Measured Life: The Times and Places of an Orphaned Intellectual* (New Brunswick, NJ: Transaction).

Institute of Contemporary Arts (2015) 'The Company', www.ica.org.uk/whats-on/ fig-2-1250-tom-mccarthy-think-tank.

International Necronautical Society (1999) 'We, the First Committee of the International Necronautical Society, Declare the Following', *Times* (14 December), p. 1.

International Necronautical Society (2001) 'Shooting History', www.necronauts. org/artsdas_events.htm (accessed 28 May 2015).

International Necronautical Society (2004) 'Calling All Agents', www.necronauts. org/report2_events.htm (accessed 28 May 2015).

James, David (2012a) *Modernist Futures: Innovation and Inheritance in the Contemporary Novel* (Cambridge: Cambridge University Press).

James, David (ed.) (2012b) *The Legacies of Modernism: Historicising Postwar and Contemporary Fiction* (Cambridge: Cambridge University Press).

Kachka, Boris (2015) 'Tom McCarthy Goes to TED', *Vulture* (12 February), www. vulture.com/2015/02/tom-mccarthy-goes-to-ted.html.

Kane, Pat (2011) 'Scotland's Independence Referendum Will See a Scotterati Recruitment Drive', *Guardian* (20 May), www.theguardian.com/commentisfree /2011/may/20/scotland-independence-referendum-pat-kane.

Kastner, Jeffrey, Tom McCarthy, Nato Thompson, and Eyal Weizman (2009) 'The New Geography: A Roundtable', *Bookforum* (April/May), www.bookforum. com/inprint/016_01/3511.

Keane, Erin (2015) 'Watch the Hypnotic Short Film Based on Tom McCarthy's New Novel *Satin Island*', *Salon* (3 February), www.salon.com/2015/02/03/ exclusive_watch_the_hypnotic_short_film_based_on_tom_mccarthys_ new_novel_satin_island.

Kemp, Peter (2010) 'A Barking Mock-Memoir', *Sunday Times* (9 May), p. 46.

Kirby, Alan (2009) *Digimodernism: How New Technologies Dismantle the Postmodern and Reconfigure Our Culture* (London: Continuum).

Koning, Christina (2007) 'Paperbacks', *Times* (26 May), www.thetimes.co.uk/tto/ arts/books/fiction/article2457660.ece.

Konstantinou, Lee (2013) 'Periodizing the Present', *Contemporary Literature*, 54:2, pp. 411–423.

Kunst-Werke Institute for Contemporary Art (2008) 'History Will Repeat Itself: Strategies of Re-enactment in Contemporary Art', http://www.kw-berlin.de/en/exhibitions/history_will_repeat_itself_strategies_of_re_enactment_in_contemporary_art_91 (accessed 28 May 2015).

Latour, Bruno (1993) *We Have Never Been Modern* (Cambridge, MA: Harvard University Press).

Lea, Daniel (2012a) 'The Anxieties of Authenticity in Post-2000 British Fiction', *Modern Fiction Studies*, 56:3, pp. 459–476.

Lea, Daniel (2012b) 'Discursive Networks and the Post-hermeneutic in Tom McCarthy and Steven Hall', *C21: Journal of 21st Century Literature*, 1:1, pp. 65–83.

Lewis-Kraus, Gideon (2015) 'Negative Capability', *Bookforum* (February/March), www.bookforum.com/inprint/021_05/14155.

Linklater, Alexander (2003) 'Scotland's Saddest Export', *Evening Standard* (31 March), p. 43.

Lipovetsky, Gilles and Sebastien Charles (2005) *Hypermodern Times*, trans by Andrew Brown (Cambridge: Polity Press).

Lott, Tim (2011) 'Good Riddance to this Unequal Union', *Independent on Sunday* (15 May), pp. 38–39.

Luckhurst, Roger and Peter Marks (1999) *Literature and the Contemporary: Fictions and Theories of the Present* (Harlow: Longman).

Lumsden, Alison (2000) 'Scottish Women's Short Stories: "Repositories of Life Swiftly Apprehended"', in Aileen Christianson and Alison Lumsden (eds), *Contemporary Scottish Women's Writing* (Edinburgh: Edinburgh University Press), pp. 156–169.

Lyall, Sarah (2014) 'An Onion of a Novel, There To Be Peeled', *New York Times* (26 November), www.nytimes.com/2014/11/26/books/ali-smith-on-her-new-book-how-to-be-both.html?_r=0.

Macfarlane, Robert (2003) 'Celebrity Knocks', *Times Literary Supplement* (11 April), p. 5.

MacLaren, Lorna (2003) 'No, It's Not about Lena Zavaroni', *Herald* (29 March), p. 14.

Mahawatte (2006) 'Gathered Time: A Curator Struggling to Understand His Past and His Wife Finds Meaning in Memorabilia', *Financial Times* (26 August), p. 31.

Mallon, Thomas (2014) 'Highbrow, Lowbrow, Middlebrow — Do These Kinds of Cultural Categories Mean Anything Anymore?', *New York Times* (29 July), www.nytimes.com/2014/08/03/books/review/highbrow-lowbrow-middlebrow-do-these-kinds-of-cultural-categories-mean-anything-anymore.html.

Mansfield, Susan (2007) 'I've Never Been Interested in Characters in Books; Human Beings Don't Interest Me Very Much', *Scotsman* (20 February), www.scotsman.com/lifestyle/culture/books/i-ve-never-been-interested-in-characters-in-books-human-beings-don-t-interest-me-very-much-1-682724.

Mansfield, Susan (2011) 'Finding His Way', *Scotsman* (14 September), p. 20.

McCarthy, Tom (2006) *Tintin and the Secret of Literature* (London: Granta Books).

McCarthy, Tom (2007) *Remainder* (London: Alma Books).

McCarthy, Tom (2008) *Men in Space* (London: Alma Books).

McCarthy, Tom (2010a) *C* (London: Jonathan Cape).

McCarthy, Tom (2010b) 'Stabbing the Olive', *London Review of Books*, 32:3, pp. 26–28.

McCarthy, Tom (2012) *Transmission and the Individual Remix: How Literature Works* (London: Jonathan Cape).

McCarthy, Tom (2014a) 'Writing Machines', *London Review of Books*, 36:24, pp. 21–22.

McCarthy, Tom (2014b) 'Words vs Images', *Aperture*, 217 (winter), p. 41.

McCarthy, Tom (2015) *Satin Island* (London: Jonathan Cape).

McCarthy, Tom, Simon Critchley, et al. (2012) *The Mattering of Matter: Documents from the Archive of the International Necronautical Society* (Berlin: Sternberg Press).

McCulloch, Fiona (2012) *Cosmopolitanism in Contemporary British Fiction: Imagined Identities* (London: Palgrave).

Mcfadyen, Siobhan (2013) 'Unionist Academics Fear SNP Ministers Are Out to Gag Them', *Scottish Express* (18 November), www.express.co.uk/scotland/443618/Unionist-academics-fear-SNP-ministers-are-out-to-gag-them.

McGonigal, James and Kirsten Stirling (eds) (2006) *Ethically Speaking: Voices and Values in Modern Scottish Writing* (Amsterdam: Rodopi).

McGregor, Jon (2003) *If Nobody Speaks of Remarkable Things* (London: Bloomsbury).

McGregor, Jon (2007) *So Many Ways to Begin* (London: Bloomsbury).

McGregor, Jon (2010a) 'Jon McGregor on Writing *Even the Dogs*', *Nottingham Evening Post* (2 February), p. 18.

McGregor, Jon (2010b) 'Jon McGregor on New Novel *Even the Dogs*', *Nottingham Evening Post* (8 March), p. 22.

McGregor, Jon (2011a) *Even the Dogs* (London: Bloomsbury).

McGregor, Jon (2011b) 'Jon McGregor's Top 10 Dead Bodies in Literature', *Guardian* (19 January), www.theguardian.com/books/2011/jan/19/jon-mcgregor-dead-bodies-literature.

McGregor, Jon (2011c) 'On Learning to Read', http://onlearningtoread.tumblr.com/post/11017277122/the-title-of-the-story-wires-is-taken-from-the.

McGregor, Jon (2012) *This Isn't the Sort of Thing that Happens to Someone Like You* (London: Bloomsbury).

McGurl, Mark (2011) 'The New Cultural Geography', *Twentieth-Century Literature*, 57:3, pp. 380–390.

Merritt, Stephanie (2006) 'The Wind Cries Mary', *Observer* (20 August), p. 21.

Messud, Claire (2007) 'When Life Caught Up With Him', *New York Review of Books*, 54:12, p. 10.

Moderna Museet (2008) 'Eclipse: Art in a Dark Age', www.modernamuseet.se/en/Stockholm/Exhibitions/2008/Eclipse---Art-in-a-Dark-Age/Artists-biograhpies/Tom-McCarthy (accessed 28 May 2015).

Morrison, Jago (2003) *Contemporary Fiction* (London: Routledge).

Mueller, Andrew (2011) 'The Life and Opinions of Maf the Dog, and of His Friend Marilyn Monroe', *Times* (30 April), p. 10.

Mullan, John (2005) 'That's Showbusiness', *Guardian* (15 January), p. 32.

Murray, Isobel (ed.) (2006) *Scottish Writers Talking 3* (Edinburgh: John Donald).

Musil, Robert (1997) *The Man Without Qualities*, trans by Sophie Wilkins and Burton Pike (London: Picador).

Nealon, Jeffrey T. (2012) *Post-postmodernism: Or, the Cultural Logic of Just-in-Time Capitalism* (Stanford, CA: Stanford University Press).

Nicoll, Ruaridh (2007) 'Torn Asunder', *Observer* (7 January), www.theguardian.com/politics/2007/jan/07/uk.scotland.

Nietzsche, Friedrich (1997) *Untimely Meditations*, trans by R. J. Hollingdale (Cambridge: Cambridge University Press).

Norquay, Glenda (ed.) (2012) *The Edinburgh Companion to Scottish Women's Writing* (Edinburgh: Edinburgh University Press).

O'Donnell, Patrick, (ed.) (2012) 'New British Fiction' [special issue], *Modern Fiction Studies*, 58:3.

O'Farrell, Maggie (2012) 'Bolts from the Blue: An Inventive, Audacious Collection Impresses Maggie O'Farrell', *Guardian* (4 February), p. 10.

O'Hagan, Andrew (1994) 'Scotland's Fine Mess', *Guardian* (23 July), p. 24.

O'Hagan, Andrew (1999a) 'Caledonia Dreaming', *Sunday Herald* (7 February), p. 1.

O'Hagan, Andrew (1999b) 'In a Class of His Own', *Times* (27 February), p. 16.

O'Hagan, Andrew (2000) *Our Fathers* (London: Faber & Faber).

O'Hagan, Andrew (2004a) *The Missing* (London: Faber & Faber).

O'Hagan, Andrew (2004b) *Personality* (London: Faber & Faber).

O'Hagan, Andrew (2005) 'The Degenerate Heart of Reality TV', *Daily Telegraph* (28 May), p. 3.

O'Hagan, Andrew (2007) *Be Near Me* (London: Faber & Faber).

O'Hagan, Andrew (2008) *The Atlantic Ocean: Essays on Britain and America* (London: Faber and Faber).

O'Hagan, Andrew (2010a) *The Life and Opinions of Maf the Dog, and of His Friend Marilyn Monroe* (London: Faber and Faber).

O'Hagan, Andrew (2010b) 'A Shaggy Dog Story about Marilyn and Me', *Sunday Times* (25 April), pp. 14–19.

O'Hagan, Andrew (2013) 'Boys and Girls', *London Review of Books*, 35:15, pp. 3–6.

O'Hagan, Andrew (2014) 'Ghosting', *London Review of Books*, 36:5, pp. 5–26; www.lrb.co.uk/v36/n05/andrew-ohagan/ghosting.

O'Hagan, Andrew (2015) *The Illuminations* (London: Faber and Faber).

Parks, Tim (2014) *Where I'm Reading From: The Changing World of Books* (London: Harvill Secker).

Petrie, Duncan (2004) *Contemporary Scottish Fictions: Film, Television and the Novel* (Edinburgh: Edinburgh University Press).

Purdon, James (2010) 'Tom McCarthy: "To Ignore the Avant Garde Is Akin to Ignoring Darwin"', *Guardian* (1 August), www.theguardian.com/books/2010/aug/01/tom-mccarthy-c-james-purdon.

Rabinow, Paul and George E. Marcus with James D. Faubion and Tobias Rees (2008) *Designs for an Anthropology of the Contemporary* (Durham, NC: Duke University Press).

Randall, Lee (2010) 'Interview: Andrew O'Hagan, Novelist', *Scotsman* (31 July), www.scotsman.com/lifestyle/interview-andrew-o-hagan-novelist-1-477337.

Robson, David (2003) 'Of Fame and Fasting', *Sunday Telegraph* (6 April), www.telegraph.co.uk/culture/books/3592360/Of-fame-and-fasting.html.

Robson, Leo (2010) 'No New Direction', *New Statesman* (13 August), www.newstatesman.com/books/2010/08/mccarthy-novel-serge-smith.

Rourke, Lee (2008) 'The Return of British Avant Garde Fiction', *Guardian* (14 July), www.theguardian.com/books/booksblog/2008/jul/14/post27?CMP=share_btn_link.

Schwenger, Peter (2008) 'The State of Inauthenticity', *Triple Canopy*, www.canopy-canopycanopy.com/1/state_of_inauthenticity.

Scurr, Rachel (2006) 'Faith of Our Father', *Times* (12 August), p. 13.

Searle, Adrian. (1996) 'Pamphlet: *Field* for the *British Isles*, Hayward Gallery, London, UK, 1996', http://www.antonygormley.com/resources/essay-item/id/108.

Self, Will (2002) *Dorian: An Imitation* (London: Viking).

Self, Will (2012) 'Will Self on Influences', *Five Books* (31 July), http://fivebooks.com/interviews/will-self-on-influences.

Shields, David (2010) *Reality Hunger: A Manifesto* (London: Hamish Hamilton).

Shriver, Lionel (2015) 'The Wolf Border by Sarah Hall', *Financial Times* (10 April), www.ft.com/cms/s/2/4db8f490-dd10-11e4-975c-00144feab7de.html.

Simon, Scott (2014) 'Art and Death are Two Things at Once in *How to be Both*', *National Public Radio* (29 November), www.npr.org/2014/11/29/367362530/art-and-death-are-two-things-at-once-in-how-to-be-both.

Slenske, Michael (2010) 'Like a Fake 19th Century Novel: Tom McCarthy's *C*', *Interview Magazine* (7 September), www.interviewmagazine.com/culture/tom-mccarthy-c.

Smith, Ali (1995) *Free Love* (London: Virago).

Smith, Ali (1997) *Like* (London: Virago).

Smith, Ali (2002) *Hotel World* (London: Penguin).

Smith, Ali (2003) *The Whole Story and Other Stories* (London: Hamish Hamilton).

Smith, Ali (2004) *Other Stories and Other Stories* (London: Penguin).

Smith, Ali (2006) *The Accidental* (London: Penguin).

Smith, Ali (2007) *Girl Meets Boy* (Edinburgh: Canongate).

Smith, Ali (2008) *The First Person and Other Stories* (London: Hamish Hamilton).

Smith, Ali (2012a) *There But For The* (London: Penguin).

Smith, Ali (2012b) *Artful* (London: Penguin).

Smith, Ali (2013) *Shire* (Woodbridge: Full Circle Editions).

Smith, Ali (2014a) *How To Be Both* (London: Hamish Hamilton).

Smith, Ali (2014b) 'Floating in the Blue... He Looked Like the Finest, Most Well Made Man Who Ever Lived', *Observer* (24 August), p. 16.

Smith, Zadie (2008) 'Two Paths for the Novel', *New York Review of Books*, 55:18, www.nybooks.com/articles/archives/2008/nov/20/two-paths-for-the-novel.

Smith, Zadie (2009) 'Two Directions for the Novel', in *Changing My Mind: Occasional Essays* (London: Penguin), pp. 71–98.

Sontag, Susan (1982) 'Notes on Camp', in *Against Interpretation* (New York: Octagon Books), pp. 275–295.

Stoddard, Katy (2010, 12 October) 'Man Booker Prize 2010: All the Winners, and the 2010 Shortlist', *The Guardian*, http://www.theguardian.com/news/datablog/2010/oct/12/man-booker-prize-2010#data.

Sturgeon, Jonathon (2015) 'Kafka and the Crash of the System: An Interview with Tom McCarthy', *Flavorwire* (26 February), http://flavorwire.com/506844/kafka-and-the-crash-of-the-system-an-interview-with-tom-mccarthy.

Swift, Graham (1983) *Waterland* (London: Picador).

Tait, Theo (2015) 'In the Ascendant', *Sunday Times* (29 March), p. 38.

Taylor, Alan (2003) 'Opportunity Knocks for a Reimagining of Lena', *Sunday Herald* (30 March), p. 10.

Taylor, Catherine (2015) 'Incendiary, Like Cordite', *Daily Telegraph* (4 April), pp. 26–27.

Tew, Philip (2007) *The Contemporary British Novel*, 2nd ed. (London: Continuum).

Timmer, Nicoline (2010) *Do You Feel It Too?: The Post-Postmodern Syndrome in American Fiction at the Turn of the Millennium* (Amsterdam: Rodopi).

Turner, Jenny (1995) 'Foreword: Culture Surfing', *Guardian* (28 October), p. 8.

Tuten, Frederic (2015) 'Tom McCarthy', *Bomb*, 131 (spring) http://bombmagazine.org/article/276933/tom-mccarthy.

Urquhart, James (2010) 'Drawing Out the Dispossessed', *Independent*, www.independent.co.uk/arts-entertainment/books/features/drawing-out-the-dispossessed-jon-mcgregor-tests-his-readers-loyalties-with-his-latest-novel-1889490.html.

Vermeulen, Pieter (2015) *Contemporary Literature and the End of the Novel: Creature, Affect, Form* (Basingstoke: Palgrave Macmillan).

Vermeulen, Timotheus and Robin van den Akker (2010) 'Notes on Meta-modernism', *Journal of Aesthetics and Culture*, 2, pp. 1–13.

Virilio, Paul (1991) *The Lost Dimension* (New York: Semiotext(e)).

Wagner, Erica (2012) 'Jon McGregor: The Best Novelist You've Never Heard Of', *Times* (14 June), www.thetimes.co.uk/tto/arts/books/article3444668.ece.

Williams, Kirsty (2006) '"A Different Kind of Natural": The Fiction of Jackie Kay and Ali Smith', in James McGonigal and Kirsten Stirling (eds), *Ethically Speaking: Voices and Values in Modern Scottish Writing* (Amsterdam: Rodopi), pp. 165–177.

Wood, Gaby (2015) 'We Have Only Galvanised the Forces of Darkness', *Daily Telegraph* (24 January), p. 4.

Wood, James (2001a) 'Human, All Too Inhuman', *New Republic* (30 August), https://newrepublic.com/article/61361/human-all-too-inhuman.

Wood, James (2001b) 'Tell Me How Does It Feel?', *Guardian* (6 October), www.theguardian.com/books/2001/oct/06/fiction.

Index

Note: literary works can be found under authors' names.

Lightning Source UK Ltd.
Milton Keynes UK
UKHW021115170519

342860UK00003B/170/P